DOCTRINES OF THE CREED

William P. Morrison

DOCTRINES
OF THE CREED

Their Basis in Scripture and Their Meaning To-day

by

OLIVER CHASE QUICK

D.D. Oxon., Hon. D.D. St. Andrews

REGIUS PROFESSOR OF
DIVINITY IN THE UNIVERSITY OF OXFORD

JAMES NISBET & CO., LTD
22 BERNERS STREET, LONDON W.1

First published May 1938
Reprinted ... October 1938
  ,,   *November 1940*
  ,,   *February 1943*
  ,,   *May 1945*
  ,,   *March 1946*
  ,,   *June 1947*
  ,,   *January 1949*
  ,,   *July 1951*
  ,,   *November 1954*
  ,,   *May 1956*

Printed in Great Britain

TO

THE MEMORY OF MY NIECE

MARY BERTHA HILL

IN WHOSE LIFE THE LOVE

OF CHRIST WAS MANIFEST

CONTENTS

vii

CONTENTS

PREFACE

IT IS IN the hope that it may prove useful both to teachers and students in the subject, and also may perhaps be of interest to a wider circle of readers, that I offer this essay in systematic theology. Systematic theology has a distinct field of its own, to which, in the Church of England at least, insufficient attention is being paid. This neglect is due in part to a failure to recognize the distinct aim of systematic theology and to a confusion of its proper subject with others, especially that of dogmatics. " Dogmatic theology " concerns itself mainly with the genesis and original significance of traditional dogma, and, in so far as it turns its attention from the past to the present, it seeks only to answer the question, What does the Church teach as *de fide* ? or, To what beliefs are the teachers and members of the Church essentially committed ? " Systematic theology ", on the other hand, asks the question, " How can we best understand and interpret as a coherent whole the doctrinal tradition of our Church in relation to that particular world in which we are now called upon to uphold the Christian faith ?

Systematic theology can only be written from the point of view of a particular Church-tradition, but it does not claim any dogmatic authority for its conclusions. The answer given to its central question is bound to vary more or less with the individual, and the variation is likely to be particularly marked in a Communion which, like the Anglican, includes widely different " schools of thought ". A man is trained in systematic theology, not by learning and accepting any particular presentation of it, but rather by exercising his powers of understanding and criticism upon some particular presentation.

This book, of which much of the substance has been delivered in the form of lectures to theological students at Durham, is an attempt to provide such a presentation with reference to the main doctrines of the Christian Creed. I am aware that there are conspicuous omissions, while some of the subjects treated will appear to many to be side-issues. But I have tried to emphasize the issues which seem to me to be of chief importance to-day, and, as an Anglican, I have also borne constantly in mind the appeal to Scripture as the supreme standard of doctrine. The lessons taught by historical criticism seem to me to require us to use this standard in a new way, but yet to emphasize, rather than to diminish, its importance and authority. If the Church is to preserve the gospel without admitting the principle of ecclesiastical infallibility, the interpretation of doctrine must always be based upon the interpretation of Scripture. I do not therefore apologize for the amount of space I have devoted to the discussion of Christian doctrine as it appears in the New Testament.

I am deeply indebted to my colleague the Archdeacon of Auckland for much sympathetic advice and encouragement, and also to Professor Dodd of Cambridge, who has most generously found time to read my book in proof and to make very valuable corrections and suggestions on details connected with Biblical scholarship.

O. C. Q.

PART I

THE CHRISTIAN FAITH IN GOD

CHAPTER I

THE MEANING OF FAITH

THE FIRST three words of the Creed, " I believe in," are perhaps neither the least important nor the least misunderstood. It will be well if, before entering upon further discussions, we can gain a clear idea of what the term " faith " means to the Christian. In the present chapter I shall try to distinguish faith from bare assent on the one hand and from spiritual vision on the other.

1. FAITH AND ASSENT [1]

Faith and assent are both kinds of belief. The difference between them is often marked by the presence or absence of the word " in " after the verb " believe ". To believe that God exists is, or may be, bare assent. To believe *in* God is faith.

There are of course many things which we believe without any thought of believing *in* them at all. We believe, in a quite detached manner, all sorts of facts which we are informed of by competent authorities. We believe, for instance, so far as modern theories of relativity still permit, that the earth is a more or less spherical mass traversing an orbit round the sun. But our acceptance of this proposition evokes in us no particular enthusiasm. And therefore to say we believe *in* the spherical shape or orbital movement of the earth hardly seems accurate, if we are using words

[1] For some further remarks on the distinction between faith and assent, see pp. 319 sqq.

carefully. On the other hand, there are many things to
believe which is a matter of intense personal conviction.
Suppose a man believes that he has discovered a cure for
a hitherto incurable disease. Naturally he will spend years
of his life trying to perfect his discovery, to convince others
of its genuineness, and to make its results available for
mankind. We should then say at once that the man
believes *in* this cure, whatever it may be, or that he has
faith in it.

The Creed then affirms *faith* both in God and what God
has done and revealed for man's salvation. And this faith
is a kind of belief quite different from bare assent. It is
conceivable in the abstract that a man should assent without hypocrisy to every clause in the Creed, and yet have
no spark of faith in anything which it affirms.

But we need not for that reason necessarily suppose
that faith in Christ or his gospel is the exercise of some
quite peculiar or mysterious faculty which those whom we
call " unbelievers " have not yet received or learned at
all to use. Doubtless that Christian faith is a gift of God
which seems to us unaccountably to be withheld from
some good men while it is bestowed upon others of vastly
inferior merit. Doubtless also, all religious faith has for
its object the unseen spiritual world which cannot be
apprehended by the bodily senses. But still I do not see
any reason for alleging that the faith whereby a man
believes in the gospel of Christ must differ, as a mere attitude of mind, from the faith whereby a man believes in
a cure for a bodily disease. The difference between the
two cases seems to lie less in the faith considered as such
than in the object of the faith. And if you contrast the
enthusiasm shown by some men in spreading the knowledge of remedies for disease with the relative lack of
enthusiasm shown by many Christians for missionary
work, the relevant question suggested is whether these
Christians really do believe in their gospel at all, and are
not mistaking for faith what is really a bare assent to
propositions. Is the Christian gospel the one sovereign
remedy for ills more terrible even than cancer ? If we
do not believe that, are we really Christians ? And if

we do believe it, why is there not more tangible evidence
of our faith ? How is it that men can still allege with
any show of plausibility that the Christian profession does
not seem to make much difference in those who make it ?

2. FAITH AND NOVELTY

Let us assume, then, that Christian faith, while it differs
radically from assent, is not a special kind of belief reserved
for Christians alone.   And let us pursue rather further the
question of its relation to its object.   Men to-day believe
enthusiastically in Communism or in National Socialism,
partly because these movements and their characteristic
doctrines appear to be new, whereas orthodox Christianity
is old.   I suggested just now that it seems hardly accurate
to say that we believe *in* the movement of the earth round
the sun.   But time was when that doctrine also was new,
and its discoverer believed in it so intensely that he was
almost ready to be a martyr for its truth.   I am not of
course suggesting that even Galileo supposed the movement of the earth to be in itself a gospel.   But his new
theory on this subject no doubt represented in his mind
a new conception of scientific method and its possibilities,
for faith in which a man might be prepared to die.   To-
day even faith in experimental science has lost its freshness.   Its method is established and will continue to be
used.   But men are coming more and more, as they accept
that method, to realize its limitations as a gospel.   Ominous
doubts of its sufficiency to lead us to the promised land
are uttered by many.   And even Communists look beyond
experimental science to a highly disputable philosophy of
history, dialectical materialism, in order to discover a
substitute for religion and a faith to live by.

The connexion of faith with novelties is not accidental.
If there can be any permanent object of a lively faith, it
must be such as to afford permanently something of the
freshness of a new discovery.   For though " in a higher
world it is otherwise, here below ", as Newman saw, " to
live is to change, and to be perfect is to have changed
often ".   And lively faith is the possession of an aim and

principle of direction which enables us to travel hopefully through ever-changing experiences, because we know that our journey has a worthy end. The Christian Creed sets before us as the object of our faith nothing less than the unsearchable love of God. It affirms that that love was once for all revealed in Jesus, who died in every circumstance of shame and horror, and rose again for men. And therefore it assures us at the same time that no experience, however terrible or repugnant, can be such that through it no fresh discovery of God's love is possible for one who has God's Spirit in his heart. Here then is the gospel which provides the truly permanent object of faith.

Nineteen hundred years ago that gospel itself was new in time. Then to say, " I believe in God the Father and in Jesus Christ his only Son our Lord " was indeed a new discovery, the discovery of a new world. St. Paul writes at times as one bewildered by the novelty of the one new thing which the clever Athenians could neither tell nor hear, the thing which had shown the weakness of God to be stronger, and the foolishness of God to be wiser, than every work of man's hand and thought of man's brain. But to-day, what we have to prove in thought and life is this, that the essential newness of the Christian revelation is not a temporal newness, which, as the centuries pass, passes itself into old age. It is as true now, as it was when the Epistle to the Hebrews was written, that " that which waxeth old is near to vanishing away ". We believe in Christianity not because it is old but because it still is new. It is the gospel of an ageless truth of which ever fresh discoveries are to be made ; and in making them our faith itself must live. Christ's call to union with himself through sacrifice will bring as fresh a revelation when the earth is becoming uninhabitable by the exhaustion of the sun, as it did when Mary cried " Rabboni " and Paul was blinded by the light on the Damascus road.

3. FAITH, DOUBT AND VISION

What then of the opposition between faith and doubt ? There is a kind of doubt which is the enemy of faith, and there is a kind which proceeds from faith, and is often a condition of its growth. The difference between the two is not easy to define in abstract terms. But there is a story in St. Matthew's Gospel which makes it clear by concrete illustration. Our Lord bids St. Peter, at his own request, to walk on the water towards him. St. Peter starts ; but when he sees the wind, he becomes afraid and begins to sink. And our Lord takes hold of him and says, " O thou of little faith, wherefore didst thou doubt ? "

Faith is essentially that which enables us to direct our effort and movement towards a goal not yet attained. No doubt faith must give us some apprehension of the goal itself. But, especially when we are speaking of religious faith, the clearness of the apprehension may vary very greatly with different persons and at different times. It may be as definite as we may suppose St. Peter's sight of Jesus to have been when he descended from the boat. Or it may resemble rather a sort of spiritual instinct or impulse analogous to what we call " the homing instinct " in birds or animals which enables them to find their way apparently without any distinct knowledge whither they are going or why or how.[1]   Or again, faith in some persons becomes more conjectural, like the guesses and calculations of some explorer who is traversing an unknown country towards a destination he has heard of by report. Faith as we know it has many degrees of clearness, certitude and perfection. But in every case the real enemy of faith is not the dimness or distance which hides the goal from sight, nor even the misgiving which may induce a man to take his bearings afresh and start along a different path, but rather that which suggests to him that there is no goal attainable or worth attaining, and that he had better abandon quest and effort altogether. Such is the doubt that is deadly, because it means the loss of hope and courage. It was when St. Peter saw the wind and was afraid that he began to sink.

Christian faith is that by which a man directs his life in the following of Christ. If he has at all realized the meaning of the Cross, he will not expect on earth any clear

[1] Cf. *Jeremiah* viii. 7.

or uninterrupted vision of his goal. Imagine, in the story about St. Peter, that a mist had blown across, as he walked on the water, so as to hide Jesus from his sight. He might still have persevered in the same direction as nearly as he could, and he might have found himself much closer to Jesus when the mist cleared, than he had been before. Like such a mist are many of the doubts and questionings which arise in the mind of any Christian who thinks seriously. They are always perplexing, and sometimes acutely distressing for a while. But when they are squarely faced, they can be passed through ; and the proof of faith is thus to face and pass through them without evasion. They are never in themselves enemies of faith, even though they fling us back for a while on a blind trust that those who seek shall find, and to those who knock it shall be opened. All sincere questioning has faith at its root. For why should we ask, if we do not believe that there is an answer to be had which is worth having ? Faith is a movement of the mind and soul towards an end. Therefore it is incompatible with two states of mind and two only : first, the doubt which makes a man abandon search in despair, and secondly, the self-satisfaction which makes him content to stay where he is. In fact, those two states of mind are nearer to one another than at first sight they appear to be. And the real faithlessness of the modern world is seen in its half-despairing, half-complacent agreement to give up ultimate questions. Most of the so-called " sceptical " philosophies collapse at the first breath of a scepticism which is genuine and thorough.

4. FAITH, CREED AND GOSPEL

It is with the Creeds as expressions of Christian faith that we shall hereafter be concerned. The Creeds have been put to various uses in the course of history. Originally they were professions of faith made by converts at their baptism, and they formed the basis of the instruction given to catechumens. By the fourth century they had also become formulæ of assent used as tests of orthodoxy for the Church's teachers. It was as a test-word, which the Arians could not accept, that the term homoöusión was introduced into the Creed of Nicea. Subsequently Creeds have also had a regular place as acts of praise in the Church's worship.

With the liturgical use and meaning of Creeds we shall not deal at all. Of their use as tests of orthodoxy we shall speak only when we come to discuss the Church's exercise of authority.[1] Our principal aim is to expound what it is that the Christian believes in as the essential content and object of his faith. We shall therefore regard the Creeds primarily as the classical expression of what Christians believe about God and Christ. As such they will furnish the framework and main themes of our discussion.

The object of Christian faith is Jesus Christ himself and the facts concerning him which the New Testament records. These facts constitute the gospel. As a human expression, however divinely inspired, of the essential content of the gospel, the Creeds are distinct from the gospel itself. And it is important to bear this distinction in mind. In the nature of the case no Christian creed could be delivered by the incarnate Lord himself. And indeed all the evidence goes to show that he carefully refrained from formulating or handing down to his followers any statements of a credal sort. His contemporaries, as later generations have been, were perplexed because he refused to speak more definitely concerning the nature of his own person and mission. The deepest reason for his reticence is not difficult to conjecture. He knew, as the greatest teachers perhaps have always known, that the truths by which men live, though their substance is conveyed through outward events, must be formulated and expressed by the inward travail of men's own minds and hearts. A merely oracular revelation cannot touch the deepest springs of man's being. It must therefore be for the disciples to say more definitely who " the Son of Man " is, and to speak the truth ever more fully as they grow in knowledge of him after his visible presence has been withdrawn. Thus the Creeds are seen to be not only human expressions of

[1] Part IV, c. V.

what it is that Christians believe in, but also expressions characteristic of the particular age which produced them. To borrow a well-known term of modern pedagogics, they are the expression-work of the early Church.

To say this is not to deny that the Creeds have permanent authority. But by insisting that the Creeds are primarily the inspired " expression-work " of a particular age, we secure for subsequent ages a freedom of interpretation which is necessary for the life of faith itself. The real and permanent object of Christian faith is, not the Creeds, but Christ and his gospel. To substitute creed for gospel is to go back from " the newness of the spirit " to " the oldness of the letter ", and to allow faith itself to be confused with that orthodoxy of mere assent which, as St. James grimly pointed out, may in principle be shared by devils. A living faith must re-express and reinterpret ancient truths, and make ever-fresh discoveries of their meaning.

Yet, even so, we can only claim to be true heirs and successors of the age in which the Creeds were composed, so long as it is the same gospel of Jesus Christ that we are interpreting anew. The element of permanent identity in the gospel will, we must hope, emerge more plainly as our discussions proceed. Meanwhile it may be pointed out, that if the permanent gospel is to be reinterpreted by faith, it is as important that the interpretation should be really fresh as that the gospel should be really the same. It is a poor sort of " modernism " which can only revive heresies which the Church of Athanasius and Augustine had already tried in the balance and found wanting. We can learn much from the heresies of all ages, and must admit the frequent unfairness of orthodox polemics. But it would be a paradox indeed, if doctrines which could not survive the criticism of the first four centuries could be hopefully resuscitated to resist that of the twentieth.

CHAPTER II

FAITH AND REASON

THERE IS a further question connected with the nature of faith which we are bound to raise, before entering upon the subject-matter of the Christian Creed itself. For upon the answer to this question depends, as we shall see, our whole method of treating our principal themes. What is the true relation of faith to reason ?

1. NATURAL AND REVEALED THEOLOGY

Scholasticism divides the truths about God and man which a Christian holds into two classes ; (a) truths of natural theology, which can be proved by reasoning from axiomatic premisses, and (b) truths of revelation, which, though not contrary to reason, are neither discoverable nor demonstrable by reasoning, and require for their acceptance faith or trust in Christ as the revelation of God. To the first class belong the being and perfection of God, the validity of the moral law, the freedom of the will, and the immortality of the soul. To the second belong the divine tri-unity, the incarnation and the atonement, and the doctrine of the Church and the sacraments. Thus, though faith is not held to be irrational, the spheres of pure reason and of faith are clearly marked out and distinguished from one another.

If we accept this demarcation of spheres, it is clear that our subsequent expositions should show a corresponding order and division. First we should seek to prove by the purely philosophical reason, without any appeal to Christianity in particular, the general truths about God and his relation to the world, and about the nature and destiny of the human soul. Then we should proceed to show what

truths the Christian revelation has added, not seeking to
prove these latter by reason or philosophy, but expounding
them as truths in which we trust on the authority of Christ
and his Church.

This apportionment of distinct spheres to faith and
reason, however, proves on examination to be unsatisfactory. There are two grounds of objection to it :

(a) If by " rational proof " we mean the cogent demonstration of logic, it is doubtful whether by such proof we
can establish any really important truth about God at all.
No doubt, if certain premisses be granted, logic can show
that a certain conclusion must inevitably follow. But
obviously the truth of the conclusion so demonstrated
remains dependent on that of the premisses. And, if
these are not to require demonstration in their turn, they
must be axiomatic or self-evidently true. Genuine axioms
are difficult to find. Many propositions that were once
accepted as axiomatic are no longer admitted to be so by
a more rigorous logic. And any real axiom, which might
form a basis for theological inference, turns out on examination to be so abstract that no conclusion of concrete
value can fairly be derived from it. In this incurable
abstractness lies the real defect of the traditional proofs
of God's being. Let us grant both the formal validity
and the truth of the old cosmological argument from
contingent to necessary being. Still, necessary being as
such seems to have little more connexion with the reality
of God than, let us say, the square root of minus one has
with a sunrise. And the moment we endow necessary
being with any concrete attributes or qualities, we find
we have gone altogether beyond the logic of our proof.
The truth is that without a certain exercise of faith we
cannot lay down the foundations on which the argument
for any important belief in God must rest. For instance,
we must *trust* our moral experience, before we can build
upon it any argument for believing in the reality of a
moral power behind phenomena. No doubt good reasons
can be given for such initial trust ; but they fall short
both of logical cogency and of axiomatic self-evidence.
And in any case even to guess at the existence of a holy,

righteous or loving God is vastly more important than to be absolutely certain of the existence of necessary being.

(b) Again, the scholastic distinction between natural and revealed theology seems to do less than justice to the organic unity of the Christian Creed. Take the two clauses, " I believe in God the Father Almighty, Maker of heaven and earth, and in Jesus Christ his only Son, our Lord." What is really left of the meaning of the first clause, if you take away from it all that is derived from the meaning of the second ? The title Father in its Christian use is wholly derived from faith in Jesus, and the Christian's belief in God's fatherhood ought profoundly to modify his conception of God's almightiness and creatorship. If, therefore, we seek first to prove what we might know of God apart from Jesus, and then to add to it what Jesus has revealed to our faith, we shall find that the whole plan ends in confusion. Indeed, the attempt to keep to such a plan has done grave harm to the traditional orthodoxy of the Western Church. Doctrines concerning God which were held to belong to natural theology have for that reason been artificially and wrongly isolated from the influence of the Christian revelation, with the result that they have been retained in a really sub-Christian form.

2. PROTESTANT IRRATIONALISM

In recent times some Evangelical theologians have been so much impressed by the objections to the scholastic distinction between natural theology and revelation, that they have attempted a quite opposite line of approach to Christian theology as a whole. Everything of value, they would suggest, in the Christian doctrine of God and man is derived from the Christian revelation ; and is apprehended by faith and not by reason. Therefore the best order of exposition is to start from the record of the facts concerning Jesus, and to draw from that source exclusively the whole content of the Christian's creed. This content is then presented as an object of faith essentially alien from everything which rational philosophy or non-Christian religion may claim to have learned or discovered. We must make up our minds that Christian beliefs are not to be judged or criticized by the general reason or conscience of mankind at all ; their truth is to be discerned only by a quite non-rational faith which is itself a special gift of the Holy Spirit.   Such a task as ours, therefore, ought to consist simply in the further exposition of what is contained or implied in the pages of the New Testament. Our chief concern should be to separate Christian theology from the adulterations of a pagan rationalism and mysticism.   Faith and reason move in such different worlds that the very attempt to relate them positively to one another is a mistake.

But this more radical opposition between faith and reason seems to be open to objections not less serious than those which cast doubt upon the doctrine of the scholastics. The objections can only be appreciated fully in the light of that further exposition of the meaning of the Christian gospel which we are presently to undertake.   But we are at least justified in treating with suspicion a theory which easily disposes of all radical criticism of Christian beliefs by assuming to start with that only those who already believe in Christianity are qualified to criticize it at all. Moreover, it may well seem a quite impossible task to purge Christian theology of all elements which have entered into it from sources external to that particular series of historical events of which the Bible is the record.   It really is not true that everything which is of permanent value in man's knowledge of God is derived from Jesus, or from biblical documents, alone.   And even from a Christian point of view it seems hardly tolerable to suppose that the whole attempt to relate Christian belief to the secular philosophies of the time, which was the work first of patristic, and then of scholastic, theologians, was from the beginning simply a sin or a mistake.   To condemn in principle the whole theological aim and method of an Origen and a Thomas Aquinas is really to condemn oneself.

In general it appears to be true that, while the error of scholasticism was to tie down Christianity to a particular philosophy, the error of much modern Protestantism has been to disparage philosophy altogether. The former sought to impose faith in the Christian revelation as a superstructure upon a base of Aristotelian rationalism. The result was that it did not allow the new revelation in Christ to penetrate into and transform the very foundations of theology. Modern Protestantism on the other hand has sought to interpret the historical revelation of God in Jesus Christ as a wholly self-sufficient basis for theology. It has thus represented Christian theology as a closed system of truth, apprehended by specifically Christian faith, which makes no appeal to the general reason or conscience of mankind and cannot in any way be judged or criticized by the principles or methods of rational philosophy. The result has been that it also limits in effect the universality of that very gospel which it seeks. to exalt by isolation.

3.   REASON AND LOGIC

The scholastic distinction between the spheres of reason and of faith identifies the sphere of reason with that of cogent logical demonstration, faith being concerned with the apprehension of truth which cannot be thus logically proved. But this distinction cuts across another which appears to be more important, viz., that between logic, as the science of accurate thinking, and reason, as that by which we apprehend the rational order of actual being. This latter distinction requires clearer statement and explanation.

The relation of logic to truth must first be examined. The use of logic can assure us that if certain premises be accepted as true, then a certain conclusion must be accepted as true also. But logic by itself can never take us beyond the assertion of a hypothetical truth : if a, then b. If all men are mortal, and Socrates is a man, then Socrates is mortal. That syllogism is an instance of strict logic. But logic cannot tell us either that all men are really mortal, or that Socrates really is a man. Nor would the logic of the syllogism be in the least impaired, if some men were in fact immortal, or Socrates were a mythical being. The proper function of logic is indeed confined to analysing the meaning of statements, so as to exhibit the necessary connexions of these meanings with one another. Logic shows us that, if we affirm two propositions, *a* and *b*, we must affirm a third, *c*, because its meaning is implied by that of *a* and *b* taken together ; and also that we cannot affirm a fourth, *d*, because its meaning is incompatible with that of *a* and *b* taken together, and so the three propositions, *a*, *b* and *d*, if affirmed together, would constitute a contradiction in terms, which is meaningless nonsense. Logic throughout is concerned with the mutual implications of the meanings of propositions, not with their truth or falsehood as such.

Now if we are in possession of premisses the truth of which is indisputable, we can by logic draw from them conclusions the truth of which is indisputable also. For the meaning of the conclusion, when affirmed as true, is implied by the meaning of the premisses when affirmed as true : and, on the other hand, to affirm as true a contradictory conclusion would be nonsensical. But in fact the deep and vital affirmations about the real nature of the world we live in are never either indisputably true in themselves or capable of being logically inferred from indisputable premisses. One such affirmation is that the universe is rationally ordered. The truth of it is both disputable and indemonstrable. It would be indeed a paradox to assert that to affirm that the universe is rational is not itself a rational affirmation. But the only alternative to the paradox is to distinguish reason from logic. And then at once the distinction of the sphere of reason from the sphere of faith completely vanishes. For it is obvious that we believe in the rationality of the universe, because we *trust* our reason. The Christian may acknowledge his faith in reason to be a reason for his faith. On the other hand, this faith in reason, which is also a rational faith, certainly cannot dispense with logic in its pursuit of truth. Vital truths cannot be discovered or demonstrated by pure logic ; but we must test and exhibit by logic the mutual coherence in meaning of the propositions which we affirm as true, in order to assure ourselves that we are not asserting propositions which contradict each other and are therefore in conjunction meaningless. Herein lies the value of the logical discipline of the mind. For though significant propositions may be false, meaningless propositions cannot be true.

4. THE MEANING OF RATIONALITY

But what does it mean to affirm that the universe is rational ? It means, I take it, that reality is throughout informed by a single principle or order and intelligibility, so that the meanings of all truths must be coherent and consistent with one another for the thinking mind, though they need not be demonstrable from one another by any process of purely logical deduction. It is on such faith in the rationality of things that the scientific search for truth depends. No doubt for a time experimental science may pursue its inquiries by the help of two hypotheses which apparently contradict one another. But, while it does so, the science must be content to regard both these hypotheses as " working hypotheses " only. It cannot seriously believe both of them to be true, so long as their mutual contradiction remains. And since the aim of the science is truth, it must ever be seeking further knowledge which will remove the contradiction.

But then we must go on to recognize that physical science does not take into account the whole of reality, or concern itself with the coherence of the universe in its deepest and widest aspects. Suppose, for the sake of argument, that the universe is using up its energy and gradually " running down ", as the second law of thermodynamics seems to suggest ; and suppose further that the process of space-time in which the universe is thus exhausting itself is the ultimate order of reality. It might then still be argued that there is nothing in all this which conflicts with the rationality of the universe as physical science assumes it for the purpose of pursuing its inquiries. And yet the conclusion we have supposed, if it is clearly thought out in all its implications, must appear utterly unintelligible to the spiritual reason and conscience of mankind. If man

with all his ideals of beauty, truth and goodness, all his
gropings after God and intuitions of eternity, has come
into being simply as the product of a physical process to
vanish again in the physical dissolution of all things, then,
from a point of view wider than that of physical science,
we must say that there appears to be no sense or intelligibility or rationality in things at all, and the universe as
known to us has a fatal incoherence at its heart : for the
moral and spiritual aspect of man's being, which is a fact
of experience as much as any other, is now made fundamentally discordant with the rest.

5. REASON AND FAITH UNITED IN CHRISTIANITY

We conclude therefore that any faith, which can interpret the ultimate order of the universe so as to make man's
spiritual nature and experience somehow coherent with
other aspects of reality, may legitimately claim reason for
its ally. And if the faith which can best perform that task
is one which recognizes a special revelation of God to man
in certain particular events, then that faith is seen to be
supremely rational. For the really rational doctrine or
theory is not one which can be logically demonstrated to
be true, but one which, when it is believed as true, exhibits
an intelligible order in the whole scheme of things and
makes coherent sense of our experience.

It must be our task, therefore, to expound the main
beliefs of Christianity in such a way as to show that these
beliefs, when accepted as true, do illuminate the order of
the universe as nothing else can.

We do not admit that Christian faith goes beyond reason.
For we do not mean by reason an activity of thought
which demonstrates truths *a priori* before the facts of
experience are considered. Reason, as we understand the
term, considers the facts and interprets them so as to make
them intelligible. Some facts give more illumination than
others. And it is our Christian conviction that the life
of Jesus interpreted as God's unique and supreme self-
revelation is uniquely and supremely illuminating to the
reason of mankind. It would therefore be absurd to pro-

ceed as though reason apart from Christianity could prove certain truths about God and man, and then faith in Christ came in to complete a knowledge which reason has left incomplete. Reason and faith are not concerned each with a distinct sphere of cognition.

On the other hand, still less can we speak as though all true knowledge of God came through faith in Jesus, and the Christian believer moved in a world of specifically religious truth which the philosophic reason is debarred from entering. On the contrary, faith in Jesus shows itself to be true by illuminating the reason and submitting to its criticism ; and the philosophy which is enlightened by that faith is simply a better, truer and fuller philosophy than one which either has not considered the facts concerning Jesus or has rejected their Christian interpretation.

We shall therefore endeavour to expound all the truths of the Christian Creed, and not some only, in the light of faith in the Christian revelation. We shall assume the truth of that revelation at the outset without proof or examination of evidence, and seek to show how it does illuminate all our thought about God, the world and human life. And we shall follow the order of the historic Creeds in considering first the more general beliefs about God in his relation to the world which Christianity did not create but enables us to reinterpret.

CHAPTER III

GOD

1. THE ESSENTIAL QUESTION AND ANSWER

BEHIND ALL questions of particular doctrines about God, and behind all arguments for and against theism, there lies the fundamental question which the modern world is asking with a new insistence : why should we believe in God at all ? what is the real value and importance of that belief which is at the centre of traditional religion ? It is well that we should attempt a summary answer to that question before entering upon more detailed discussions amid which we may otherwise lose sight of the wood for the trees.

The essential answer can indeed be given in a few sentences. Belief in God, as Christians understand it, is the conviction that the destinies of the world, of the human race and of individual men, are ultimately controlled by the eternal and living will of goodness which, because it is eternal, is utterly stedfast, invariable and unfailing. In less directly personal language, God is the alpha and omega of all things, the source from which they proceed, the end towards which they move, the unity in which they cohere. To believe in the one eternal God alone gives us the right to speak and think of the universe as being really the universe at all. For if there be no eternal reality above and beyond the changes and chances of temporal succession, " the universe " itself is found to be but a phrase fashioned by man for his convenience, which, if it be taken to denote objective reality, merely falsifies the limitless multiplicity and variety of particular events extending for ever into the darkness of the unknown. To believe in the goodness of the eternal alone enables us to hope that the tiny efforts any of us make after righteousness and truth can have any abiding consequence or value.

For, if there be no eternal reality, or if the eternal be indifferent to good and evil, the same result of dissolution and extinction will wait on all our achievements in the end.   Only look far enough ahead, and selfishness and self-sacrifice, sin and holiness, delusion and enlightenment will all come to the same thing.   From such a conclusion belief in God affords the only possible deliverance, if we think coherently at all.   Apart, therefore, from all the logical proofs of theism, apart from all doctrines of particular revelation and from all enlightenment of mystical experi-ence, the mind of man in its most clear-sighted moments will always retain the substance of belief in God, simply because any real rejection of it involves consequences which are intolerable alike to reason and to conscience. It is exceedingly difficult to say what particular value the belief possesses.   For the question is rather : if the belief be taken away, what value in anything is left ? [1]

2.   A HISTORICAL COMPARISON AND CONTRAST

" These are brave words," the sceptic will reply, " but how is it, then, that so many of the keenest and most influential intellects of our time reject your belief as obsolete and worthless ? "   This further question is very pertinent, and we must acknowledge its force before we attempt an answer.

Compare the situation of civilization to-day with that of the Greco-Roman world during the later days of the Roman Empire.   Then, as now, the foundations of society were threatened with collapse under the assault of anti-Christian and barbarian forces.   So far there is resem-blance.   But in the reaction of civilized men to the danger there is a startling difference.   Under imperial Rome the best minds of the age turned to an other-worldly religion for hope and consolation.   This was true not only of Christians but of pagans also.   Stoic and neo-Platonist philosophers were as religious and as other-worldly as St. Augustine himself.   The darkness of the outlook for

[1] A very forcible exposition of this line of thought is to be found in Père Sertillanges, *Dieu ou Rien ?* (Paris, Flammarion).

human society upon earth caused the finest and most
cultured minds to turn inward in order to cultivate that
life of the spirit which is above time and place. But now
it is quite otherwise. Men do not believe in an eternal
world at all. Where religion is valued, it is valued largely
because it is thought to be effective as a means either of
bringing about changes in this world which are desirable,
or else of preventing changes which are not. Considered
strictly as truths, the central doctrines of religion are losing
their appeal to the human mind. Why ? Certainly not
because men to-day are more content with contemporary
circumstances than were their forefathers. Certainly not
because the danger of relapse into barbarism is substantially
less now than in past ages of civilization. The main
reasons seem to be two :

(a) The first is the belief which the last century established in general progress and evolution, a belief shared,
though with important differences in form, by Marxists,
nationalists and humanitarians. To all alike the history
of life on this planet is a story of constant development
from lower to higher, and the development seems bound
somehow to continue. There is indeed no more profound
difference between the mind of the ancient and that of
the modern world than that which is to be found in the
attitude of each towards time. The ancients never enter-
tained seriously the notion of general progress. They
never saw any reason to think that what comes later in
time must be better than what comes earlier. They
usually put the Golden Age in the past, and if they did
occasionally indulge in utopian hopes of a good time
coming, the hope was based on the expectation of some
divine intervention, and not on the operation of any
natural law. But now almost everyone has a belief in
general progress firmly rooted at least in his subconscious
mind. Almost everyone is convinced that much better
times for all are coming or can be made to come. To
reformer and revolutionary alike—and which of us is not
either one or the other ?—time is the bringer of all good
things, though some, it would appear, think that his slow
footsteps need occasionally to be hastened by a judicious

application of bombs and poison-gas. As to what will happen ultimately they refuse to inquire. The ultimate future seems too far off to be of interest. The prospect of some better age to come in a few generations provides faith and hope enough to carry them through the present. To ask what reason there may be for this apparently quite uncritical trust in time brings us to the second cause of the disfavour into which other-worldliness has fallen.

(b) It is the new control which man by experimental science has won over nature and is continually extending. The result of it is a quite new consciousness of power which has convinced our generation that human destiny is in human hands. However great may be the dangers, men are sure that they can and must escape them by the use of their own resources. Here is the great reason why traditional piety and belief in God make so little appeal to the modern world. Salvation must lie in some political or economic gospel. For man can do everything that can be done at all by the knowledge and equipment which science puts ready for his use. No doubt the saints of old dreamed of another world, because they lacked the scientific apparatus necessary to build heaven upon earth. They may be excused for meditating upon God's ways, when there was no broadcasting station to fill the silence with propaganda. In the twentieth century we have more efficient methods of redeeming the time. We can afford to trust the future because there is no limit to what man can do with it. It is this new Titanism of man which has thrust God out of mind and blinded our eyes to the ulti- mate ends and issues of human living.

3. THE FRUITS OF MODERN GODLESSNESS

Yet it is becoming increasingly evident that modern godlessness must bring what ancient heathenism used to call a nemesis upon its head. When men have abandoned all belief in an unchanging and eternal authority over human life, they can reach no agreement as to what ulti- mate end they ought to pursue, or by what means it is right to pursue it. Where there is no agreement on such

matters, the appeal is inevitably to force. Accordingly it
is to the use of force, physical and psychical, that the
adherents of the new gospels betake themselves. But
even the modern world is not allowed to forget that those
who take the sword perish with the sword, since force
constantly begets force in opposition to itself. And therefore the majority of us live in terror of war, civil, inter-
national or economic, which as experience has shown must
under modern conditions bring disaster to all and victory
to none. Of course co-operation alone can save us. But
where is the power that will enable us to co-operate ?
Government control of press, wireless and education is the
modern answer to that question. But official propaganda,
however perfect its organization, can only deceive the
citizens of one state at a time ; and a policy of too systematic lying can but increase in the end the very confusion
it sought to remedy.

We said just now that when belief in eternal realities is
abandoned, men can reach no agreement as to what ultimate end they ought to pursue or by what means it is
right to pursue it. Let us notice more exactly what is
actually happening in both respects.

First, as to the end. Man's destiny being in his own
hands and no authority set over him, what end should
he live for, what future ought he to make for himself ?
Some say that the supreme end is the establishment of
a classless society. Others say that it is to make one
nation or race dominant over others. Forthwith we have
the rival religions of Communism and Nationalism arrayed
against each other. What court is to decide between
them ? There can be no appeal to any eternal principles
of right or justice or truth. For these are rejected by
both sides. " Philosophy ", said Lenin " is a partisan
affair," and his followers say the same of justice. And
there at least the Nationalists wholeheartedly agree with
them. The only difference is that their " philosophy "
and " justice " are partisan on the other side. Nothing
can arbitrate but force. And when the guns and bombs
and poison-gas have done their work, will it much matter
which side says it has won ?

Secondly, as to the means. If you believe in an eternal
and divine principle of right and goodness, the means you
take to achieve your good end must be the expression of
that same goodness and morally appropriate to it. If the
end is a divine kingdom of righteousness and peace and
love, the means you take to move towards it must be
themselves the appropriate expression of a righteous,
peaceable and loving spirit. For the end you seek is set
by eternal principles which lay their authority upon you
now. But if you believe only in some *future* good as the
end, there is no reason why your choice of means should
be thus limited. Love and truth and freedom may be
the goal for the future : hatred, lies and oppression may
be the policy for the present. Why should not the classless society, which is the Marxist's heaven, be sought by
deliberately creating the ruthless dictatorship of the prole-
tariat backed by the methods of the Ogpu ? Why should
not the noble civilization of the Nationalist's dream issue
from an utterly sordid persecution of the Jews ? Once
men have thoroughly rejected the thought of the divine,
the other-worldly and the eternal, they will inevitably
think that they can justify the blackest crimes in the
present, because their result will be some glorious Utopia
in the future. It is perfectly possible to gather grapes
from thorns and figs from thistles, when there is no eternal
law which decrees that thorns and thistles must bear less
desirable fruit. Clearly Jesus did not understand the
principle of dialectical development.

4. THE CHRISTIAN BELIEF

Christians think otherwise. St. Paul's teaching at this
point makes a particularly instructive contrast to that of
some modern missionaries. He also looked for a glorious
age in the future. The Kingdom of God, he said, is
righteousness and joy and peace in the Holy Ghost ; and
no doubt he was thinking primarily of a future world.
But he did not mean that Christians might now hasten
its coming by violence and fraud. For the Kingdom was
God's ; and therefore it was not future only, but eternal.

Therefore again he who would enter it fully in the future, must begin to enter it now by living according to its law of love even in face of suffering persecution and apparent failure. There is indeed a bringing of good out of evil, of which the Cross of Christ is the sacrament ; but the Christian " dialectic " depends on the eternal consistency of God's love.

We need seek no further to exhibit what is to the Christian the essential meaning and value of belief in God. It is not the mere clinging, for comfort and guidance, to the orthodoxy of the past : the Christian must never forget that the Son of God himself appeared out of the Nazareth which the orthodox despised. It is not a bulwark against revolution. Modern society, however different from that of the first century, is still far too like the world which the New Testament condemns not to stand in need of a revolution at least as drastic as any Communist could wish. Belief in God is the conviction that we may enter now into communion with that living and eternal will of goodness which, because it is above the changes and chances of time, alone can give meaning to their movement and order them towards an end.

CHAPTER IV

MAN'S THOUGHT OF GOD

BOTH THE Apostles' and the Nicene Creeds teach us to think of God as revealed in three great attributes —fatherhood, almightiness, creatorship. These attributes have a common characteristic which they share with all, or almost all, the names which we use to describe God's being and nature : they derive their primary meaning in our experience from the activity not of God but of man. Fatherhood denotes primarily a human relationship. The notion of creatorship takes its primary content from man's work in making. And, though it is true—if we may ignore certain extravagances of Freudian psychology on the subject of the infant-mind—that no human being outside a lunatic asylum would claim to be almighty, yet our primary understanding of might or power itself is given to us in the achievements of our own hand and brain. Therefore, at the very outset, our attempt to interpret the Christian Creed is confronted by the problem of anthropomorphism. Is the God of Christianity a god made in man's image ?

1. TRADITIONAL CHRISTIANITY NOT ANTHROPOMORPHIC

It is from this suggestion that most of the sceptical attacks on the Christian doctrine of God derive their destructive force, at least in the judgement of ordinary men. Christian orthodoxy, it is alleged, thinks of God simply as a human person imagined on a much vaster scale. Such, we are told, is the deity Christians really profess to believe in, if they are honestly loyal to their faith. But this whole way of thinking about God has become impossible for the modern mind. Modern science has shown convincingly that even as a mental being man may no longer assume that he occupies any place of central importance in the universe. And to suppose that the power behind the universe has any special affinity to man's nature at all is quite illegitimate. The whole notion of God as Father, Creator and almighty Ruler is therefore no better than a fantasy. The Christian Creed is but a nursery tale which mankind has now outgrown.

If apologetics were our main concern, there are many lines of reply to this criticism which we might elaborate.[1] Our purpose, however, is not to argue in defence of the faith, but to explain it. It is therefore more relevant to point out that the charge of anthropomorphism, when brought against the doctrine of the trained theologians of the Christian Church, can hardly be substantiated.

It is true that the theology of the Old Testament, whatever may be said of the later and more philosophically minded Rabbi's, is in a high degree anthropomorphic. Jehovah is represented as thinking and acting like a greatly magnified human sovereign. Even the explicit warnings against a too literal anthropomorphism which are frequent in the Old Testament are themselves evidence that such warnings were needed, and that the Jewish mind was too prone to think of Jehovah as though he were a man. The implications of Christ's own teaching we shall consider presently. But the other great formative influence in the theology of the Catholic Church was the tradition of Hellenic philosophy and mysticism. And this influence from the first counterbalanced and corrected the anthropomorphic tendency of Judaism, chiefly through the teachings of neo-Platonic mystics. Neo-Platonism insisted that God's being and nature could only be truly expressed in negative propositions, since God is beyond and above all beings properly so called. Hence patristic theologians constantly recognized the need for a reverent agnosticism to qualify all affirmations about God. This agnosticism, based on the ground that God transcends all human powers of knowing, is particularly strong in the two great doctors of the Western Church, St. Augustine and St. Thomas Aquinas. According to St. Thomas we

[1] See, e.g., B. H. Streeter, *Reality*, cc. I and II.

can indeed know certainly by the light of reason that God is the eternal ground of all being, and in him all perfections are realized. But even these affirmations do not imply any positive knowledge of God as he is in himself, but only of the relation of complete dependence in which we and all things stand to God. Even by the revelation of grace, which gives a higher knowledge than that obtained by the natural reason, we cannot in this life know of God *what he is*.[1] St. Thomas's teaching is summed up by saying that we do not know what God is, but only what he is not, and the relation of all things to him.[2] If the theologian still uses about God language derived from human thought and action, he must do so only in the same way as a Copernican astronomer still speaks of sunrise and sunset although he knows that such terms are, when strictly considered, inaccurate. There could not be a more complete mistake than to suppose that modern science first showed Christian theology that man's mind must not fashion God in its own image.

2. THE REAL DIFFICULTY

But our main concern is not to defend traditional theology against the criticisms of the ill-informed. We must determine more precisely for ourselves in what sense terms, which have their primary reference to human activities and relations, are applicable to God. The question has to be faced at the outset, if we are to gain any clear idea of what we mean by affirming credal statements about God to be true.

Men are fathers, men are mighty, men are makers. But no magnifying of human fatherhood, power or creativity could give its true meaning to the affirmation, I believe in God the Father almighty, Maker of heaven and earth. Such magnification could only give us the conception of a superman. And a superman, however much we emphasize the prefix *super*, would still not be God. Moreover, whatever Christian faith has meant by asserting the Lord

---

[1] *Summa Theol.*, Pt. I, Q. 12, Art. 13.
[2] *Contra Gentiles*, Bk. I, c. XXX, *ad fin.*

Jesus Christ to be God and man, it has certainly not meant to attribute to him anything like superhumanity. As we shall see more clearly later on, any such interpretation of the doctrine of the incarnation would simply destroy its value and significance.

Again, it is no help to say that we apply human attributes to the Godhead in a merely " symbolic " sense. The point at issue is not whether the attributes are symbolically used (of course they are !), but how far and in what way they can be said to symbolize a truth. And it is still more dangerously confusing to suggest that these attributes, though in plain prose they are applicable only to man, may be poetically true of God. The truth which is *proper* to poetry consists in its peculiar power to give vivid expression to human feelings and imaginations. Literature has poetical truth in so far as it does express vividly a human imagination or emotion which can be shared and appreciated by other men. Prose becomes poetical in so far as it affords such expression. Poetry becomes " prosy " in so far as it fails to do so. But the true opposite of poetry, as Wordsworth long ago pointed out, is not prose but science. Now, if you ask whether a poem, which vividly expresses human imagination or emotion, expresses also some further truth about reality, you are dealing with it no longer as poetry but as science in the broadest possible sense of that term, in which it may be held to include scientific history, philosophy and theology, as well as what is commonly known as natural science. Thus, Milton's *Paradise Lost* undoubtedly has the truth of great poetry, but what degree of theological truth it may possess is obviously a different question altogether. In the same way, the dramatic truth of Shakspere's *Julius Cæsar* is independent of its historical accuracy.

Now no one doubts that anthropomorphic language about God, such as that which we often find in the Old Testament, is poetically true, in the sense that it vividly expresses religious imaginations and emotions of man which are shared by all who respond to its appeal. And in the same way the language of the Christian Creeds, with all its sacred associations, inevitably stirs our feelings and

convinces us of its poetic truth.   But the precise question
we now have to ask is this : how are these credal statements true in a manner other than poetical ?   Granted that
it is true poetry to speak of God as the Father Almighty,
Maker of heaven and earth, in what sense is this true
poetry true theology also ?   What is the truth symbolized,
and how is the symbolism to be rightly understood ?

3.   THE SOLUTION OF THEOMORPHISM

In order to answer that question we have to make a
great assumption or hypothesis.   We call it an assumption
or hypothesis, since its truth cannot be demonstrated by
deductive logic from more elementary or axiomatic principles.   We may equally well call it a venture of faith.
But we do not mean that it is irrational or even beyond
reason, if we distinguish reason from deductive logic.   Its
rational justification lies in its power to throw light upon
all our experience and to help us to interpret that experience as a coherent whole.   The assumption or hypothesis
or venture of faith is this : that ideas of God, including
anthropomorphic ideas as well as others, only enter man's
mind and experience at all, because man's being has its
source and ground in that being infinitely other than his
own, and yet inclusive of it, which the human word God
properly denotes.   The word God does not denote any
idea of God, but the reality of which the human mind can
frame no adequate idea at all.   Yet an idea of God is
only possible to man, because man's being is dependent
upon God's.[1]
In the beginning, God.   That is the grand and primary
affirmation of the Bible.   And, if it is true, then it follows
that every process whereby man reaches any sort of idea
of God, is not a process which man initiates : it is but a
response which God has enabled him to make.   " It is
said ", wrote Voltaire, " that God made man in his own
image : man has retaliated."   Those words, written in

[1] The statement above represents what I take to be the truth
expressed by the so-called " ontological proof " of God's being,
at any rate in its Cartesian form.

irony, indicate the truth towards which anthropomorphism really points. If man makes a god in his own image, his action in doing so is still a retaliation, a response, only possible because the initiative does not lie with him, but with the God who made him in the image of the divine. This is the hypothesis of theomorphism.

Starting from that hypothesis, we shall have no difficulty in explaining anthropomorphism, nor even in finding in it a certain value. God, we shall say, gave man all his natural capacities and powers and faculties of acting and knowing, so that, as the apostle said, he might feel after and find God himself. Man must rise towards the knowledge of the true God by enriching and seeking to explain his experience both of himself and of his surroundings. And the worship of a fully man-like God is at least a better and a truer worship than that of the definitely sub-human forms of being which idolatry, ancient and modern, has often represented as divine. And yet we must insist that no imagination of a being endowed with human and super-human attributes and powers, however magnified, can give us a positively true conception of the Godhead. It is not even accurate theology to say that God is greater than man, however much greater. For " greater " is a comparative term ; and between God and man there is, strictly speaking, no comparison. Still, there is something in man which gives him a true indication of what God is.

We can perhaps best explain as follows what that something is. Man, according to our hypothesis, cannot be an absolute or ultimate originator, author or authority. His very notions of absolute origination and authority are not notions of anything which exists in himself. And, inasmuch as he has no experience of what it is to be an absolute originator or authority, these notions are to him primarily negative. They mark man's sense of his own inadequacy and limitation. Yet to be conscious of limitations is in some manner already to transcend them. If man were not at all an originator and an authority, he could have no consciousness of his own limitations in those respects. But, being in fact a relative and partial originator, and wielding relative and partial authority, man has in that experience a hint of that absolute divine origination and authority on which his own, in their limitation, are dependent.

Thus, in recognizing our limitations we recognize our dependence upon God as the being not thus limited. St. Thomas Aquinas taught at the same time that we cannot know God as he is in himself, except by negations. Nevertheless, to negate our limitations, when we think of God, is not a pure negation, even though we can have no clear conception of the positive truth. And we need not be afraid of affirming that we rightly and truly predicate of God the highest human attributes, if we remember that such attributes, as for instance fatherhood, power, and creatorship, are in man but dim hints and reflections of the one perfect being from whom humanity itself proceeds, towards whom it aspires, and before whom it bows its head in worship. We do not in any way make human fatherhood, power and creatorship the standard by which we are to judge of the divine. That is the error of anthropomorphism. But we insist that human fatherhood, power and creatorship themselves teach us, if we think about them deeply enough, that they are not self-sufficient or self-explanatory, but point beyond themselves to an Author, an Authority, and a Power from whom they come and in whom their truest meaning is found.

4. THE RELEVANCE OF CHRIST'S PARABLES

And, now that we have reached our conclusion by a process of abstract reasoning, do we not find that it is essentially the same way of relating human experience to the Godhead which our Lord taught in his parables ? Consider the three parables which follow one another in the fifteenth chapter of St. Luke : the Lost Sheep, the Lost Coin, and the Prodigal Son. Remember that the characters in all three are natural, even ordinary, human beings, not heroes or supermen chosen to represent God because of their difference from others. It is natural for the ordinary man or woman to take trouble to find lost property and to rejoice over success. It is natural for the ordinary

father to welcome home the lost son even when he returns
destitute, broken and ashamed. " Likewise I say unto
you there is joy in the presence of the angels of God . . ."
What does it mean ?   Not that there is an apparently
rather far-fetched and dubious analogy between the particular actions of certain individuals and certain other
actions which faith may symbolically or poetically attribute to God ; but rather that the instincts of care for
property and of parental love, which are deep in the
common heart and nature of mankind, are themselves of
divine origin, and reflect at an infinite distance something
which is true first and last of the relation of all things and
persons to God, who is the author and owner of all.   It is
not that God is like a man, like the shepherd, or like the
house-wife, or even like the father of the prodigal.   To
interpret the parables so is to begin to make them into
allegories, which they are not.   The point is rather that
certain relations, which exist in common experience between a man and his property or his children, have their
true ground and significance in relations of things and
persons towards God, which they help us to conceive truly
even under conditions of human limitation.   Human
ownership and fatherhood have their truest meaning and
value as parables of God, parables to which the human ear
and eye may nevertheless be deaf and blind.   Believe
that, and human life begins to make sense at last.

5.   A MODERN ILLUSTRATION

In conclusion, let us consider one illustration of the way
in which the line of thought so far suggested may be applied
to modern perplexities.   During recent years it has been
maintained by some psychologists that the idea of God as
father is a projection of the human mind.   During infancy
and childhood the human being is entirely dependent upon
parental care.   This dependence generates an instinctive
temper or disposition which the adolescent finds it impossible to throw off when the parental care is withdrawn,
and he or she has to face the world without it.   In such
circumstances the human soul subconsciously seeks to

compensate itself for its loss by imagining a heavenly parent who will guard and guide it all the days of its life. The obvious inference from these facts constitutes to some minds a grave obstacle to belief in God. But consider the matter in the light of the Christian hypothesis as to the relation of man to God. There is no reason to dispute any of the facts alleged by the psychologists, not even the fact that the notion of the heavenly father is really a projection due to the subconsciously felt need of the earthly father. But we shall put God first and last in the whole process. And we shall say that God is teaching man about himself and drawing him towards himself, first by giving him experience of the human parent's care, and then by withdrawing it, so that by his sense of need he may learn to depend on his father who is in heaven. It is by making what the psychologist calls projections, and by learning through experience their inadequacy and their truth, that man grows in the knowledge of God whose image he bears. It is only because God is there from the beginning that man has any power to project any ideas upon heaven at all. God, as man speaks and thinks of him, is no doubt always in some sense a projection of man's mind. But that can only be true because man is first a creature of God's mind and bears the image of his heavenly father and creator within himself.

CHAPTER V

GOD AS CREATOR

W E HAVE now to consider severally the different attributes of God in which the Christian Creed expresses our thoughts about him. But we must first acknowledge one difficulty which springs from this very necessity of separate consideration. It is the limitation of the human mind which splits up the perfection of God's being into different attributes so that we may direct attention first to one and then to another. But inevitably by doing so our thought sets asunder things that in God are indissolubly joined.

1. DIVINE SIMPLICITY

Even in the case of a human personality we are conscious that we mar the unity of the whole, when we separate, let us say, our account of a man's family-life and dealings with intimate friends altogether from his professional or public activities. For it is essentially the same man who is manifested in all. Yet in the case of a man, the separation is to a great extent justified, though in proportion to the man's greatness and goodness we feel that the justification is diminished. The man enters many different fields of activity and thought, and he can only live in one at a time. Therefore the separation is justified. Yet it is a weakness and imperfection in his character, if a man shows himself in his office a quite different person from what he is in his home. The character of the best and greatest men is rightly felt to be indescribable, precisely because the description of such a man's varied characteristics and activities, because it can only take them one by one, is unable to convey the total simplicity of the impression which his whole personality made upon those who knew him well.

The perfection of God's nature surpasses all human thought and knowledge, not only in its infinite variety, but also in the absolute simplicity in which the variety coheres. God, as scholastic theologians remind us, is not just wise *and* powerful *and* loving, even in a supreme degree. In him perfect wisdom, power and love are *one*, and the unity in which they cohere is also his creative and redeeming will. The efforts which we make to suggest what God is by speaking of his various attributes, are at best somewhat like an effort which might be made to suggest the character of some great chorus by humming successively the parts assigned to the several voices. The defect would be of a double nature. The humming would fail to reproduce the quality of the several voices. And the separate rendering of each part would break up the unity of the harmony which is the very essence of the chorus itself.

The illustration is of course exceedingly crude. But it may indicate the sort of difficulty which confronts us when we try to speak of God successively as creator, father, almighty and the like. Yet the insurmountable difficulty need not altogether destroy the value of our attempt. The attempt, if we recognize its inadequacy, may train the spiritual ear to hear what language cannot utter.

2. THE PROBLEM OF THE FIRST CAUSE

We will begin then with the thought of God as creator. What do we mean by affirming that God is maker of heaven and earth ?

In answering that question it is convenient to start from a provocative assertion made by a well-known modern writer : " Darwin's *Origin of Species* is to-day a good deal more profitable as theology than the first chapter of Genesis." To see the confusion of thought in this statement is to understand the difference between a theological doctrine of creation and a scientific doctrine of origins. Natural science is concerned with the causal order of events as they actually happen and have happened in space and time. This order, as it is traced backwards, brings us to certain primitive events which we may believe to have been the origin of life, or of the earth, or of the solar system or the stars.   As to the nature and succession of these events it is doubtless true that the authority of such experts as Darwin is to be preferred to that of the author of Genesis.   But theology is not interested primarily or chiefly in the question of temporal origins, even when it is stating its doctrine of creation.   It is interested primarily and chiefly in the end or value of what has been created. In other words, it is only because of its interest in the final cause of things that theology is interested in the first cause at all.   Now on the question of final cause, in any absolute sense, natural science has nothing whatever to say.   Biology can indeed point out the relations of structure to function in organisms, and chemistry the peculiar adaptation of the terrestrial atmosphere which is needed to sustain life.   Biology can even go further and show that man may in the future control the development of his own species in hitherto undreamed-of ways.   But if you question the end and value of life itself, natural science is simply dumb.   But just at this point, Genesis speaks with no uncertain voice.   " God saw everything that he had made, and behold it was very good."   That is the reason why " in the beginning God created the heaven and the earth ".   And to vindicate the belief that the world has a divine value the theologian attributes to it a divine origin.   The value of the ultimate end must reveal the ultimate source.   But when we speak of " ultimate source " in this theological or metaphysical sense, it is obvious that we are speaking of something altogether beyond the series of spatio-temporal events with which alone natural science can deal.   " Thou madest us for thyself," wrote St. Augustine, " and our hearts are restless till they find rest in thee."   It is because the Christian believes himself to have been made for God, that he believes also that God made him.   And the belief so grounded cannot be upset by anything that natural science may discover about the temporal origin of mankind.

Thus it appears that the expression " first cause " is ambiguous in meaning.   It may denote simply the event which comes temporally first in a causal series of events.

Thus we may say that the falling of a spark is the first cause of a conflagration. When the expression is used in this sense, " first causes " in the universe are investigated by natural science rather than by theology ; and Darwin is more authoritative than Genesis. On the other hand, " first cause " may denote the *explanation* of a process or series of events, i.e., that which causes it to exist as its reason or ground. Thus we may say that man's appreciation of music is the first cause of the construction of pianos. In this case it is obvious that the first cause is not itself a member of the series of events which constitutes the process explained. The appreciation of music is not one of the events which constitute the construction of a piano. It exists both before the process of construction begins and after it has ended. And in such a case the first cause is one with the final cause ; for it is only purposive processes which can be thus explained. It is in some such sense as this that theology affirms God to be the first cause or creator of the world. Theology in its doctrine of creation takes us beyond the events of the process of world-history altogether to something which is in a fundamental sense their origin, because it directs the whole and explains it in terms of a value realized in its end.

Imagine a race of intelligent beings who are excellent craftsmen but are tone-deaf and have never heard of music. Imagine further, that in some way they find a musical instrument and examine its constitution and method of manufacture. They might understand it well enough to be able to make a duplicate for themselves. But they would still be no nearer to understanding what was the real origin and purpose of the instrument. If the world has any purpose or final cause, Darwin may still need Genesis to help him in his account of origins.

But, it may be said, the analogy is not a fair one. A musical instrument, as for example a piano, is a mere instrument : it exists for a purpose outside itself. The music is not in the piano, although without the piano the music cannot be played. The non-musical people, therefore, whom we have been imagining never get into contact with the music at all, and are studying a quite different

object, the piano. On the other hand, the theologian and
the scientific expert, in so far as each is concerned with the
world of nature, are both studying the same object, though
perhaps with different interests and from different points
of view.

If this is a valid objection, it can easily be met by a
slight change in our myth. Let us suppose that our non-
musical people were made sufficiently familiar with music
to analyse the physical characteristics of the sound, and
the method by which it was produced, while still remaining quite untouched by its æsthetic quality. They might
then learn everything about the music except the reason
or end of its composition. And in that case they would
be as little able as ever really to explain its origin.

3. TWO HUMAN ANALOGIES FOR CREATION

There are, it seems, two main types of human analogy
which theology can use to help our minds to think truly
of the relation of God to his created world. There is,
first, the analogy of the maker of instruments or machines,
the craftsman or mechanic ; and there is secondly the
analogy of the creative artist. We must remind ourselves
once more of the limitations under which we use such
analogies. We must not be taken to suggest that God
is *like* a craftsman or an artist. That would be to fall
into the error of anthropomorphism. Our intention is to
proceed on the hypothesis that, because man is made in
God's image, man's relation to that which he makes is
grounded in and points towards the relation of God to
his creatures. At the same time we remember that man,
because he is a creature, can have no experience nor any
adequate conception of that absolute creation which is
properly divine.

Now we may notice at once that it is the work of the
creative artist which must give us relatively the fuller
analogy of the two. The reason is that the work of the
artist necessarily includes in some degree the work of the
craftsman, whereas the converse does not hold. No artist
can be an artist without being to some extent a craftsman

also, whereas the craftsman, if we understand by that word the maker and manipulator of instruments, need not necessarily be an artist at all.   It must have been an artist in music who first invented a musical instrument.   Afterwards, no doubt, musicians and composers use instruments which they have no skill to make.   But still the composer remains a craftsman in musical technique.   The æsthetic imagination which is the creative artist's peculiar gift is not by itself enough for artistic creation.   We all recognize that some great artists excel in sheer force and originality of imagination, and others in technical skill.   But without having something of both a man could not be an artist at all.   On the other hand a skilful maker and manipulator of instruments or machinery need not necessarily have any æsthetic gift.

It has been a defect at least in the more popular theology of the Jewish-Christian tradition that in interpreting its doctrine of divine creation, it has attended too exclusively to the analogy of the craftsman and neglected that of the creative artist.

4.   THE ANALOGY OF THE CRAFTSMAN :   ITS DEFECTS AND
VALUE

It is not unnatural that some analogy of craftsmanship should be the first which occurs to the mind of man when he contemplates the marvels of the world he lives in and regards them as the work of the divine creator.   In the book of Job, for instance, it is the utterly astounding skill of God's handiwork, rather than any æsthetic value or moral purpose in it, which has evidently impressed itself upon the author's mind.   Modern craftsmanship consists largely in the making of machinery.   And nature revealed itself both to the scientific and to the theological inquirers of the eighteenth and nineteenth centuries as a vast working mechanism.   In some ways man finds himself in a position not unlike that of the unmusical people we were imagining just now, who could appreciate the skilful mechanism of the piano, but not the value of the end which it was de-signed to serve.   Some scientific experts, indeed, recognizing their inability to answer the question why the wonderfully intricate order of nature should be such as they find it to be, have used this ignorance as an argument against the belief that it proceeds from any designing or purposive intelligence at all. But the religious man, who prefers the hypothesis that the order is designed to realize an end, the value of which he can only in very small part appreciate, would seem to have at least as good reason to show for his alternative. Yet so long as he allows his theology of creation to be confined by the analogy of the machine-maker, it will be gravely defective, and that especially at two points :

(a) If we think of nature in its relation to God after the analogy of an elaborate and skilfully constructed machine, we naturally suppose it to be finished and complete at the first moment when it begins to work, and we may conceive it thereafter to work by itself, save for occasional interventions on the part of its maker. Thus a clock or watch, if we may borrow one of Paley's celebrated illustrations, is finished before it begins to go, and then it goes automatically, except for occasional interventions which are needed for purposes of winding or of repair. But in its theological application this way of thinking tends inevitably towards a false kind of supernaturalism. For it is a false supernaturalism which would teach that God's activity in the created world is to be looked for mainly in occasional acts which are to be conceived of as interventions from without into its ordered working. It is precisely because Protestant orthodoxy at least was tending to a supernaturalism of this kind, that the physicists and biologists of the last century found it so easy to rest in a philosophy which regarded nature as a simply automatic mechanism, and saw no need for divine activity at all.

(b) Again, the craftsman and mechanic make instruments, things for use, intended to serve a purpose outside themselves. And in the case of instruments but little of the soul of the maker is expressed in what he makes. Not much of the watchmaker's individuality can be expressed in the products of his labour. And modern machinery has greatly diminished what chance of self-expression the craftsman once enjoyed. It is therefore no matter for surprise if a science, which has studied the constitution of the world as though it were an instrumental mechanism, should find but little of the creator's mind expressed in it. It is indeed to be expected that such a science should be able to characterize that mind only as that of a mathematician. The conclusion only proves that a student wholly interested in pianos or in sound-waves may forget the music.

Nevertheless in the relation of man to his instruments and machines there is something which does really inter- pret the relation of the divine creator to his world.   Man has been inspired to make machines because he finds in nature a working mechanism which has been made.   And as the purpose of an instrumental machine lies outside the actual constitution and movement of the machine itself, so the ultimate end of this created world lies outside all those uniformities of ordered change and movement which constitute its own actual being. Perhaps the deepest truth which this analogy has to teach us about divine creation is that this world of our present experience, with all that it may reveal to us of God, remains nevertheless *instrumental* to his ultimate purpose in creation. It is designed to achieve an end beyond itself, which, so long as we are in this world, we cannot fully appreciate or apprehend.   At present we ourselves are instruments in the great craftsman's hand.   What he is doing with us we cannot fully know.   Yet we can know that we are instru- ments adapted to some great use of which, however dimly, we may guess the nature, and so ourselves co-operate towards God's end.   Therefore we are not instruments merely ; and so the analogy breaks down.   But still it has its partial and characteristic truth, which in regard to human life has never received a more profound expression than in Browning's poem *Rabbi ben Ezra*.

5. THE TWOFOLD VALUE OF CREATIVE ART

We have a different set of ideas in our minds, if we take as an analogy for divine creation the work, not of an inventive craftsman or mechanic, but of a creative artist.

The work of art exists not for use but for admiration. Its value, that is to say, is in itself ; it is not instrumental to an ulterior end. Further reflection seems to show that this inherent value of the work of art is essentially twofold. It consists partly in what the work of art directly *reveals*, partly in what it indirectly *expresses*.

This distinction requires explanation. First let us consider what is meant by the revealing character of the work of art. The creative artist works primarily in order to see, hear, or perceive more clearly the æsthetic values which are latent in the world of common experience, but become patent only when his own hand, directed by his imaginative insight, has fashioned a fresh object to embody them. In this sense the artist's primary aim is revelation. The painter works that he may see, the composer that he may hear, the poet that he may perceive with perhaps a more inward sense. Before the artist has actually set himself to fashion something, he apprehends, as a rule, but dimly what the finished work will display. As the work proceeds, the vision becomes clearer ; often the work itself seems to take charge of him, and to demand some alteration of his original design.[1] But when the work is complete, it reveals to him what all the while he had been striving to see clearly. Having once seen it, the true artist will very likely lose interest in that particular work, and proceed to another. But what the great artist has revealed once for all to himself, his finished work continues to reveal to others also. And it remains to those others a source of joy and wonder which does not grow old.

But, secondly, the great work of art not only reveals, it also expresses. It expresses, that is to say, the qualities and the genius of the artist himself. Probably the greatest artists do not work in order to express themselves. Their interest is mainly in the perception of values outside their own personalities. Hence their self-expression is indirect. But none the less they stamp their own characters upon their art. True, Shakspere is so intensely interested in

[1] G. K. Chesterton somewhere wrote of Watts that he went on painting because of the word of truth and meekness and righteousness, and *his right hand taught him terrible things.*

the human world which he observes, that his plays give us little direct indication of his own personal views or judgements. He infuses such personal vitality into the very varied characters he creates, that they give a strange effect of impersonality in their creator. In this respect Shaksperian characters are the exact opposite of those puppets of the modern stage which appear to be mere mouthpieces of the dramatist's complicated dissatisfaction with the world he lives in. Yet none can doubt that only a mind of the deepest insight and sympathy could have produced Shakspere's plays. Shakspere's personality remains a baffling mystery just because the expression of it in his art is at once so indirect and so profound.

Because art is in this way essentially expressive, every great work of art has a certain individuality and relative perfection, so that it cannot be reproduced with improvements by later hands. It is in this respect that artistic creation differs most obviously from mechanical invention. There are flaws in Botticelli's drawing; but no more skilful draughtsman of later days could really improve one of Botticelli's Madonnas in copying it. On the other hand, Stephenson's locomotive, the Rocket, has been improved upon by subsequent generations of engineers in a way which might leave Stephenson himself speechless with admiration. We cannot to-day reproduce the excellence of much ancient art, though we could easily reproduce ancient machinery if we cared to waste our time in doing so. Leonardo da Vinci painted " The Last Supper ". He also invented the wheelbarrow. " The Last Supper " is badly damaged, and nothing can restore or replace it. Wheelbarrows, no doubt, with some improvement on Leonardo's original design, are turned out by the million and used everywhere. But it is not in them that Leonardo's soul still lingers.

6. THEOLOGICAL APPLICATION OF THE ANALOGY FROM ART

Let us pass on to the theological application of our analogy, remembering the double value of art both as revelation and as expression. The true artist, we sug-

gested, works primarily in order to see or perceive clearly.
" God saw all that he had made," wrote the author of
Genesis, " and, behold, it was very good." Dare we
emphasize the parallel ? In one way, no doubt, we dare
not. We must not attribute to God the longing and the
sense of need which drive man to fashion out of the world
on which his life depends something which may more
nearly satisfy his æsthetic soul. God creates, not to supply
his own need out of what is beyond himself, but rather
from pure love of creation and out of the riches of his
own eternal being. Every human analogy at this point
inevitably breaks down. Yet something in the artist's
essential aim and motive may bear the true image of the
divine. We may at least believe that there is a joy for
God in the contemplation of the beauty of his own works.
Their value is in themselves ; and in the recognition of
the value is the only answer to the question why they
were made. Again, we said that what the creative artist
has revealed to himself, he reveals at least in some degree
to others also ; for others also have the artistic capacity
to appreciate what only the artist can create. And if
God has indeed made man in his own image, he has done
so not only that man being pure in heart might be able
to see God, but also so that man according to the tiny
measure of his capacity might see what God sees of beauty
and acknowledge its goodness. Perhaps in every great
achievement of human art some artist has seen more
divinely an aspect of what God has made. And, as Rudyard Kipling has suggested with great discernment, there
may be for all of us something of the same quality of
creative joy in the love we have for deeply familiar places
which we see for that reason with a truly original insight.

> God gave all men all earth to love,
>   But, since man's heart is small,
> Ordained for each one spot should prove
>   Belovèd over all ;
> That, as he watched creation's birth,
>   So we, in god-like mood,
> Might of our love create our earth
>   And see that it is good.[1]

---

[1] Rudyard Kipling : *Sussex*.

The second point we noticed was that the work of art expresses the soul of the artist.   When we are thinking of God, there is no longer any distinction possible between what his work reveals or displays, and what it expresses of his own mind and nature.   For what God creates, he does not make out of any material which he finds existing outside or beyond himself.   All things depend for their being on him, the creator of all.   And, since he creates out of the infinite resources of his own being, all things in various manners and degrees of perfection express him.   It is thus that the artistic analogy leads us towards a conception of divine immanence which the analogy of the craftsman or machine-maker could not suggest.

And at this point the difference which we noticed between the self-expression of Shakspere and that of some modern dramatists may have a theological value.   Shakspere at first sight seems not to be expressing himself at all, and his own personality remains an enigma.   The moderns, on the other hand, seem to be doing little else than express themselves, and we are left in no doubt as to what they think and feel.   But the truth is that Shakspere's greatness manifests itself in the self-repression which allows his characters and situations, as it were, to speak for themselves uninterrupted by his own personal comments.   His creative mind is immanent in them all, and we can only reach its own essential thought and feeling by a deeper appreciation of the meaning and value of the drama as a whole.   In the modern play, on the other hand, the dramatist's comment on life is obvious, and the situations and dialogue give an impression of having been specially constructed to convey it.   In such cases the author's mind is less truly immanent in the play as a whole, and seems rather to mar its dramatic quality by continual interruption from outside.   Perhaps such an illustration may help us a little way towards understanding how it is that a world which we affirm to be in all its points an expression of the divine mind should nevertheless often seem to a superficial view entirely to conceal it.   It is true to say that God is expressed in the parts ; yet it is truer to say that he is expressed only in the whole.   And it is precisely the final wholeness of creation that we cannot see. It is for that reason that we are so often obliged to think of ourselves as but instruments in God's hands designed by him to serve a purpose as yet unrealized. Yet the analogy of the instrument, right and true as it is up to a point, can never give us the whole truth of the relation in which we and the world of created being stand towards our creator. Moreover, Christians believe that in Jesus Christ God's whole purpose for mankind stands once for all revealed and accomplished. And God's Spirit through Christ dwells in our hearts. God's self-expression in his works is infinitely more mysterious than Shakspere's. Yet by his living Spirit he is infinitely nearer than Shakspere to our souls.

7. THE VALUE OF TIME IN CREATION

Again, the analogy derived from art helps us to a fuller understanding of the function of time in God's creation. If we think of the world of nature as a vast machine, we naturally suppose it to be completed from the first moment when it begins to work. It is thus that we explain the order and reciprocal adaptation of all its various parts and members. To conceive of nature as of a machine in the making, which does not as yet work at all, would explain nothing. No doubt when a machine is finished, it still needs time to work and to produce the results for which it was designed. But, generally speaking, the less the time needed, the better the machinery. In the working of a machine time means just delay, and the object of the maker is to speed up the machinery until the desired result is produced as nearly instantaneously as possible. And therefore, as soon as we regard nature as a divinely constructed mechanism, we inevitably ask, why does it take so long in producing its results ? Why do the mills of God grind so slowly ? Is it because the creator has to learn and acquire skill as his work proceeds ? Does he have to wait to improve the anthropoid into man, for the same sort of reason that man himself must wait to improve the Rocket into the modern railway-engine ? Such an hypothesis of course destroys the very notion of God altogether.

But the analogy drawn from art enables us to see further. The value of the work of art is in itself, not in an ulterior result which its working produces. And human works of art not only take time to produce, but also require time as an essential condition or constituent of their completed beauty. Drama and symphony are fashioned out of the stuff of time, and could not exist apart from it. A master-piece of architecture is built *in* time rather than *on* it. Yet a great medieval cathedral derives its essential grandeur from the historical developments and changes which have expressed themselves in its stone. If then we regard nature and even man himself as being in some sense a work of God's art, can we not see more clearly that development through time may be essential to the goodness of the creation ? Even primitive forms of life, now extinct, may have value, not merely as means to the production of higher and later forms, but also as very subordinate con-stituents in the beauty and meaning of the whole as it appears to God. The gradualness of creation need not be a necessity laid upon God by an intractable material which he could not immediately master. It may belong to the perfection of his method in achieving his purpose. It may be necessary to that purpose that the earth should bear fruit of itself, first the blade, then the ear, then the full corn in the ear, and finally the harvest. Without the gradualness of the process, the perfection of the final whole would not be attained.

If this be so, we must affirm that God's creative work is continuous through time and, from our point of view in time, is not yet complete. According to the record of the Fourth Gospel, such in fact was our Lord's own teaching. We there read that the Jews persecuted Jesus, because he had healed a cripple and made him carry his bed on the sabbath day. " But Jesus answered them, ' My Father worketh hitherto, and I work.' " In other words, there can be no sabbath-rest for God, while evil remains to be overcome, and perfec-tion still to be achieved. The six days' labour of creation spoken of by the author of Genesis is still unfinished.

Yet in one sense the work of creation is complete in the ascension of Christ. There is a great difference between the Jewish Sabbath and the Christian Sunday if we consider both as symbols. Prophetically the book of Genesis affirmed God's rest on the seventh day when creation was finished, and prophetically the Jews kept sabbath on the last day of every week. But the first day of the week has always been the holy day of the Christian Church. Why ? Historically, no doubt, because on that day Christ rose from the dead ; but that is not the whole reason. In Christ as the first-fruits, to use Pauline language, manhood became perfectly what God intended it to be, and in so doing it rose from the dead and passed behind the veil which hides the eternal from the temporal world. Henceforth, therefore, the Christian is not one who only strives on and on, looking for a distant goal, a rest at the end of the working week. No doubt such striving and pilgrimage still constitute one aspect of his life. He cannot forget that " the whole creation ", and his own natural manhood as part of it, " groans and travails in pain together until now ", or, as the modern poet writes :

> To get the whole world out of bed,
> And washed and dressed and warmed and fed,
> To work, and back to bed again,
> Believe me, Saul, costs world of pain.[1]

The Christian knows it, and therefore, like the Jew of old, he still looks for the life of the world to come. But his faith has another dimension also. He looks back on the perfection once for all achieved in Jesus, and up to the already glorified manhood in heaven. Whither his Lord is gone, he knows the way. And therefore Sunday has ceased to be for him the symbol only or mainly of an everlasting day of rest which will dawn when work is over— that endless sabbath the prospect of which used to frighten Victorian children hardly less than its alternative. Sunday to the Christian is the symbol of creation perfected in the victory of Christ. In Christ, God's whole work of creation and redemption is complete ; yet in Christ's members, still living in this world, it remains to be achieved.

[1] John Masefield : *The Everlasting Mercy.*

CHAPTER VI

THE FATHERHOOD OF THE CREATOR

IT MAY be said that in considering human analogies to help our thought about the divine Creator we have so far still neglected the nearest analogy which our experience affords. We have made mention only of man's creative work in the realms of matter and imaginative fiction. But if we ask what within our experience is the most effective force in fashioning personality, we must answer that it is the influence of other personalities, and that the most truly creative influence is that which is directed by love. It is such influence from parent, teacher and friend which really makes the character of a man. We are anything but ready-made personalities from the moment of birth. It is our environment, above all the environment of other souls, which draws out of every man what he is capable of becoming; and it is largely in proportion to the love he finds in that environment that a man will realize his capacities of spiritual growth. In every moment of our mutual converse we are in a very real way creating one another.

1. THE CREATIVE QUALITY OF LOVE

If, then, we are to think of God as the true creator of souls, we shall naturally follow the author of the Book of Wisdom and think of him also as their lover. The human love whereby in social life we make each other must have its source in God's love, which is the creative environment of us all. And love enables us to conceive a form of creation in which the very nature of the creator can go forth into the creature, in such a way that the creature itself can share the creator's work. For, in proportion as another's love creates a soul, it communicates to it its own living essence. The parent's love makes the child's character only by itself passing into the child and being, as it were, born again in him. And if in truth God's love creates us, we can then without any assertion of independence for ourselves lay claim to some share in the creative activity which is derived from him alone as its source.

No doubt there is profound truth in the thought just indicated; but the truth needs guarded expression. When we speak of the relation of the human artist or craftsman to what he makes, we are speaking of his relation to something which belongs to a lower order of reality than himself. On the other hand, when we speak of the love of human parent for child or of friend for friend, we are speaking of a relation between two beings of the same nature and order of reality. And the creative power of this love seems to depend on such equality or identity of nature; for it presupposes a capacity in the object of love for loving response. But man is not of the same nature as God. It is no doubt for this reason that orthodox theology has hesitated to use the analogy of parental love as an aid to understanding the significance of divine creation. The Creed speaks of the only-begotten Son of God, of one nature and substance with the Father, who because he is begotten is not created. The created children of God are of a quite inferior order of being to the only-begotten Son: they are children not by nature but by grace. The dependence of the creature on the creator is of a quite different kind from the dependence of the son on the father. It seems then that we cannot find in the creative influence of man's love on man an analogy for the creative power of God's love on his creatures.

But again this negative conclusion only yields a half-truth. Man is unique among creatures in being made in God's image, and through God's grace in Jesus Christ he is capable of receiving a true sonship, so that Christ himself can be called in a figure the first-born among many brethren. Christ's manhood is itself created, and as man Jesus Christ is himself inferior in nature to the Father. Yet he became human that we might become divine; and the Christian who in Christ has been begotten again

as a child of God is no longer a mere creature and nothing
more. Moreover, this rebirth is only possible because
man was originally made in God's image. That is to
say, man had from the beginning in virtue of his own
nature an inherent capacity for being united with the
only-begotten Son and for becoming through that union
divine, as the limb of a material body is human through
being the organ of the mind or spirit of a man. It is
this inherent capacity of man, not destroyed by sin,
which is made an actuality through the incarnation and
the atonement.

We can therefore hardly be wrong in saying that natural
human love at its best is the clearest mark of the divine
image in man, and the sign of his capacity for a status
higher than that of a mere creature. And though the
analogy drawn from love as a relation between man and
man is defective when applied to the relation between
man and God, inasmuch as it ignores the gulf between
creature and creator, yet we shall rightly expect to learn
from it something of the divine creator's relation to the
human creatures which bear his image.

We will inquire, therefore, more precisely what we may
learn from it. In so doing we pass inevitably from the
thought of God as creator to that of God as Father. It
is true that the concepts of father and creator are in our
minds quite distinct, and, as applied to a man, they are
to some extent incompatible with one another. The
human father is only in a limited and partial sense the
creator of his child ; just as the human creator is only in
a limited and partial sense the parent of what he makes.
But if both fatherhood and creatorship in man are themselves dim and partial reflexions of the transcendent
reality of God, it is not absurd to suppose that God can
fashion a creature capable of a filial as well as a merely
creaturely response to his will. That this supposition is
indeed the truth is what Christian faith and experience
affirm. And it argues want of reason as well of faith to
pronounce the Christian experience an illusion, because
the intellect cannot find concepts which adequately express
its content or remove its mystery.

2. THE DISTINCTION BETWEEN AGAPE AND EROS

The Swedish theologian, Professor Anders Nygren, has recently helped us to see how we may think of God's love as that of one who is both Creator and Father. In his book, *Agape and Eros*, he calls fresh attention to the difference in meaning between the two Greek words which we translate by the same English word " love ". *Eros* and *agape*, he argues, are respectively the dominant ideas which characterize two great types of religion. Eros-religion is the product of the Hellenic mind at its best. Plato and Aristotle, and perhaps Plotinus also, are its great exponents, and Plato the greatest of all. Agape-religion is pure Christianity. In the theology of the Church elements of agape and eros have been intermingled and confused with one another, even in the concept of *caritas*. But in their proper and essential meaning the two terms remain radically opposed to one another ; and Christianity has not been enriched, but rather adulterated, by the admixture of an eros-religion derived from an alien source.

The contrast thus drawn between eros and agape is not only of great importance in itself, but also very relevant to our present subject. Its essential point is this, that while eros is man's way to God, starting from man's sense of spiritual need, agape is God's way to man, starting from God's free goodwill. According to Nygren agape is essentially creative.

This [he writes] is the deepest reason for the spontaneous and uncaused character of God's love. The love of which we are thinking is God's love, and God is the creator. It is not that God loves that which is in itself worthy to be loved ; but, on the contrary, that which in itself is without value acquires value by the fact that it is the object of God's love. Agape is the direct opposite of that love which is called out by the worthiness of its object and so may be said to be a recognition of the value and attractiveness of its object. The man whom God loves has not any value in himself. His value consists simply in the fact that God loves him.[1]

---

[1] *Agape and Eros*, p. 54.

As thus stated, the opposition of eros to agape seems open to criticism. To say that that which is in itself without value acquires value by the fact that God loves it, suggests that we can at least conceive it to have existed before God loved it, and in that condition to have been entirely without value, although created by God. This is probably not what Nygren means to say. He means that God's love for the creature both created it and gave it value as by a single act. But in that case he ought not to have said that the creature as it is in itself is value-less. For it is impossible to distinguish even in thought between a thing as it is in itself and a thing as God created it, except perhaps in so far as the thing has been corrupted by evil since its creation. Nothing can be itself at all apart from its relation to God ; and it is this same relation which gives it both existence and value. We must not make a separation either between the existence and the value of the creature, or between the creative activity of God which gave the one and his love which gave the other. It is in man as he is in himself that we must look for the value which God's love has given him.

We must therefore restate Professor Nygren's antithesis. And we shall find its primary ground, not in the simple opposition of God's love to man's, but rather in an opposition between two kinds of love in man, one of which reveals God's love more directly than the other and affords an indication of a love in God in which the perfections of creative power and fatherhood are one. The words eros and agape may very aptly stand for these two kinds of love ; and we may also cordially agree with Nygren that Christ alone has revealed to us the true meaning of the difference between them. Agape in its Christian usage is in effect a new term coined to represent a fresh idea. And it is a defect in language, due to a defect in spiritual insight, which compels us to use only one word in English, where Greek-speaking Christians of old felt the necessity of two.

Eros is essentially the love which springs from desire and the sense of need. In its psychological and biological origins no doubt it is closely connected with sex. But, as Nygren points out, the developed meaning of eros is by no means confined to what is sexual. In Plato and his followers it is sublimated into what is really a new emotion, as spiritual and other-worldly as any human emotion can be. It becomes a hunger and thirst after the beatific vision and after the righteousness and purity of heart which alone can exalt a man to heaven. Yet still it is closely connected with man's sense of his own needs and defects. If eros is called divine, it must be principally because God is its *object*. For in God himself there can be no eros. He can have no sense of need or defect, or desire anything because his own nature lacks it. Thus Aristotle taught that, although God sets the whole world in motion as being the object of its eros, he himself in the eternal enjoyment of his own perfection has no knowledge of the strivings of the imperfect world towards him. Aristotle stops short of any doctrine of creation properly so called. According to him, God exercises influence upon the world not by any action of his own upon it, but only by the desire of the world for the perfection realized in himself.

But there is even within human experience a very partial and rudimentary realization of another kind of love also. It is this which the New Testament has taught us to call by the name of agape, and in its pure form it is essentially divine. Human agape is never without a considerable admixture of eros. But this need not prevent us from recognizing the essential difference between the two even within human relationships themselves. The difference may be shortly stated by saying that whereas in eros desire is the cause of love, in agape love is the cause of desire. I may begin by loving a person because I desire him, because he gives me something I need, because he has some special attraction for me, or because I recognize in him some peculiar quality which stirs my admiration. So far this is eros-love. But, as I get to love him deeply and truly, I find that I love him more and more not simply for my own sake, but for his. And this love of a person for his own sake is really another kind of love. It is not caused by any desire of mine, nor does it seek directly any satisfaction of my desire. Rather it is the cause of a new desire in me, a desire purely for the good of my friend. In such love we begin to have a hint already of the nature of God's love for man.

Now if we look for traces of this agape-love among men at the most simply natural level, it is in the father's love for his child that we shall find them in their clearest form. The love which draws man or woman towards a member of the opposite sex is mainly based in the first instance upon their need of one another. The same is true in a less degree of friendship ; and even the mother has naturally more need of the child than the father, a fact which tends to make the mother's love at once more devoted and more possessive than the father's. The father's love, as a natural phenomenon, is perhaps less intense than any of the others ; but it also has naturally more of the peculiar quality of agape, in that it is less caused by any instinctive need, and is more purely a love of a person for his own sake, which issues naturally in a simple desire for that person's good. And in a special way the father's love illustrates the creative quality of agape. For the father especially loves the child not only for what he is but also for what he can help him to become.[1]

If we could imagine the love of one who loves men purely for their own sake, and not because of any need or desire of his own, purely desires their good, and yet loves them wholly, not for what at this moment they are, but for what he knows he can make of them because he made them, then we should have in our minds some true image of the love of the Father and Creator of mankind.

3.   LOVE IN GOD AND IN MAN

Among the peoples of the world the Jews have always been pre-eminent for the strength of their parental affec-

[1] Perhaps it is because in natural human relationships eros needs to be completed with agape, that the Church has taught that in normal circumstances marriage ought only to be contracted by those who are willing to have children. The coming of children is not of course the only opportunity, but it is the most natural and normal opportunity, for agape to supervene upon eros.

tion. Among them the impulse of sex has been subordinated to the love of offspring in a remarkable degree.
This national or racial characteristic cannot be unconnected with the fact that through them the full revelation
of God's fatherhood has been given to mankind. We
may see here one reason why the Saviour was, according
to the flesh, a Jew. Our Lord's greatest parable of the
divine agape is the story of a natural father's love. For
we miss the whole point of the story of the Prodigal Son,
if we suppose that in it the father acts in any supernatural way. It is indeed remarkable how inevitably
our Lord seems to turn to the parental instinct in order
to express God's disposition towards his people. " O
Jerusalem, Jerusalem, that killeth the prophets and
stoneth them that are sent unto her, how often would
I have gathered thy children together, even as a hen
gathereth her chickens under her wings."

Certainly then we shall not understand as fully as we
may the Christian doctrine of God as creator, unless we
think of the creator also as the father. Aristotle was
profoundly right in attributing eros to the world and
not to God. God does not love from any sense of need
or defect in himself, or because of the perception of any
value in another. But Aristotle was wrong in concluding
that therefore God cannot love his imperfect world at all.
Perhaps because he was a Greek and not a Jew, he missed
the obscure hint which exists, even within human relationships, of a love which is not caused by any desire to have
something that it now lacks, nor by any recognition of
value or merit in another, but is simply the spontaneous
outflowing of goodwill causing the desire that another
should enjoy all good. This absolutely uncaused love in
God is, as the Christian believes, the ultimate *raison
d'être* both of man's existence and of every true value
which his life possesses. It is the same love which by
the cross of redemption brings to fulfilment in spite of
sin the original purpose of creation. And man the creature
can recognize and cling to its divine grace and power,
because in his own nature its creative work has left traces,
never entirely effaced, which make him capable of such

response. If Christians alone can address God as Abba, Father, in the true and full meaning of the word, nevertheless the fullness of that meaning itself involves the faith that all men can recognize and accept the gospel of God's fatherhood in Christ as the saving truth.

We must still, however, acknowledge a final difficulty of understanding. Agape, it has been suggested, is the highest and divinest love, and in human nature are found the traces of it which enable us to recognize it as divine. In itself it is God's love for man. But what of man's love for God? Is not this the highest of which man is capable? And yet must it not be essentially eros, since it cannot but arise out of man's need for God? Man cannot will God's good, nor reciprocate towards God the agape which he receives. And then, if so, does it not follow that man's love for God is self-regarding, inasmuch as it arises from man's sense of his own need for God?

We must, I think, say that the highest love of which man is capable strictly as a creature is the eros for God, and that this eros at every stage short of complete fulfilment is in a manner self-regarding. For man's very self-abasement before God still makes him think of his own unworthiness and imperfection, even while he longs to lose himself in adoration of God. It is precisely the deepening sense of this tension which makes the religious man cry out for an atonement. Nevertheless, the absolutely highest thing in man does not belong to him simply as a creature, but as the bearer of God's image which gives him the capacity for rising above what is strictly the creature's level. That highest thing is not man's love for God, but divine love in man, the image of that love which in Christ communicated itself to man up to the utmost capacity of human nature to partake of it. "Herein is agape, not that we loved God, but that God loved us." Man cannot directly reciprocate that love to God. Only Christ the Eternal Son can love the Father with the Father's own love, and we in Christ can only realize and understand our own incapacity to do the same. But we can manifest God's agape within us towards one another. "We know that we have passed from death into life, because we love the brethren." And we can forgive one another as God in Christ forgave us.[1]

Nevertheless, we may say that in the fulfilment of heaven eros is swallowed up in agape. For in the self-surrender of complete thanksgiving (and thanksgiving is man's proper recognition of God)[2] man's concern with his own needs and defects vanishes away. He no longer needs anything when he has finally given himself to the giver of all. All things are his, when he is God's.

[1] For Caietan's different solution of this problem, see Newton Flew, *The Idea of Perfection*, p. 239.

[2] See Rom. i. 21.

CHAPTER VII

DIVINE OMNIPOTENCE

TRADITIONAL DISCUSSIONS of divine omnipotence suffer from the assumption that the difficulty of the doctrine lies in the meaning of " omni- " and not in the meaning of " -potence ". St. Thomas Aquinas explicitly starts from this assumption : [1] " All confess," he writes, " that God is omnipotent ; but it seems difficult to explain in what his omnipotence consists, for there may be a doubt as to the precise meaning of the word ' all ', when we say that God can do all things."

1. THE MEANING OF " POWER "

St. Thomas next proceeds to argue that omnipotence can only operate within the sphere of things that are in themselves possible. Some things are possible in themselves, but impossible for creatures of limited power. These things man cannot do, but God can. But there are other things which are impossible in themselves, because the very idea of them involves self-contradiction —as, for instance, the making of a square circle, or the

[1] *S.T.*, Pt. I, Q. 25, Art. 3. One of the objections, which St· Thomas himself states, argues that, since God has made the wisdom of this world foolish by showing those things to be possible which the world judges impossible, therefore human ideas of what is intrinsically possible are no valid criterion of what God can or cannot do. He does not however state or meet the opposite form of the same objection (which is far more damaging to his own doctrine) that, since we do not know what is and what is not intrinsically possible, many things may be really impossible for God which we judge to be possible. St. Thomas might no doubt meet this difficulty by appealing to the authority of God's own word in the gospel ; but it is sufficient at least to show that his doctrine of divine omnipotence, as a truth of natural theology, is worth very little.

creation of a being with freedom of choice who is unable to choose wrong. Such things even God cannot do; though it might be truer to say that they cannot be done, than that God cannot do them, since the impossibility implies no real restriction of God's power. According to St. Thomas, therefore, the doctrine of divine omnipotence means that God can do everything which is intrinsically possible.

But St. Thomas has not stated the real problem, and therefore his solution is worth little. It is evident that with our imperfect knowledge we are unable to say, except within very narrow limits, what is and what is not intrinsically possible, and which of our highest hopes may turn out to involve self-contradiction. It would therefore be no logical contradiction of St. Thomas's doctrine of divine omnipotence to say that the promises of the gospel are incapable of fulfilment.

The truth is that the value of the doctrine of divine omnipotence lies, not in enabling us to maintain that in some sense God can do everything possible, but in assuring us that certain things are possible for God to do, that the eternal salvation of men and the final victory of good over evil are not idle dreams. In other words, what we need to know is not in what abstract sense God can do everything, but what is the actual nature and effect of God's power. It is really idle to talk about power at all except in relation to the concrete nature of a thing or person who is powerful. The word " power " by itself conveys no definite idea whatever to the mind. We must discuss the character and quality of God's power before the doctrine of his omnipotence can become really significant.

Let us then make a fresh start by examining the meaning of the word " power ". There seem to be three principal meanings which the word can bear:

(1) It may mean only *capacity* or potentiality, δύναμις in the Aristotelian sense. Thus we may say that heat has the power of melting ice, or that ice has the power of being melted under heat. In this sense power is as much passive as active, and an omnipotent being would be one which is omnicapable, i.e., capable of every kind of action,

passion, motion and change. This definition sounds less
applicable to God than to primary matter as Aristotle
conceived it, a being purely indeterminate which might
be the subject of all possible determinations. Certainly a
human character which is as yet unformed and immature
may be said to have a greater variety of capacities or
potentialities than one which is already stable. But
clearly such multipotence, if we may coin the word, would
be a sign of weakness, not of strength. And we may at
least follow St. Thomas Aquinas in excluding this sense
of the word power from anything we mean when we
speak of the omnipotence of God. There would have been
no need to mention it at all, if the traditional theology
of the Western Church had not translated the Greek word
παντοκράτωρ by the Latin *omnipotens*. It is the ambiguity
lurking under the Latin word *potentia* (corresponding in
this respect to the Greek δύναμις), which has led to the
ridiculous notion that " an omnipotent God " ought
somehow to mean a God who is capable of being or doing
any conceivable thing. No sane theology ever intended
to affirm anything of the kind.

(2) In a second sense, the word " power " is equivalent
to " physical force ", as when we speak of " horse-power ".
Exact scientific definitions of force are apt to be unintelligible to the layman, but we know at least roughly
what we ordinarily mean when we use the word. We
mean the impulse to motion, or the restraint of motion,
in material bodies ; and we usually measure the amount of
force by the amount of change produced in relation to the
resistance encountered. To talk about an almighty or
omnipotent force would be nonsense. For force by itself
cannot control anything at all, nor does it even *act* in the
proper meaning of that word. A volcanic eruption produces certain conspicuous changes in material bodies, but
it cannot be said to control the effects of which it is the
cause, and in the interaction of material bodies the distinction between action and passivity is always relative
and to some extent arbitrary. Therefore force is from
one point of view essentially powerless, until it is directed
by some power other than itself.

(3) In the third sense, " power " means power to control or the ability to achieve purpose. Clearly this is the meaning which we mainly intend when we speak of the power or might of either man or God. Almightiness or omnipotence is then the attribute of one who can make all things serve his will or achieve his purpose in all things. What he does is necessarily determined or, if you will, limited by what he purposes or wills to do. A power which may do anything whatever, or a mere force which nothing can resist, is by definition purposeless, and therefore impotent. By affirming belief in an almighty being we must mean to assert that there is a purposive will controlling all events or phenomena, and able in the end to subdue all things unto itself. Can we further determine the nature or character which must be attributed to this purposive will, if our belief in its existence is to be at least intelligible ?

2. POWER AND CREATIVITY

We may, I think, say at once that the almighty will must be creative and not destructive. The purpose of the almighty must control the world so as to make something out of it, something which has positive value in his sight. To control the world so as merely in the end to destroy it, or make nothing of it, could fulfil no intelligible purpose whatever : such an end would be a confession of failure which cannot be attributed to almightiness. Many things in the world may no doubt be destined for destruction, at least in respect of their own proper existence, in order that the almighty purpose may fulfil itself by this means. Christians indeed have usually held that this whole world of our present experience in space and time is ephemeral and must pass away with all that is within it. But to suppose that it must all be simply destroyed, so as to end in nothing and to produce nothing of enduring value out of its transience, would be to contradict the belief that an almighty power controls it. If power be essentially purposive, creative power is inherently greater than destructive. Almighty power has a positive end in what it does. And, if in the long run evil is inherently destructive and good creative, it will follow that the purpose of the almighty will must be a purpose of goodness.

3.　POWER AND FORCE

With this conclusion in mind, let us next examine more closely the relations which we find in our experience to exist between the power of creative and purposive control and that other kind of power which we call force. So long as our own purposive control is being exercised over material things, we find that it must work by using force ; yet the real power displayed is not in the force itself, but in the intelligent direction of it. The wonderful power which we acknowledge in the building of Durham Cathedral consisted not in the mere force which heaved vast masses of stone to great heights from the ground, but in the purposive intelligence which used force to shape and to move them into certain positions in which they form a structure of transcendent beauty. And when we come to consider the power which men as intelligent and moral beings exercise over one another, we find that the usefulness of force or physical compulsion is much more restricted. Those whose power over human minds has been strongest and most creative have in general tended to dispense with force altogether. Most of the great personalities whose influence over character and culture has been deepest have been wholly men of peace. No doubt in statesmanship and sometimes in the founding of a new religion, such as Islam, force has had its part to play. But in general we find that the effect of force in controlling human personalities is negative, and that to be obliged to resort to it is a sign, not of strength, but of weakness. We can, it is true, prevent each other by force from doing what otherwise would be done ; we can shut men up in prison, or take away their lives, and so prevent them from doing anything more at all. We can also often induce them to do what otherwise they would not have done by making them afraid of the force they may suffer if they do not. Nevertheless, it is not the strong government which has to declare martial law and call out the military to keep order. It is when the authorities of a state are weak and society begins to be really afraid of its criminals, that judges use force more drastically, and sentences of death or flogging become frequent. Moreover, history provides interesting evidence of the comparative impotence of force in human affairs. We do not yet know, it is true, what will be the ultimate effect of the great communist revolution in Russia; but on the whole the great conquerors and revolutionaries have produced far less change in human culture and civilization than the prophets, saints, sages, and the pioneers of science, even though the discoveries of the latter have often been used by lesser men for the manufacture of weapons of destruction. It is interesting to reflect that you and I have only heard of Nebuchadnezzar because the despised and outcast Jeremiah has immortalized him.

It is true, no doubt, on the other hand, that modern experts in biology and surgery hold out to us the prospect of a complete remaking of human character by forcible or mechanical means. It would be foolish indeed to ignore the possibilities of change thus indicated. But on examination it would seem that the most which even the most wisely scientific use of force can achieve is the removal of certain material hindrances which now stand in the way of mental and moral development. No manipulation of man's bodily organism, however drastic or skilful, can of itself supply the creative or educative power which fashions the soul of man into the true greatness of which it is capable.

4. THE OMNIPOTENCE OF LOVE

The more deeply we consider the matter, the more surely we shall come to rest in the conclusion that love, understood in the meaning which the New Testament gives to the word agape, is the greatest creative power in human life. And if we may suppose that, as Christians believe, agape is the clearest reflection in the created world of the divine will which directs it towards its end, we gain a quite fresh understanding of what almightiness may mean, and a fresh assurance that the Christian belief in the omnipotence of God is no extravagant dream, but a profoundly reasonable faith.

The justification of this statement is really the task of Christian theology as a whole, and it should appear more plainly as our discussions proceed. But we may notice at once one or two general considerations which are immediately relevant to the arguments about the nature of power just put forward.

One difficulty popularly urged against the Christian faith takes the form of a dilemma, that we might perhaps believe either in a God who is perfect love and goodness or in a God who is omnipotent, but that to believe in a God who is both is impossible. This dilemma rests on a radically false conception alike of God's love and of God's power and of the relation between them. The unreflecting mind tends to identify love simply with a tender emotion, and power with the use of force. It then pictures to itself a loving and almighty God as one whose love would use gentle methods so long as there remained any hope of their success, but whose power would be held in reserve to intervene with decisive force as soon as gentleness had proved finally to be ineffective. Thus God is naïvely imagined after the analogy of a schoolmaster who keeps a rod in his cupboard for use in the last resort. When facts seem to make it evident that such an analogy is utterly misleading, it is concluded that God cannot be both loving and almighty.

But the Christian revelation at least shows that a different conclusion is possible. It declares that the strongest power in the world is that of agape itself, which does not work by force to achieve its highest purpose or win its greatest victories. The Cross is the power and the wisdom of God. And if St. Paul speaks truth, our whole conception of God's omnipotence must be transformed. The supreme manifestation of divine power is in no terrific theophany which compels man either to obedience or to destruction, but in the complete self-sacrifice of Christ which has overcome evil by suffering, made atonement for sin, and opened the kingdom of heaven.

And dimly we can see even by the light of reason that such a power has at least possibilities of omnipotence to which no other could conceivably make good a claim. For this power converts even suffering itself into something active and creative, and makes the very forces of evil, even through the apparent completeness of their triumph over it, nevertheless subserve its own purpose of good. Christians for this reason find the chief subject of their praise and thanksgiving in that very event which they also hold to be the blackest crime in human history, viz., the crucifixion. When we consider as symbolic of what God's power can do the presence of dice, scourge, hammer and nails in the east windows of our churches, we begin faintly to apprehend the nature of a power which is indeed almighty, the power which can make of sin and death opportunities for the sacrifice which redeems and conquers.

But one warning we must remember. The omnipotence of God is indemonstrable by any logic, because the power of love can only be truly apprehended from within, or rather by those within whom it already dwells. Selfish people can never understand it ; and most of us have to learn with difficulty to recognize a new sort of power, before we can judge of the truth of God's almightiness as Christian saints have believed it. It is to those who believe, says St. Paul, that the Cross is the power of God. It can be no matter of surprise to a Christian that many even intelligent people should reckon him either a fool or a hypocrite when he says that he believes in God the Father Almighty.

PART II

THE INCARNATION

CHAPTER VIII

THE JEWISH BACKGROUND OF CHRISTOLOGY

UP TILL now we have been dealing in general terms with the main ideas about God which the Christian creed presents to us, without attempting to distinguish within these ideas that element which is derived from God's historical revelation of himself in Jesus Christ. We have in fact said almost nothing about history. The moment, however, we pass to the next words of the Creed, " and in Jesus Christ his only Son our Lord ", history inevitably comes into the foreground of our thoughts. Whatever different views may be held about the truth of the Incarnation, the doctrine of the divinity of Jesus Christ has a definitely historical origin, which the general doctrine of God has not. And, that being so, we must first try to discover as clearly as we can what the doctrine of his divinity meant to those in whose minds it originally took shape, before we can go on to determine what it means or ought to mean to us to-day.

1. THE PRIMARY RELEVANCE OF HISTORY

What are our primary data for such an historical interpretation of what the Creed affirms about Jesus Christ ? The first obvious fact is that all the framers of Christian creeds have believed themselves to be affirming nothing that is not either explicitly asserted, or at least directly implied, in the New Testament. Nowhere among Christians could any doctrine of the person or work of Jesus have been maintained which was acknowledged to be in conflict with the evidence of scripture. The New Testament therefore must be the starting-point of our interpretation. But, in the next place, it is obvious also that the New Testament doctrine of the Christ, however securely it may be based upon fact, is not a mere statement of fact, but is itself a work of theological interpretation. The authors of the New Testament affirmed, and the authors of the Creeds repeated, that Jesus is the Christ, the only Son of God, the Lord of Christians. It may be that all these titles were derived in fact from the lips of Jesus himself; yet still the meaning of these titles, as the first disciples understood them, was not derived from Jesus only, but also in part from the ideas which men had had in their minds about God, Lord, and Christ or Messiah, before Jesus came. In acknowledging a unique relation between Jesus and God, they did not understand this relation to be between Jesus and one who, apart from Jesus, was simply an unknown, an x. On the contrary, the disciples, as soon as they became preachers, assumed that their hearers already shared with them some notions about Godhead, Lordship, and Messiahship, which, though they would have to be radically changed in the light of the new gospel, were at least true enough to be made the starting-point of its interpretation. Therefore, if we would know what the New Testament means by its doctrine of Jesus as Christ, Lord, and Son of God, we must begin by examining the ideas which the titles must have suggested to those who first heard them applied to him.

2.   THE CONTRAST BETWEEN HEBRAIC AND HELLENIC IDEAS OF GOD

Principally we must direct our attention to characteristically Hebrew ideas of God and of his relation to the world ; and, inasmuch as the Christian faith quickly came into direct contact with the Greco-Roman civilization which encircled Judaism, we must compare and contrast these ideas at every point with those which were current in Hellenic religion and philosophy.

(1) The most obviously distinctive characteristic of Hebrew theology is its belief in God's guidance of history. We owe the familiar idea of Providence to the religious legacy we have received from Israel. It is right to emphasize the difference between the catastrophic view of history which we find in the Bible, and the evolutionary view which was the discovery of nineteenth-century humanism. But the two views have at least this much in common, that both interpret history as a series of caused and causative happenings which lead up to a great dénouement in which the significance of all is seen. To the Jew, Jehovah was essentially the living God who acted in history and controlled the issues of events. In his religious philosophy history itself is the story of God's mighty acts, wherein God achieves his purposes for the vindication of his chosen and the punishment of those who disobey him.

A striking illustration of the Hebraic point of view in theology is to be found in the prophetic teaching about idolatry. Belief in the universal rule of Jehovah the creator, which we find already in Amos, does not seem to have led immediately to the inference that other gods were simply non-existent ; and in the end a pure monotheism was attained by arguing, not directly the unreality of heathen deities, but rather their ineffectiveness or impotence. They are " things that cannot profit or deliver ". Thus, when their nonentity is finally declared, the declaration takes the curious form of identifying the heathen god with the mere inactive piece of wood or stone of which his image was fashioned. Prophets and psalmists simply deride the idols as lifeless bits of stuff : they do not denounce them as symbols of false ideas. They do not seem even to consider the possibility of the idol symbolizing anything at all.

In direct contrast with this way of thinking stands the philosophical and mystical religion of Greece, which comes nearest to Christianity in Platonism. To this religion all things in the world are more or less adequate symbols, which partly reveal and partly veil an unchanging divine reality which to the seeing eye shines through them. Such a religion, as Brunner points out,[1] gives men a sense of a divine being which, though as the universal ground of all things it may be called creative, is yet in absolute repose. Its manifestation is found, not when it acts in particular events to manifest itself, but when certain hindrances to the perception of its reality have been removed. Revelation then is due to a subjective process in the human mind : it is like opening the shutters that the light of morning may stream into a darkened room : it is not the act of God, but the unfolding of the soul God-ward. God is not conceived as the doer of mighty works who fulfils his promise or purpose against all opposition, but as the eternal and changeless perfection, imperfectly imaged in phenomena, and revealed to those who know how to look behind them.

(2) A further aspect of what is really the same contrast is found when we consider the way in which knowledge of God is attained and the character of saintliness. In the Old Testament the true knowledge of God is neither mystical nor contemplative nor theoretic : it is essentially a practical and obedient response to the will of the living God. Knowing God means loyalty to his commands. It is based therefore on hearing or hearkening to God's word. The religious leader in Israel is the prophet in whose ear God speaks and who faithfully reports his message to the people that they also may hear and do it. The greatest of all the prophets is Moses, who received and declared the law of the covenant which contained God's permanent commands for Israel. To Elijah on Horeb God is revealed as " the still, small voice ", which gives definite directions. True, there are many descriptions of prophetic visions in the Old Testament ; but the vision is always interpreted by a divine voice conveying a definite message, and the main summons of the prophets from first to last is to hear the word which the Lord has put in their mouths. It is the later apocalyptists who rely mainly upon vision ; and, as the pseudonymous character of their writings shows, they

[1] *The Mediator*, p. 23.

did not claim to speak with the direct authority of the prophet.   Their visions were enigmatic even to themselves ; and they did not dare to proclaim, " Thus saith the Lord."

On the other hand, to the Platonist knowledge of God was essentially a clearer vision of the eternal reality behind phenomena ; the end of action was the attainment of the spiritual or intellectual sight in which the saint might dwell for ever in the world beyond time and space and change.   The famous simile of the cave in Plato's *Republic*, while it appeals to one whole side of man's religious nature, is almost typically un-Hebraic.   It is significant that except in the most primitive parts of the Old Testament, where God is represented as appearing in bodily form, the true knowledge of God is a hearing rather than a seeing.   Although the vision of God's face may belong to the hope of a redeemed world-order,[1] the conviction prevails that for sinful man to see God would be death.   " Hearing God " is the Hebrew way of expressing that less open and direct communion which is all that man can attain to in this world.   The author of 1 Samuel calls attention to the fact that " he that is now called a prophet was beforetime called a seer ".[2]   It is interesting to notice that in Greek religion an opposite development occurred.   The primitive prophets or prophetesses of the oracles became discredited, and religious authority passed to philosopher-seers.

(3) The last point in our contrast between Hebraism and Hellenism is concerned with the doctrine of salvation.   To the Hellenic mind "salvation" consisted in the inward union of the individual soul with the eternal and divine reality. Since this salvation was an individual achievement and the divine was conceived as the changeless unity behind all the changes of external things and events, what happened in history could be of no essential importance to the attainment of the goal.   The science of the Greeks usually regarded the time-process as consisting of an endlessly

[1] On this whole subject, see Kirk, *The Vision of God*, Lect. I, esp. pp. 10–14.
[2] 1 Sam. ix. 9.

revolving series of enormously long cycles which in the
end led nowhere. To the Hebrew, on the other hand,
salvation was essentially connected with Jehovah's fulfilment of his covenant-promises to his people. In the
earlier documents of the Old Testament the content of
this promise is believed to be the assured possession of
the Holy Land in the fullness of prosperity and peace.
It was the disloyalty of Israel which continually delayed
the complete fulfilment of the promise, although the
temporary splendour of the Davidic Empire gave some
hint of what the fulfilment might be. Meanwhile Jehovah
was obliged to deal with his people by way of punishment
rather than reward. Even when the Northern Kingdom
has been destroyed by Assyria, the people of Judæa
carried captive to Babylon and the Temple demolished,
the Jews never gave up hope of salvation to come. At
times, indeed, prophets and psalmists seem to speak as
though Jehovah recompensed the individual righteous
man with temporal prosperity. This theory of salvation
obviously raises more difficulty than it solves, and there
is plenty of evidence in the Psalms and in Job that the
difficulties were keenly felt. But in Jewish thought as a
whole salvation never became a matter simply of rewarding
individuals or even families. God's promise had been
made to his people Israel ; and, whatever might be said
of Israel's sin and its inevitable consequences, the Jew
felt deep in his heart that, if Israel as such were never
finally saved or delivered at all, Jehovah himself would
be convicted of failure : his choice of Israel would come
to nothing in the end, if his promise rested on conditions
which must remain for ever unfulfilled. Such a result
was to the pious Jew unthinkable. Its unthinkableness
is manifested again and again in different ways all through
the Old Testament, and again and again it leads to assured
prophecy, running counter to all apparent indications of
fact, that somehow and somewhen a blessed age will
dawn when Israel will be clearly shown to be God's people
indeed, and be satisfied with the goodness of the Lord.

3.   THE MESSIANIC HOPE

It was this conviction, obstinate or inspired, which gave rise to what immediately concerns us in interpreting the title Christ, viz., the Messianic hope.   The form of this hope, though not always vague, was variable in the extreme.   There was never any doctrine of the Messianic age or kingdom defined as orthodox.   The hope seems to have originated in the expectation of the pre-exilic prophets that a great conqueror and king of David's line would one day arise to restore David's empire in a yet more glorious and enduring form.   Later on, the author of 1 Maccabees seems to find many characteristics of the Messianic kingdom in the righteous and peaceful rule of the priest Simon Maccabæus.   But often a much more distinctly supernatural note sounds in prophecies of the future blessedness of Israel; and as time went on this note was more and more accentuated.   Moreover, in addition to the strictly Messianic expectation of an anointed king of David's line, there arises a hope of a different kind, that God by a great intervention of his power will bring this world or age to an end, that there will be a universal judgement of men associated with a resurrection of the dead, and that thereafter a new world or age will come into being, in which the righteous will be rewarded with everlasting bliss. We find hints of this expectation already in the later passages of the Old Testament,[1] and it was developed by later apocalyptists who wrote after the canon of the Old Testament had been closed.   Sometimes the visions of apocalyptic ignore the personal Messiah altogether, or substitute for him, as does the Book of Enoch, a supernatural figure called the Son of Man.   Sometimes the two kinds of expectation are combined; the Messiah's kingdom is represented as immediately preceding the end of the world, his reign is associated with miraculous prosperity and signs of divine power, but the general judgement and resurrection of the dead do not occur until its close.

Amid all this confusing variety of prophetic word and apocalyptic dream, it is manifestly impossible to arrive

[1] E.g. Isa. xxiv. to xxvii., and Dan. xii.

at any one clear or consistent picture of pre-Christian belief about the Messiah. What is indisputable is that at the beginning of the Christian era there was a wide-spread popular belief among the Jews, a belief however admitting great variety and by no means universal, that the Messiah, the God-appointed redeemer of Israel, might appear at any moment. As to the most generally accepted characteristics of the Messiah's person and work, three points are of special importance :

(1) Although God would raise him up to fulfil his promises to his people, the Messiah was never thought of as himself personally divine. He was to be a human king, of David's line according to general belief, who was to reign over God's people on this earth. It is true that the words of Psalm ii., " Thou art my Son ", etc., were usually interpreted as referring to the Messiah, but in the Old Testament both Israel and David were spoken of as God's sons with no suggestion that they were other than human.[1]

(2) The Messiah's work was to be primarily the salvation or deliverance of God's people from their earthly foes and alien oppressors, so that they might live in righteousness, peace and prosperity.

(3) The Messiah's coming was associated with a miraculous intervention of God declared in works of supernatural power, and more vaguely also with the end of this world or age and the inauguration of a new world-order.

The first two characteristics of the Messianic hope, in a spiritualized form without definite allusion to an earthly conquest or sovereignty, are exactly and beautifully described in the Benedictus. And in these familiar verses, we may notice all three marks which we have seen to be characteristic of Hebraic religion in contrast with Hellenic. Here there appear clearly the thoughts, (1) of the living God of Israel who works through history, (2) of God's will revealed and his final action foretold in the prophetic word, (3) of salvation as the fulfilment of God's promise to deliver his people from their enemies, that they may serve him in righteousness and peace.

[1] See Exod. iv. 22 ; 2 Sam. vii. 14, and cf. Hos. xi. 9.

CHAPTER IX

THE PRIMITIVE DOCTRINE OF THE INCARNATION IN JEWISH CHRISTIANITY AND ST. PAUL

THE NEW TESTAMENT gives us primary and direct evidence of the impression made by the life of Jesus Christ upon the first generation of Christians. In estimating that impression we have constantly to remember that the original disciples were Jews, and that the background of their thought consisted of those Jewish ideas about God, the world, and man which we have already tried to describe in outline.

1. THE FULFILMENT OF MESSIANIC EXPECTATION IN JESUS

The original message of Christian preachers was that " Jesus is the Christ " or " The Christ is Jesus ", and they sought to prove this identification from the scriptures of the Old Testament. What did this preaching mean to those who gave and those who accepted it as truth ? Although on the one hand Jesus was affirmed to be really the Messiah of Jewish prophecy and apocalyptic, yet on the other hand the idea of Messiahship was deeply changed by the affirmation that the Messiah was none other than Jesus of Nazareth.

Clearly the Christians believed that in Jesus all the promises of God were fulfilled.[1] " For howsoever many are the promises of God," wrote St. Paul, " in him is the yea." And this belief already involves an enlargement of pre-Christian conceptions of Messiahship. For the Messiah's office had been variously conceived, and it was a new idea that everything that God had ever promised to

[1] On this point, see Dr. A. E. J. Rawlinson's *The New Testament Doctrine of the Christ*, pp. 15 *sq.*

75

his people should be bestowed through his sole agency. Not only were all the passages of the Old Testament which had been commonly given a Messianic interpretation now referred to Jesus, but others also, not previously thought to be Messianic at all; and moreover Jesus was to be the inaugurator to the new world or age, which had hitherto been only doubtfully and confusedly connected with the advent of the personal Messiah.

But the two lines of expectation meet and find fulfilment together in Jesus, only because Jesus himself has originated a new way of thinking about the Messiah's work and person. The resurrection was the basic fact on which the Christian gospel rested. It was the resurrection which justified once for all the claim that Jesus was indeed the Messiah, and also that, being now alive in heaven, he would come again to bring this world to an end and establish the glorious world to come. But the notion that the Messiah would make a preliminary appearance on earth to die and rise again, before he came finally in manifest power as king and judge of men, was a notion wholly new to the Jewish mind, though Christians strove to show that the Old Testament had predicted this also in language never before understood. And this new notion, distinctive of Christianity, revolutionized the whole Jewish conception of Messiahship. The proof lies in the plain fact that the preaching of a crucified Messiah was to orthodox Judaism a scandal.

2. THE FORGIVENESS OF SINS AND THE DIVINITY OF CHRIST

Why had the Messiah made this preliminary appearance to suffer a shameful death ? The Christian answer is not doubtful; it lies at the centre of the earliest and most universal tradition, and it is contained in five momentous words, *for the forgiveness of sins.* God's glorious covenant-promises to his people must somehow be fulfilled. But God is righteous, not only in his faithfulness to his promise of glory, but also in his punishment of sin; and Israel remains too sinful to receive the glory promised. Such was the conviction which had cast its shadow over the hopes of the earlier prophets, and darkened the minds of the later apocalyptists, until their visions of the end often became pictures of gloom and terror for man, even more than of victory for God. For the pious and conscientious Jew there seemed to be no way out of the impasse. But the Christian declared confidently that the way out had been found; God had opened it himself. God has sent the Messiah Jesus both to declare his free forgiveness to all who receive him and also to give his own life as an accepted offering for the sins of all. Henceforth all without exception who would become loyal followers of this gracious Messiah, might for ever lay aside their fears of the last day, and wait in eager hope for his appearance in triumphant glory to bring this world to an end and complete their redemption.

There is no doubt of the intense reality of this gospel of forgiveness from the very beginning of the Church's life. In the primitive stories which are preserved for us in the earlier chapters of Acts we find the apostles, directly after Pentecost, offering free forgiveness to the very men who shared responsibility for the shameful death of Jesus. From any point of view it is a startling attitude in the followers of a rejected and condemned claimant to Messiahship. But we must notice what a change in the conception of the Messiah's office is involved.

(a) The Messiah of popular expectation was a conquering hero of David's line. The " Zealots " expected him to be a nationalist Mahdi, and their fanatical hatred of Rome had caused more than one serious disturbance. The Zealots of course were extremists; but they were extremists only because they laid extreme emphasis on one aspect of the general Messianic expectation. The notion of a Messiah whose primary aim was forgiveness, and who put aside all methods of political agitation as a temptation of the devil, was unheard of.[1] And, once accepted, it

[1] Of course, if the term " Messiah " is understood to include the purely supernatural figure who fills the Messianic rôle in some apocalypses, the question of temptation to political agitation cannot arise in the case of such a Messiah.

changed the central idea of that deliverance from enemies in which Jehovah's salvation was to consist. There was no longer any question of a deliverance from earthly enemies which was to issue in a kingdom of earthly prosperity for God's chosen. The more spiritual Judaism, which had always felt that sin was the real enemy from which deliverance was needed, was completely vindicated in a quite unlooked for way.

(b) But a further and more important result follows. In the theology of the Jew forgiveness of sin was God's prerogative alone, and belief in its exercise was always more of a pious hope in God's mercy than an assured conviction of pardon actually bestowed. Jesus had gravely offended the orthodox by authoritatively and unconditionally absolving the sinner with the simple pronouncement, " Thy sins are forgiven "[1]; and his disciples regarded themselves as commissioned to do the same, to declare God's free and absolute forgiveness to all who believed in the name of Jesus. But this very claim in itself set Jesus above prophet, priest, the Mosaic Law, and even Messiahship as it had been generally understood. As the mediator of a new and absolute forgiveness from God, Jesus was set forth as the possessor of a strictly divine authority. It was, we may reasonably conjecture, as forgiver of sin, and saviour from the wrath which was its penalty, that Jesus first stood forth in Jewish eyes as a divine person. Thus it was through the realization of atonement that Jewish Christians felt their way towards a full doctrine of the incarnation. Non-Christian Jews might think of the Messiah as a judge administering God's law, perhaps not without mercy. But God alone, the author of the law, could absolutely forgive.

[1] See Mark ii. 5 *sqq.*, Luke vii. 48 *sq.* Critics question whether Jesus ever made such a claim. But, if he did not, the unquestionable belief of the primitive Church seems difficult to account for.

3. ST. PAUL'S DOCTRINE OF CHRIST'S DIVINITY

The sequence of thought which, as we suppose, led the Jewish mind towards recognizing the Godhead of the Messiah Jesus becomes apparent in St. Paul. St. Paul's whole Christology rests upon the fundamental conviction that in the earthly life, death and resurrection of Jesus Christ, God had accomplished a supreme act of grace for the deliverance of men from the otherwise inevitable consequences of their transgressions of his law. " Grace " to St. Paul meant primarily the free love of God coming forth and manifesting itself in action towards men ; and Jesus Christ was, as it were, its personification. He was therefore emphatically not a miraculously righteous and holy man who by his life and death had succeeded in propitiating an outraged and wrathful deity. Nor was he just the perfect human saint whose goodness mirrored in human nature the eternal and infinite love of God. This latter thought, which belongs to a later Christianity, may well contain truth, but it is certainly not Pauline. St. Paul's thought about the atonement is as far from that of Abelard as it is from that of Anselm. It is characteristically expressed in language which presents the life of Jesus as the act of the living God working mightily in love for the deliverance of his creation from bondage to sin and death. " God was in Christ reconciling the world to himself." [1] " In this God commendeth his love towards us in that while we were yet sinners, Christ died for us." [2] And this thought of the atonement, which begins by identifying what Jesus himself did, and not merely what was revealed in Jesus, with what God did to redeem mankind, ends inevitably in a doctrine of the incarnation. For the person who is Jesus Christ, being in some sense distinct from God the Father, comes nevertheless to be identified with one in and through whom the one God has always acted and will always act towards his people and his world. The Christ by whom we are forgiven and justified is the same person who will appear in glory to exercise God's final judgement. Therein lies the assur-

---

[1] 2 Cor. v. 19.   [2] Rom. v. 8.

ance of perfect salvation. And it is the same person
again who was the spiritual rock from which the Israelites
drank in the wilderness when God delivered them from the
Egyptian bondage and led them towards the promised
land.[1] And, if by Christ's work Christians are created
anew through forgiveness and made inheritors of the new
world, the original creation also must have be̶̶ ̶n̶e̶d̶
through the agency of the same person in wh̶
final purpose is revealed and is being fulfille̶
Irenaeus says, " It is the same hand through̶
creates and completes." [2] So, St. Paul write̶
there is one God the Father of whom are all ̶
we unto him, and one Lord Jesus Christ, thr̶
are all things, and we through him." [3]

The remarkable sequence of statements in the first
chapter of Colossians makes explicit the order of St.
Paul's Christological thought as we have been trying to
expound it. First, Jesus Christ is " the Son of God's
love ",[4] i.e., the Son who is the living personal expression
of God's love, and actuality of his grace. Secondly, it is
he " in whom we have our redemption, the forgiveness of
our sins " ; by this fact his sonship is revealed. Thirdly,
he is " the image of the invisible God, the first-born of all
creation . . . all things have been created through him
and unto him ; and he is before all things, and in him
all things consist " or cohere. These metaphysical affirmations about the relation of Christ to the universe are
inevitable inferences from the truths previously stated,
which are the immediate content of the Christian experience or revelation ; and in the following verse St. Paul
passes on at once to assert that by his resurrection Christ
becomes the " first-born " of the new creation as he was
also of the old. The fundamental thought is that, when
the distinction is made between God as active originating
creator and man and the world as creatures, Christ must

---

[1] 1 Cor. x. 4.   [2] *Adv. Hær.*, V, 16, 1.   [3] 1 Cor. viii. 6.
[4] Col. i. 13. It makes little difference if we take the words to
mean primarily " the Son who is the object of his love ", υἱὸς
ἀγαπητός. St. Paul probably chose an ambiguous expression to
convey both ideas.

appear on the divine side of the dividing-line.[1] And
this truth was first revealed in the fact that Jesus
Christ is himself the forgiver, justifier, and redeemer of
men, who wholly in obedience to the Father's love, and
yet wholly of his own love also, gave himself up for
them.

And so we come to that difficult passage which has the
most direct bearing of all upon St. Paul's doctrine of the
incarnation :

Have this mind in you which was also in Christ Jesus (or,
more probably, show towards one another that same mind
which is yours in Christ Jesus), who, being originally in the
form of God, counted it not a prize to be on an equality with
God, but emptied himself, taking the form of a servant, being
made in the likeness of men ; and, being found in fashion as
a man, he humbled himself, becoming obedient unto death,
even death on a cross : wherefore also God highly exalted
him, and gave unto him the name which is above every name,
that in the name of Jesus every knee should bow of beings
in heaven, on earth, and under the earth, and every tongue
confess that Jesus Christ is Lord to the glory of God the
Father.[2]

St. Paul here affirms that Christ Jesus was originally
that is, before he was born on earth, " in the form of
God ". The word $\mu o \varrho \varphi \acute{\eta}$ does not mean " form " in the
sense of an " appearance " which may be superficial or
illusory (the word for that is $\sigma \chi \tilde{\eta} \mu a$), but " form " in the
sense of " essential shape or character ". The Christ there-
fore was from the beginning a divine person. But, St. Paul
goes on, he did not treat equality with God as a $\dot{a} \varrho \pi a \gamma \mu \acute{o} \varsigma$.
This word properly means " something snatched ", " spoil "
or " booty " ; and its use here only becomes intelligible
when we perceive that St. Paul is drawing as complete
a contrast as he can between the action of Christ, the
second Adam who redeems mankind, and that of the first

---

[1] Cf. Heb. iii. 3.
[2] Phil. ii. 5–11. The word $\varepsilon \dot{v} \varrho \varepsilon \theta \varepsilon \dot{\iota} \varsigma$ (" being found ") in v. 8
is additional evidence against the view that the whole passage
contains no reference to any pre-existence of Christ.

D.C.   G

Adam, who caused its fall.[1] Adam, being originally in
the form of man, counted it a prize or booty " to be as
God, knowing good and evil ", and, in snatching at the
prize, he fell, and dragged mankind down with him.
Christ, on the contrary, being originally in the form of
God, did the exact opposite ; he denuded and humbled
himself to the uttermost, and being therefore exalted, he
raises mankind to life with God.   The central thought is
an elaboration of that expressed in the words, " Ye know
the grace of our Lord Jesus Christ, that, though he was
rich, yet for your sakes he became poor, that ye through
his poverty might become rich." [2]   In both passages we
trace the same underlying conviction that by his earthly
life and death Christ Jesus expressed not only the Father's
love and grace towards man, but also and equally his own,
and this is the reason why his pre-existent divinity must
be asserted.   " The name which is above every name ",
interpreted by the quotation from Isaiah [3] which follows,
must be Adonai (translated κύριος), which in the Old
Testament is the title of Jehovah as the covenant-God.
" The *name* of God " in the Old Testament commonly
stands for the glorious character and power of God as
manifested to men by his mighty acts.

In this whole passage St. Paul is not writing in the
precise and carefully chosen phrases of scientific or metaphysical theology.   He is preaching an ethical sermon
with the help of a more or less pictorial contrast between
Adam and Christ.   Nevertheless, there can be no doubt
that he believes the contrast to be profoundly true.   And

---

[1] I take this illuminating suggestion from Dr. Rawlinson's *The
New Testament Doctrine of the Christ*, p. 134.   But I cannot agree
with him that St. Paul identifies Christ as the second Adam with
" a heavenly man " who existed from the beginning.   The teaching found in 1 Cor. xv. does not seem to me to support this idea
at all.   The *new* manhood, in which Christ is there spoken of as
ὁ ἔσχατος or ὁ δεύτερος 'Αδάμ, only begins with the resurrection
or, possibly, with the birth of Jesus.   St. Paul's whole point is
that it comes *after* the manhood of the first Adam, i.e., after in
time.   Gore (*The Holy Spirit and The Church*, p. 279) could " find
no trace of the pre-existing Man in the New Testament ".

[2] 2 Cor. viii. 9.   [3] Isa. xlv. 23.

if we draw out, with the help of a term which subsequent orthodoxy made definite, the theological doctrine which St. Paul's language seems to imply, we may interpret his meaning thus : whereas before his self-humiliation Christ had the *nature* of Godhead, in the exaltation which followed the humiliation he received also the *name* of Godhead, so that all may worship him as they worship the Father. That St. Paul did definitely, if one may be allowed the expression, rank Jesus with God, is abundantly clear from evidence which extends all through his epistles. In at least one other passage, besides that just quoted, he applied to Christ Old Testament language which in its original context was used of Jehovah.[1] But not less striking is the way in which in almost all his epistles, from the earliest onwards, he mentions God the Father and the Lord Jesus Christ together as the source of grace and peace, and in one such prayer he actually puts first the name of Christ.[2]

Such language is indeed startling on the lips of a Jewish monotheist. No doubt it could never have been used at all so soon after the death of Jesus, if Christians had not remembered words of his own, such as are recorded in the synoptists as well as in St. John, which imply his unique relation to the Father. But St. Paul does not expressly appeal to any words of Jesus in order to justify his faith and doctrine as to his divinity ; and in any case it must have been the total impression and experience of the personality of Jesus rather than any particular sayings, which settled such a faith and doctrine in the minds of the apostles and evangelists. If then we may translate into more modern terms the inner logic of the process which impelled the Jewish mind, against rooted presuppositions of its theology, towards the doctrines of Christ's Godhead and of the incarnation, we may perhaps express it thus without serious misrepresentation. The expected Christ of Jewish tradition was to vindicate the majesty of God's law as a divinely appointed sovereign and judge, delivering the

[1] Rom. x. 13 ; Joel ii. 32.
[2] 2 Thess. ii. 16, cf. 1 Thess. iii. 11. In both passages the two names of God the Father and the Lord Jesus govern a verb in the singular.

righteous and punishing sinners. Christ Jesus, on the other hand, had first and foremost brought to earth the gospel of God's love and free forgivene 3 towards all men. Now God, the absolute sovereign, might in principle vindicate the majesty of his law by appointing and empowering a representative to act vicariously in his behalf. But in the nature of things forgiving love can only be effectively revealed *in person*, not by proxy. Forgiveness on the lips of a mere representative or messenger can never really carry conviction. Because the message of love can only be conveyed in person, therefore Jesus Christ must be personally God ; for he *has* conveyed it, and shown unmistakably in so doing that the divine love, which is his gospel, is not only the Father's but also his own.[1] Once the message has been conveyed thus in person, it becomes the task of apostolic men to proclaim it. That which God in Christ has done and revealed is the substance of the *kerygma* with which St. Paul, and others with him and after him, are entrusted as ambassadors for Christ. But the gospel itself loses its essential content, if Christ is no more than an ambassador for God. The crucifixion does not bring the message of a forgiving love which suffers only by proxy. If it be true that Jesus suffered vicariously for men, still he did not suffer vicariously for God. The person who suffered in Jesus and as Jesus was the eternal Son of God's love.

True, the wrath of God remained in St. Paul's mind a terrible reality, working itself out in the misery and destruction which must inevitably by the operation of God's laws fall on the heads of those who disobey them, and finally on those who reject the gospel. But to St. Paul Jesus Christ had once for all revealed that the personal

[1] As Dr. J. O. F. Murray has pointed out (*Jesus according to S. John*, p. 261), it is a striking fact that in the Fourth Gospel Jesus speaks only once directly of his own love to the Father, and that in immediate reference to the Crucifixion. He goes to Gethsemane with the words on his lips " That the world may know that I love the Father " (John xiv. 31). To St. John therefore the Cross is the expression, not even only of God's love to man, and certainly not of man's love to God, but of the love which is eternal within the Godhead.

attitude of God to sinful men is not the wrath of outraged majesty, but the love which seeks at all costs to save them from the wrath which they are drawing down upon them-selves—and to him " at all costs " meant the cross of God's Son.[1]

4. JESUS AS REPRESENTATIVE OF THE TRUE ISRAEL

There is, however, another and quite different line of Christological thought about Jesus, also apparently having its starting-point in Judaism, which must not be neglected. From the beginning the Christian community regarded itself as the true Israel, the people of God which inherited the promises made to Israel under the old covenant.   Now Dr. Rawlinson has pointed out [2] that

of the terms and titles which in Biblical literature are bestowed upon the Messiah all or most are as capable of being applied to the Church (whether Jewish or Christian) as they are of being applied to the Christ who is Lord of the Church.

Dr. Rawlinson proceeds to illustrate the truth of this state-ment in respect of the titles, " Christ ", " Prophet ", " Priest ", " King ", " Son of God ", " Son of Man ", " Servant of God " ; and he concludes as follows :

The Messiah or the Christ, according to each of these several conceptions of him, is the fulfiller of the hope, or the realization of some aspect of the ideal, of the elect nation, the people of God. We might be tempted to say that the Messiah fulfils Israel's hope through the actualization of Israel's ideal.

It was the common belief of post-exilic Judaism that it was the sin of the people which delayed the fulfilment of God's promises. The Messianic feast was postponed, because " those who were bidden were not worthy ". And many scholars have been tracing and emphasizing the thought in the New Testament that the complete apostasy of the old Israel, manifested in the rejection of Jesus, left

[1] See Dodd's note on Rom. i. 18 in his edition of that epistle (Moffatt Commentaries).

[2] *Op. cit.*, pp. 20 *sq.*

Jesus himself the Messiah as the sole representative of the true Israel of God, who because in his perfect righteousness he represents Israel as God's beloved Son and Servant enables God's promises to be fulfilled to the Christian Israel which owns him as its head. Such is the thought which seems to underlie the very primitive title $\pi a\tilde{\imath}\varsigma$ $\theta\varepsilon o\tilde{v}$ (servant or child of God) applied to Jesus in the early chapters of *Acts*, and also perhaps the description of Jesus as simply $\delta\ \delta i\varkappa a\iota o\varsigma$ in St. James.[1] It is also suggested in the whole story of St. Mark's Gospel, possibly in its use of the title Son of Man,[2] and certainly in its emphasis on the increasing isolation of Jesus, as first the religious authorities, then the multitudes, and finally his own disciples turn against him or forsake. In St. Paul again some sort of identity between Christ and the spiritual or redeemed Israel is presupposed by the great antithesis between Christ and Adam in Romans.[3] No doubt the idea in St. Paul's mind is different from that suggested by the title $\delta\ \delta i\varkappa a\iota o\varsigma$. He regards Christ as the representative and head of the redeemed society of his followers rather than as the one perfectly righteous individual who by fulfilling the law had obtained the promises on behalf of all God's people. This latter way of speaking attached too high a value to legal righteousness to be congenial to St. Paul. Nevertheless the philosophy of history sketched in Romans,[4] which shows how God's selection of chosen vessels successively narrowed itself through the disloyalty of the chosen people until it rested on the one individual Jesus Christ, by whom all alike, having been previously rejected for sin, were now redeemed through faith, is thoroughly in accord with St. Mark's picture of Jesus as the completely isolated Messiah. And, if St. Paul's great conception of the Christian society as " in Christ " was mainly based on the new spiritual experience of Christians, he was at least helped to express it by the suggestions of the Old Testament and later Jewish thought, that the

---

[1] v. 16 ; cf. also 1 John ii. 1.   [2] See Dan. vii. 14, 18.
[3] C.V., where see Dodd's notes.
[4] Admirably expounded by Dodd, *op. cit.* See especially pp. 183–7.

individual Christ might be regarded as the true representative of the Christ-nation, or, conversely, that the nation
might be personified in the individual figure of the Christ.
Behind all such ideas of course there lies the ancient notion
of social solidarity, according to which the eponymous
ancestor or hero is identified with the nation, tribe, or
family called by his name.

5.   THE ORIGIN OF THE DOCTRINE OF THE TWO NATURES IN CHRIST

We have traced two different and, in a measure, opposite
lines of thought by which the Jewish-Christian mind sought
to give expression to the impression which the work and
life of Jesus had made upon it.   On the one hand, Jesus
was, not merely the instrument, but in the fullest sense
the personal agent, of God's great act of love for the forgiveness and redemption of man.   This was the thought
which led to the doctrine of his pre-existent deity.   On the
other hand, Jesus was the sole perfect representative of
human righteousness and obedience to God's will, and,
having been raised from death and exalted by God, he has
become the head of the new Israel, which after his example
and " in him " serves God in filial obedience and inherits
the promises.   Considering these two lines of thought
together both in their opposition and in their unity, we are
confronted at once by the theological problem which a
few centuries later the Church defined by the orthodox
dogma of two natures in one person.   However that
problem is to be solved, and whether or no it is capable
of any full solution in this world, it begins to take shape
the moment Christian faith becomes distinctly conscious
of itself.

CHAPTER X

GENTILE INFLUENCES AND ST. PAUL'S "CHRIST-MYSTICISM"

N O DOUBT it seems strange at first sight that St. Paul, "the apostle of the Gentiles", native of Tarsus, and ready to become all things to all men if haply he might save some, should in his letters to Gentile Churches have expressed his thought for the most part in a characteristically Jewish way.

1. ST. PAUL NOT A HELLENIZER

It is not surprising that critics of the late nineteenth and early twentieth centuries should have endeavoured to prove that his teaching about the person of Christ was really a Hellenization of an originally Hebraic gospel. But in the judgement of the best modern scholars that attempt has broken down. For instance, Bousset's elaborately defended theory that the title κύριος or Lord, as applied to Jesus, is of Gentile, not Jewish, origin comes to shipwreck on the Christian watchword " Marana tha " used in Aramaic by St. Paul writing to the Greeks.[1]

The radical Hebraism, however, of St. Paul's theology, both in content and manner of expression, becomes more

---

[1] 1 Ccr. xvi. 22. The watchword is a prayer meaning " Our Lord, come ", a prayer repeated in the closing words of the New Testament. The origin of the title Marana, our Lord, in its application to Jesus is probably to be found in the Christian use of the Messianic Psalm cx. 1, quoted by Jesus himself in Mark xii. 36. It does not of itself imply essential Godhead, nor was Psalm cx. understood by the Rabbi's to refer to the Messiah as a divine person ; but the prayer, " Marana tha ", could only have been uttered by men who felt a devotion to the exalted Christ which was indistinguishable from worship. (On this whole subject, see Rawlinson, *The New Testament Doctrine of the Christ*, Appended

intelligible when we remember that every Jewish community in the Gentile world had attached to it a number of Gentiles who followed the Jewish religion as closely as they could without being circumcized and becoming proselytes.   These Gentile adherents were known as " Godfearers " (οἱ σεβόμενοι τὸν θεόν), and it was from them that the majority of the first Gentile converts to Christianity were made.   The Septuagint was the Bible of the early Gentile Churches, and many of their members had been already familiar with it when they first heard the gospel.

2. ST. PAUL'S ENCOUNTERS WITH GENTILE MISCONCEPTIONS

Nevertheless, it is clear both from Acts and 1 Thessalonians (where St. Paul reminds his readers that they had now turned *from idols* to serve the living God), that some converts came into the Church direct from heathenism. And there is plenty of evidence in the Epistles that some of St. Paul's teaching was specially directed to those whose heathen misconceptions hindered their understanding of Christianity.

As we have already noticed, the central characteristic of the religious philosophies of the Greco-Roman world was their tendency to conceive the ultimate Godhead, not as a power personally active in human affairs and historical events, but rather as the unchanging unity and ground of being behind phenomena.   This fundamental difference in the conception of the Godhead has throughout the Church's history caused a tension in Christian theology between Hellenic and Hebraic elements, which constantly becomes

Note I.)   To this day in the Apostles' Creed " our Lord " remains as the title of personal devotion given to Jesus by his followers. The title " Christ " connotes essentially a God-appointed *office*. Jesus is *the* Christ, the fulfiller of God's promises to his people, the king who is to reign over the earth.   But he is *our* Lord, i.e., the object of the personal, freely given, loyalty and devotion of Christians.   In acknowledging the risen Jesus as both God's Messiah and their own Maran, the first Christians were beginning to discern, though not yet actually asserting, his full Godhead. (See Acts ii. 36.)

apparent in the great controversies of the faith and remains with us to-day. It is indeed a tension between
opposite truths which constitutes the central problem of
Christian metaphysics. In St. Paul's time, however, the
presuppositions of the Hellenic mind had certain consequences in Gentile religion which were definitely incompatible with the faith of the gospel. We must now par-
ticularize some of these consequences, and show how St.
Paul strove to meet them.

(1) The Gentile conception of Godhead was readily
compatible with polytheism. For the divine supra-sensible
unity was partly veiled and partly revealed or immanent
in all manner of phenomena ; and it was therefore easy
for the mind to present to itself the multitudinous deities
of the pantheon as quasi-phenomenal symbols of, or
emanations from, the ultimate Godhead. Thus particular
religious societies might devote themselves to the cult of
a particular deity, without in any way claiming exclusive
or catholic authority for that cult or its object. A deity
so worshipped would be called the Lord ($\varkappa \acute{v} \varrho \iota \sigma \varsigma$) of his
worshippers. And the terms " god " and " lord " in such
connections came to be very cheaply used. Different gods
could be readily identified with one another, when convenient, and new deities, or deities with new names, easily
admitted on a level with the rest. When the Athenians
heard that St. Paul was preaching about Jesus and
Anastasis, they supposed he was initiating people into the
worship of two new minor gods, male and female, to which
they were very ready to give a welcome.[1] Against all
such empty toleration the Jew set his doctrine of the
jealousy of Jehovah. And St. Paul the Christian has to
remind his Corinthian converts that " though there be
that are called gods whether in heaven or on earth, as
there are gods many and lords many, yet to us there is
one God the Father, of whom are all things and we unto
him, and one Lord Jesus Christ, through whom are all
things and we through him ".[2]

(2) A further consequence of Hellenism in religion was
that immortality became the chief characteristic, or differ-

[1] See Acts xvii. 18.   [2] 1 Cor. viii. 5 *sq.*

entia, of deity. From an early period Greek literature had spoken of the gods as the immortals ; and to popular thought the only definite feature of the ultimate Godhead, which is the ground of being, is that it must abide for ever, while phenomena change and pass. Thus, while in Judaism the fundamental contrast between God and man represented God as holy and man as sinful, the corresponding contrast in Hellenism lay rather between divine immortality or eternity and the mortality or transiency of men. But there was a widespread belief in the pagan world that, although the body was wholly subject to death, there was a higher element in man's being which at least had the capacity of rising to a diviner level. In St. Paul's time it was the chief aim of personal religion among the pagans to give man such communion with deity as would ensure the immortality of his soul or spirit. It is evident that Gentiles, for whom the attraction of Christianity lay in the surer or more substantial hope of immortality which it offered, would be likely to grasp eagerly, and also seriously to misunderstand, St. Paul's gospel of the new and heavenly life which was the gift of God in Christ Jesus.

Some of the Thessalonians, carried off their feet by the doctrine of Christ's resurrection and the approaching end of the world, seem to have taken St. Paul's teaching to mean that henceforth Christians would not be subject to physical death, and their whole faith was shaken when some of their number died. St. Paul reminds them that they are not worshippers merely of some divine being, such as those in pagan myths, who had died and risen again, but followers of a historical man who had actually endured physical death in order to be exalted. That is the ground of their true hope. " For, if we believe that *Jesus* (not Christ) died and rose again, even so them that are fallen asleep in (lit. through) Jesus shall God bring with him." [1]

[1] 1 Thess. iv. 14.   The Epistle is clearly addressed in the main to men who had been converted straight from paganism to Christianity.   St. Paul's eschatological teaching would have been much more likely " to go to the heads " of such men than of those who

At Corinth, where St. Paul had made a much longer stay than at Thessalonica, the misunderstanding seems to have been of a much less elementary sort.   Kirsopp Lake [1] must surely be right in conjecturing that some, if not all, of those Corinthians who denied or questioned the resurrection of the dead, were nevertheless inclined to rest upon some mystical doctrine of an immortality secured to the Christian soul here and now by participation in the sacraments.   Such a belief would have been thoroughly in line with the teaching of pagan mystery-religions.   One main point then in St. Paul's celebrated illustration of the seed [2] is to bring home to these semi-pagan believers that that which is truly spiritual must come *after* that which is natural.   The Christian hope is for a future transmutation of the physical body in the completed triumph of Christ. Meanwhile Christians must be content to bear the image of the earthly and natural, even to the grave if need be, and to persevere in the moral conflict against its tendency to sin.   They must not rest in the security of an immortality already possessed, as though the fight were over. For the sting of death is sin, and we must conquer sin before we can be secure from death.   Death is the last enemy that shall be destroyed.   Its destruction marks the final triumph of the last Adam who, through death, has become life-giving spirit.

(3) A third consequence of the Hellenic conception of divine being was the belief that salvation or union with God is attainable by man through some sort of initiation, combined with an ascetic discipline, whereby the human spirit wins a mystic vision of supersensible realities, and in this way detaches itself from dependence on the body. It is an error derived from this source which St. Paul appears to be combating in Colossians, although the Colossian heresy seems also to have contacts with a kind

by close contact with Judaism had already been made familiar with Jewish expectations about the end of the age.   That something of this kind had happened is clear from other indications in 1 and 2 Thess.

[1] *Earlier Epistles of St. Paul*, pp. 215 *sqq.*
[2] 1 Cor. xv. 35–58.

of Judaism which had come under Gentile influence.   St.
Paul meets it by insisting that the one mystery of God,
now manifest in the Church, is Christ himself, whom St.
Paul proclaims " admonishing every man and teaching
every man in all wisdom that he may present every man
perfect (or fully initiated) in Christ ".   St. Paul means
that there is behind the gospel no esoteric way of salvation
which belongs only to the specially enlightened few.[1]
The Epistle brings home the same essential lesson in
another way by reiterating that really Christian life consists in loyal membership of, and labour for, the whole
Church which is Christ's body, and not in the private
enjoyment of wonderful experiences attained through a
special ascetic discipline.   Such, for example, must be the
main point of the obscure passage in the second chapter,
which warns the Colossians against the man " who dwells
in the things that he has seen (i.e., in mystic visions), and
holds not fast the head, from whom all the body increases
with the increase of God ".[2]   St. Paul's whole warning
against false mysticism in this Epistle may be summed up
in Herrmann's words, " When the mystic has found God,
he has left Christ behind." [3]

3.   ST. PAUL'S " CHRIST-MYSTICISM "

In the foregoing cases we have traced the characteristic
influences of Gentile religion mainly in the misunderstandings and heresies which St. Paul had to meet rather than
in any teaching of his own.   But what of the theology
which St. Paul derived from his own spiritual experience ?
Can we not discern leanings towards Gentile mysticism
in his thought of his own union with the risen Christ ?
St. Paul of course was himself a mystic.   But his
" Christ-mysticism ", as it has been called, has peculiar
features which exhibit it as the mysticism of a Hebrew

[1] See Col. i. 25–9.
[2] Col. ii. 16–23.   It makes no difference to the meaning if in
v. 18, St. Paul really wrote (according to another reading) " dwells
in the things that he has not seen ", i.e., with his bodily eyes.
[3] *Communion of the Christian with God*, p. 30.

Christian, whose mind and spirit never lost contact with the national religion which had been their preparation for the gospel. In nothing is that truth more evident than in St. Paul's insistence that Christian life and faith consist in the hearing and obeying of a divine message or word of God rather than in the seeing of any spiritual vision. " The hearing of faith " and " the obedience of faith " are characteristic phrases of his, and the whole content of the Christian revelation is summed up for him as a εὐαγγέλιον or κήρυγμα, tidings which he is commissioned to proclaim. This emphasis on the heard and spoken word is certainly connected with the fact that in St. Paul's mind the whole truth of Christianity is bound up with the occurrence of certain historical and quasi-historical events which are in the profoundest sense acts of the living God, viz., the crucifixion and resurrection of Jesus, and his future appearance in glory at the end of the world. The mystic who penetrates to the direct vision, necessarily ineffable, of eternal reality can have no need of a revelation mediated by particular historical events. For, to put the same point in other words, his whole religion is based on the revelation, or unveiling, to the inward eye of the one divine reality which endures unchanging behind all things. But to St. Paul the gospel is not a mere revelation, in this strict sense, at all. It is not primarily an unveiling of the eternal unseen, but tidings of what God in Christ has done, is doing, and will do. Thus for St. Paul, God's self-revelation is necessarily mediated by historical events ; for the revelation is itself in the first instance the divine act by which Christ came to die on the cross and rise again for men. And St. Paul still looks forward to the last great act of the drama of redemption, when " the (natural) creation itself shall also be delivered from the bondage of corruption into the glorious liberty of the children of God ". And St. Paul goes on to speak of Christians, who in the gift of the Spirit have the first-fruits of the redeemed life, as groaning within themselves as they wait and long for that full and final sonship which will come to them with the redemption of the body. On this hope, he says, rests the salvation which they have already received. The

final end of redemption is hoped for and not seen ; for
what is seen is present, and can no longer be the object
of hope.   But the Christian, hoping for what he does not
see, waits for it with stedfast endurance.[1]

It is therefore quite untrue to say that St. Paul's vivid
consciousness of the spiritual presence of the exalted Christ
makes him in the last resort indifferent to the historical
events connected with Jesus of Nazareth.   This suggestion
is due to the attempt to classify St. Paul's mysticism as
belonging to a type from which in fact it is alien.   In St.
Paul's thought redemption consists in a great series of
divine acts, all equally essential to its consummation.   In
the preparatory stage we have the call of Abraham and
the giving of the law through Moses.   In redemption
proper the first act is the life and death of Jesus followed
by his resurrection and ascension.   These are finished and
belong to the past.   They have now become the message
or *kerygma* which Christians must hear and accept through
faith.   In the present is the communion of the Holy Spirit
wherein Christians themselves have been spiritually raised
to a new and heavenly life, are being united to their living
Lord, and are bringing men of all nations into their fellowship.   In the future is the final consummation when Christ
will appear again in manifest glory, all his enemies will
be destroyed, and the whole creation will be transfigured
and transformed.   Each of these stages is essential to
the divine plan of redemption, and the realization of
each depends on a divine act.   Final salvation cannot be
attained by any until the final day has come for all.

It is true that St. Paul is not much concerned to go
back and trace again in detail the life of Jesus which is
over.   Others can tell that story.   It is enough for him
to be sure that he who was in the form of God did take
upon him the form of a servant for the redemption of
mankind.   The present reality for him is the guiding
presence of the living and exalted Christ.   And he does
therefore tend to find in the historic life of Jesus only the
veiling of that divine glory which was first revealed through
the resurrection.   But it is equally true that St. Paul does

---

[1] Rom. viii. 21-6, paraphrased.

not apprehend the exalted Christ chiefly through spiritual
vision, although he is sure that once at least he has seen
him.   It is something much more like spiritual audition
on which St. Paul normally relies.   Even when, as he
believed, he was " caught up into paradise ", he does not
say that he saw things eternal and ineffable, but only that
" he heard unspeakable words which it is not lawful for
a man to utter ".[1]   And the antithesis is not unimportant.
For what St. Paul finds in his present communion with
Christ is not the vision of God or of all things in God which
would be the final satisfaction of his spiritual longing.
What he finds again and again is the word of comfort,
admonition and guidance for himself and for others on
their earthly pilgrimage.   It is no accident that all the
visions described in the New Testament, outside the Apoca-
lypse, are primarily directive visions, where what is heard
is definitely more important than what is seen.[2]   This
characteristic expresses their nature and function.   They
are not regarded primarily as privileges or marks of attainment granted to those who have reached a special degree of
spiritual insight, but rather as messages to guide the conduct
of the recipient and very often to be communicated to
others.   It is a fundamental thought in the New Testament
that he who hears and obeys a divine message received
through another may be on a spiritual equality with him
to whom the message came.   " He that receives a prophet
in the name of a prophet shall receive a prophet's reward." [3]   For, as St. Paul puts it, it is the edifying of the
whole body through the diverse gifts of individuals that
constitutes the divine purpose, and those who have only
the humbler gifts are not less members of the body.   And
all this emphasis on hearing rather than seeing is connected
in St. Paul's theology with the thought that all Christians
and the whole Christian body are being gradually led
onward and upward through toil and struggle and a dark-

[1] 2 Cor. xii. 4.   In any case St. Paul regards *this* experience as
a special and abnormal privilege.
[2] The vision of St. Stephen at his death (Acts vii. 55) is not an
exception which disproves the rule.
[3] Matt. x. 41.

ness which has only begun to break, towards a glory not yet seen which remains to be revealed in the last great act of God. " Now I see in a mirror darkly, but then face to face." [1] " The night is far spent ",[2] but it is not yet gone. Meanwhile the spiritual ear can hear the Christ more plainly than the eye can see. Communion is still at best indirect. " Brethren, I count not myself yet to have apprehended . . . I press toward the mark for the prize of the high calling of God in Christ Jesus." [3] All the religious associations which have formed themselves about the words " call " and " calling " have their historical origin in the characteristically Jewish conviction that in this world God communicates with man through the hearing of a summons rather than through sight.

I am not forgetting the tremendous language which St. Paul also uses about his personal union with the risen Christ. " I have been crucified with Christ," he writes, " yet I live ; and yet no longer I, but Christ liveth in me." [4] But here surely St. Paul is thinking, not so much of his own conscious communion or communication with his Lord, as of the Lord's activity through him. St. Paul, indeed, cannot speak of his own absolute union with Christ in this way, without remembering at once that there is still something lacking, an open vision still withheld. And so immediately after the words quoted he adds, " And that life which I now live in the flesh I live in faith ", not sight. The great phrase " to be in Christ " means to St. Paul not primarily what we call " a mystical experience ", but rather active membership in that new-created manhood, the manhood of the new age, of which Christ is the head, but which cannot attain to the full glory of its communion until the body also is redeemed.

First, the Christ veiling his glory in the form of a servant crucified for men : next, the word of atonement and forgiveness, and Christ speaking in the half-darkness to the spiritual ears of believers whom he guides : finally, the day broken, and the Christ seen face to face in a wholly transfigured and glorious world. Such are the essential

---

[1] 1 Cor. xiii. 12.
[2] Rom. xiii. 12.
[3] Phil. iii. 13 *sqq.*
[4] Gal. ii. 20.

stages of salvation through Christ in the theology of St.
Paul. We shall never understand either St. Paul's mysticism or his doctrine of the incarnation, until we grasp the
truth that to him all of these stages, and their sequence
upon one another, are equally essential to God's plan.

CHAPTER XI

THE CHRISTOLOGY OF ST. JOHN

IN ATTEMPTING to interpret the theology of the Gospel and First Epistle of St. John we are confronted at once by difficulties due to the uncertainty of their author-ship. It is impossible to disregard the question of author-ship altogether, since our interpretation of the author's essential meaning must be very different from the tra-ditional interpretation, if we suppose him to have been a Christian mystic or visionary of the early second century to whom the historical facts, as such, of the life of Jesus were of no essential importance. On the other hand, a critical examination of the problem of authorship would be obviously out of place in a work such as the present. I must therefore content myself with stating dogmatically a broad hypothesis as to the authorship of these books, which seems to me to be required in order to make their teaching intelligible.

1. THE DOUBLE AIM OF ST. JOHN'S TEACHING

We will suppose that the author, whether he was John the son of Zebedee or not, was at the time he wrote one of the last survivors, perhaps actually the last, of those who had seen Jesus in the flesh. This hypothesis will give us a key to the purpose with which the books were written, and in the light of which their theology is to be understood.

(1) At the time St. John wrote there was, we will first assume, much questioning among the less philosophical and more literal-minded Christians about the second coming of Christ. Some were relying upon a supposed promise of Jesus himself that he would return in glory before the whole generation of those to whom he spoke had passed away. St. John himself did not believe that this promise

was ever made, at any rate with the meaning it was supposed to bear, nor did he, in all probability, believe that
the second coming would ever take place in the literal way
in which the imagination of these simple-minded Christians
depicted it.   He knows therefore that his own approaching
death will bring a sore trial to their faith.   He is afraid
that many will be caused to stumble when he himself passes
away and the world still goes on.   Accordingly he desires,
before he departs, to set forth a permanent record of
Christ's life and teaching, which will show once for all that
the eternal truth revealed in him does not depend on any
second coming to bring the world to an end before a stated
period of time has elapsed.   He wants to make it clear
that the popular belief is based on a misunderstanding of
the whole revelation which Jesus brought.   But he knows
also that he will not achieve his aim of saving men's faith
by direct and controversial denials which would in fact
do more harm than good.   A new constructive work is
needed which will help those whose faith is in danger to
gain a deeper insight into the truth that is in Jesus.

(2) Secondly, we must suppose, there is another danger
of a quite different kind threatening the faith of other
Christians.   The false esoteric mysticism, which St. Paul
began to combat in Colossians, has by this time assumed
a more definite shape and become a formidable enemy of
the gospel.   It has already passed into the gnosticism with
which orthodoxy was in conflict all through the second
century.   The adherents of this heresy did not believe in
any literal " second coming " ; but neither did they believe
that at the first coming the Son of God had really been
incarnate or actually suffered in human flesh.   They seem
to have imagined that some divine spirit or emanation
from the deity had come upon the man Jesus at his baptism
and left him before the passion.   But really what happened
exactly in the case of Jesus or any other historical person
did not essentially matter to them.   For the whole phe-
nomenal and material world was in their view either evil
or unreal.   In so far as it was real at all, its existence could
not be due directly to the creative act of God, but was
to be accounted for by an elaborate theory of divine

emanations, in which the pure spirituality of the divine being was gradually debased until at last matter could be formed.   According to this doctrine it was unthinkable that God should reveal himself in the flesh, still more that he should suffer in it.   Salvation and immortality for man were found in the reascent of the spirit that was in man towards the pure spirit which was properly divine. This ascent could only be achieved by progressive separation of the spirit from the flesh ; and the proof of the reality of this separation was found in the mystical vision or knowledge, attained through ascetic discipline, in which the spirit appeared to function independently of the body. According to gnosticism, the life of Christ might have been some mysterious theophany, or else Jesus might have been the greatest of all human mystics or gnostics, but there could have been no incarnation of God.   Such a doctrine, St. John well knew, though it avoided all the crudity of eschatological beliefs derived from Judaism and made a strong appeal to the more refined souls in the Christian community, was nevertheless more fundamentally opposed to the Christian gospel of redemption than any expectation of a sudden rending of the heavens at the Lord's return.

St. John therefore had to contend both with the popular Hebraic adventism which relied upon supposed predictions of Jesus, and with the mystical Hellenic gnosticism which disparaged history altogether.   His aim was to use both his historical knowledge and the fruits of his spiritual meditation in order to present a witness which would show Jesus to be the full and final revelation in the flesh of God's eternal love and truth.   Against the adventists he emphasizes the finality of the revelation which has already been given.   There is no need to look anxiously for any future event which will reveal the Christ in any glory different from that already consummated through his crucifixion.   The event of his first coming in the flesh has already revealed the full eternal meaning of judgement and of resurrection.   The Holy Spirit's work is to interpret that revelation to Christians and to unite them with the living Christ who was incarnate, rather than to pin their faith to something which has not yet happened.   On the other hand, against the gnostics St. John would bring out clearly the vital fact that the full and final revelation of God was in the flesh. The truly spiritual knowledge of God therefore does not consist in any purely inward or mystical experience in which the spirit of man is separated from his body ; and for the same reason it is entirely inseparable from love manifested in simple external charity towards the brethren. Belief and conduct, theory and practice, to St. John are one. The truth itself is something which must be outwardly done in order to be inwardly known.

We will now examine more closely these two aspects of St. John's teaching in order to see what is the essential doctrine of Christ's person which lies behind them. It will help us at each point to mark the characteristic difference between St. John's presentation of Christian truth and St. Paul's.

2.   THE SECOND ADVENT IN ST. JOHN'S CHRISTOLOGY

St. Paul's mind clearly retains the Hebraic cosmology of two worlds or ages, the present world of sin and struggle and the future world of righteousness, peace and communion with God ; this world is to be ended and the next world brought in by a catastrophic act of God which will include the reappearance of Jesus in glory, a universal judgement, and the transformation of the whole of material nature. Nevertheless, even to St. Paul the coming of Christ has, as it were, confused the temporal boundary between this world and the next. His cross and resurrection have enabled the spirit of the Christian to attain already by faith to the next world, of which the risen manhood of Christ is itself the first-fruits. Spiritually the Christian has already risen from the dead and lives with the life of God's new creation in Christ Jesus. On the other hand, in so far as he still has a mortal body subject to decay, death, and the lusts of the flesh, the Christian still lives in this world ; his communion with the risen Christ is indirect and incomplete ; he waits for the future parousia to complete his redemption and his sonship.

In St. John the Hebraic idea of the new world to be inaugurated at a future date, together with the future judgement and resurrection, seems to have withdrawn altogether into the background. It is doubtful whether there is any great cosmic event of that nature to which St. John looks forward. It is significant that whereas St. Paul writes, " The night is far spent and the day is at hand ",[1] St. John goes so far as to say, " The darkness is passing and the true light already shineth."[2] In St. John the contrast between present and future worlds (αἰῶνες) seems to be almost wholly merged in the contrast between the evil world (κόσμος) which passes away, and the eternal truth of God which has been revealed in the midst of the darkness by Christ, himself the way, the truth, and the life. To St. John everything in this created world which is according to God's will, partakes of the truth and therefore abides. On the other hand, this same created world, apart from the manifestation of the Son of God within it, is under the dominion of evil, and is therefore evanescent and perishing. Before the incarnation the Word was from the beginning God's agent in creation, and " the light that lighteth every man " ; but in a sinful world he was not clearly revealed, and there was no clear discrimination possible between the good and the evil, or between the saved and the perishing among mankind. Then in Jesus the Word himself became flesh ; there was a clear manifestation in outward fact of God's grace and truth. Forthwith judgement takes place. Everything that is really good and true in human life is attracted to Jesus and finds its eternity in him. Everything else rejects Jesus, and thereby suffers condemnation. Men must discriminate themselves by taking one line or the other.[3]

Moreover, the resurrection of Jesus does not seem to be regarded by St. John mainly as the promise of a resurrection of Christians into a new-created world at a future day. Rather it is the sign and assurance of the true abidingness of everything that is born of God and therefore

---

[1] Rom. xiii. 12.　　　　　　　　[2] 1 John ii. 8.
[3] See John i. 1–3 and 9 ; iii. 16–21.

triumphs over the transitoriness of the world.[1] And in this matter St. John seems to wish his readers to understand that Christ's revelation supersedes the popular Hebraic eschatology. For when Martha says of Lazarus, " I know that he shall rise again at the last day", Jesus at once replies, " I am the resurrection and the life. He that believeth on me, though he die, yet shall he live ; and whosoever liveth and believeth on me shall never die. Believest thou this ? " I do not think that our Lord's words to the Pharisees in the fifth chapter of the Gospel are inconsistent with this interpretation of St. John's meaning. For here Jesus is addressing Jewish opponents, not his intimate friends and disciples, and St. John may well be suggesting to his readers that the words here uttered, like those about the destruction of the temple, bear one meaning to Pharisees and another to true believers. It is possible that St. John understood " the coming forth of those in the graves " to be a pictorial description of the awakening of souls to accept or reject the light. Indeed, it is difficult otherwise to understand the words, " the hour cometh and now is ".[2] Similarly, in the sixth chapter the saying, " I will raise him up at the last day " (also addressed to non-believers), is carefully balanced by the words, " Verily, I say unto you, he that believeth on me hath eternal life." [3] On the whole it does not seem that St. John himself understood the expression " the last day " to refer to a historical or quasi-historical event which was still in the future when he wrote. Probably he would have said that " the last day ", in so far as it was a historical period of time, began with the gift of the Holy Spirit to the disciples. It cannot be without significance that the word " hope ", whether as substantive or as verb, which is so characteristic of St. Paul, only occurs once in the Johannine books.[4]

Yet it would be absurd to suppose that St. John does not look forward to any future when Christians at last will enter fully into the joy of their Lord, and their communion

---

[1] See 1 John ii. 17 ; v. 4.
[2] John v. 25–9. See ii. 19 for the words about the temple.
[3] John vi. 40 and 44.   [4] 1 John iii. 3.

with him and with the Father will be consummated. He does not believe that the Christian has so perfectly attained eternal life already that there is nothing left to hope for. Rather his real hope is that the Christian, advancing in communion with his Lord, will follow him to a " place " or plane of being, where the Son of God eternally is. " If any man will do me service, let him follow me ; and, where I am, there shall my servant be." [1] And again, " In my Father's house are many mansions . . . And, if I go to prepare a place for you, I come again (present tense) and will receive you unto myself, that, where I am, there ye may be also. And whither I go, ye know the way." [2] God's universe is here pictured as consisting of many mansions or abodes, some closer to God's presence and glory than others. This world of our present earthly experience is one of them, and one far removed from the highest. Yet the Son entered and tabernacled in it for a time, in order to reveal God's love in the flesh, without surrendering that eternal communion with the Father which is the life of heaven itself. The Son did not abide long in the earthly mansion. He left it, when his mission was fulfilled, in order to take the manhood he had assumed up to the highest, and to enable those who believe in him to follow. He has thus become the living way. But when he spoke of coming again and receiving his disciples unto himself, he did not, according to St. John's thought, refer to any external or catastrophic event at the end of history. He was referring in the first instance to the gift of the Paraclete who would guide them into a clearer knowledge of himself and a deeper understanding of his words and works than was possible for them before he had been glorified through the cross. St. John would teach us that the disciples were raised to a higher " mansion ", a more direct communion with Christ, when the Paraclete was given. But there is a further hope still. Its fulfilment will be a complete transformation of Christians themselves wrought through the final manifestation to them of Christ as he eternally is in his unity with the Father. " It doth not yet appear what we shall be ; but we know that, when

[1] John xii. 26.　　　　[2] John xiv. 2-4.

(lit. if) he doth appear (or, it doth appear), we shall be like him, because we shall see him even as he is." Meanwhile we know already that we are God's children. Further speculation is idle.[1]

It is evident that in regard to eschatology St. John's outlook is on the whole less Hebraic and more akin to Hellenism than St. Paul's.

3.   THE INCARNATION VERSUS GNOSTICISM

It is otherwise when we come to consider the second aspect of St. John's teaching, that aspect which confronts and opposes the Gnostics. St. Paul had met gnostic tendencies by insisting on two great principles : (*a*) that Christian life means the service of the whole community which is Christ's body, and that any doctrine of an inner circle of enlightened persons within the Church who possess an esoteric knowledge, is an offence against the Christian conception of the fellowship of love ; and (*b*) that in this present world all Christians, since they still live in the flesh, must be content to walk by faith, not sight, and look forward in hope to full vision in the world to come.

But in this matter St. John changes the Pauline emphasis. He insists that to those who, while still on earth, have been born again, the flesh is the very medium in which the glory of the eternal Word has been revealed. " The Word became flesh and we beheld his glory." [2] Though the coming of the Paraclete brings a closer fellowship with Christ than was possible before his ascension, still the

---

[1] 1 John iii. 2. The reference to " a last time " and the coming of Anti-Christ in 1 John ii. 18 *sqq.*, would seem to be an example of what has been called " the transmuted eschatology " of St. John. Just as, in the Gospel, the judgement and " the second coming " are shown to be not just events in the future, but rather present experiences in the life of the Church, so with the coming of Anti-Christ also. It is already " a last time ". Anti-Christ has arrived, and has begun his activities in the person of false teachers who deny Christ's coming in the flesh. The real promise of Christ is not a dated second coming, but the eternal life which is his present gift through the Spirit. The Christian's salvation is to abide in the fellowship of that life, and to let happen what will.

[2] John i. 14.

believer who has seen Jesus in the flesh has seen the Father, and there is no other vision of God possible for man until the final manifestation when the Christian will see his Lord even as he is. " No man hath seen God at any time : God only-begotten, who is in the bosom of the Father, he hath declared him." [1] Meanwhile the closer communion is to be sought and shown, not in the cultivation of mystical experiences, but in the keeping of the commandments of Jesus, of which the supreme commandment is to love the brethren. The greatest fruit of the life of Jesus is the communication to man of that love in which the Father is eternally united to the Son. The motive of the passion was that the world might know that the Son loved the Father and obeyed his will.[2] And the proof of the presence of that love among Christians is their relief of one another's bodily needs.[3]

At this point, then, St. John's opposition to gnosticism is perhaps more radical even than St. Paul's. There is no eagerness to shake off the fleshly body as though it clogged the wings of the spirit. There is no hint even of a longing " to depart and be with Christ, which is very far better ".[4] The desire to be with Christ and the duty to do Christ's work on earth are no longer felt as even possibly conflicting or competing claims. According to St. John, it is precisely as he follows Christ in the flesh and walks even as he walked, that the Christian has eternal communion with his Lord, and so waits for whatever may be to come with a quiet confidence which feels no strain either of hope or fear. As we read St. John attentively, we recognize that we are in the presence of a spiritual experience which has no parallel elsewhere. It has neither the anxious looking forward (ἀποκαραδοκία) which is characteristic of the Hebrew, nor the reliance upon a purely inward or intellectual spirituality which is characteristic of the Greek. It unites the Greek's sense of the abiding eternal with the Hebrew's recognition of the value of that which is outward, bodily, and practical. It seems

---

[1] John i. 18, according to the reading of R.V. Margin. Cf. xiv. 9.

[2] John xiv. 31.   [3] 1 John iii. 17.   [4] Phil. i. 23.

to spring from a faith so sure that God's eternal love has been manifested in the flesh that it is content to wait in that same flesh until in God's good time this world, already known to be passing, has finally passed.

It is true that several of Christ's sayings in St. John's Gospel either make or imply an antithesis between flesh and spirit,[1] but in every case the meaning of the antithesis is plain from the context.   The Spirit, not the flesh, is the source of true life ; natural processes of themselves cannot produce what is spiritually living.   On the other hand, what God's Spirit quickens is not merely the spirit of man but also the flesh so as to make it the expression and instrument of spirit.   Thus the fundamental opposition is not between spirit and flesh (as it was sometimes to St. Paul), but rather between the fellowship of God's children whom the Spirit has quickened into life, and the world outside which has no true life at all.

4.   THE ESSENCE OF JOHANNINE CHRISTOLOGY

What, then, are we to say as to the essential features of St. John's Christology ?   We shall perhaps see them most clearly by again comparing St. John's thought with St. Paul's.   By both apostles Jesus who was crucified under Pontius Pilate and rose again from the tomb is identified with the divine person who was God's agent in creation and whose full glory will be openly and directly manifested at the end of the world.   But by St. Paul the earthly life of Jesus is valued for what it has effected rather than for what in itself it reveals.   To him it is as it were the first step in the divine action for the forgiveness and justification of men.   Its importance therefore is found mainly in its results.   One of those results is the reception by Jesus of " the name above every name ", which manifests him, only after the ascension, as fully divine.   The incarnation is the precedent condition of that revelation rather than the revelation itself.   St. Paul's thought follows this order, because he reaches belief in the incarnation through belief in the atonement.   St. John, on the other hand, values the

---

[1] John i. 13 ;   iii. 6 ;   vi. 63.

earthly life of Jesus mainly and primarily for the revelation which it conveys in itself of the eternal communion of love between the Father and the Son.   True, for St. John also the incarnation is decisive in its effects.   Its effects are indeed in one way presented as more finally decisive by him than by St. Paul.   But for St. John those effects are the effects of a revelation in the earthly life, whereas for St. Paul the revelation is itself one of the effects of that life. St. John gives us no theology of the atonement.   But he clearly regards the taking away of sin as one effect of the revelation of divine love consummated in the crucifixion. In this way he may be said to reach belief in the atonement through belief in the incarnation.

This central contrast in the theology of the two apostles may be illustrated in many different ways.

(a) Whereas St. Paul's characteristic word is grace, St. John's is truth.   To St. Paul the earthly life of Jesus is primarily an act of divine grace, to St. John it is a declaration of divine truth.   To St. Paul that act of grace has done its work ; it is a thing of the past, and henceforth we are to know Christ no more after the flesh.[1]   But for St. John the coming of the Paraclete can never supersede the knowledge of God historically incarnate in Jesus.   The Paraclete's work is rather to bring to remembrance what Jesus had said, and to interpret the true eternal meaning of his words and deeds.

(b) Again, it is significant that all through St. John's Gospel there is a suggestion that the words of Jesus, himself the incarnate Word, are somehow more important even than his works.   " The words that I speak unto you are spirit and are life." [2]   It is a higher way of salvation to believe in the truth of his words, than to believe " for the very works' sake ".[3]   And though the words are for ever unique, the works are not.   " The works that I do shall ye do also, and greater works than these shall ye do, because I go to my Father." [4]   Indeed, in St. John's

---

[1] 2 Cor. v. 16.   It is clear, however, from the context that the phrase " after the flesh " qualifies the verb " know " rather than the substantive " Christ ".

[2] John vi. 63.   [3] John xiv. 11.   [4] John xiv. 12.

record it is clear that the deepest purpose of Christ's mighty works themselves is to be signs, i.e., to have the value of words, revealing his relation to God. Everything that happens in the gospel-story is regarded by St. John as in this way symbolic. There are no parables on our Lord's lips here, because his whole life is presented as, in one sense, parable. But only in one sense ; for St. John would utterly have repudiated the notion that his record is " symbolic " in the modern sense, i.e., that it is truth embodied in a tale, a tale which would be not less true if it were myth or fiction. To St. John the historical fact, the real flesh, of Jesus is the only medium of the true revelation of God's love.

(c) Finally, St. John's Gospel conveys the impression that in his inmost being the Son of God, though truly incarnate and truly suffering and dying, had yet in a sense never left the Father's side. The repeated and solemn use of the present tense by Jesus when speaking of his own essential life and being cannot be accidental.[1] Christ's true life, so St. John seems to teach, is always in heaven. The heavenly communion between the Father and the Son is not really interrupted, it is only manifested, because the Son tabernacles in the flesh.

We may perhaps sum up the differences between St. Paul's theology of the incarnation and St. John's by saying that to St. Paul the earthly life of Jesus is the supremely effective act of God's love, to St. John it is its uniquely true symbol or expression. When Christian thought has succeeded in doing justice to both aspects of the truth together, Christology will be complete.

NOTE ON ST. JOHN'S PROLOGUE

The Prologue to St. John's Gospel is obviously a crucial passage for the understanding of his doctrine of the incarnation. The main difficulty for exegesis is to determine at what point St. John passes from speaking of what has always been true from the beginning of history to what first became true

---

[1] See, e.g., John vii. 34 ; viii. 24, 28, 58 ; xi. 25 ; xii. 26 ; xiv. 3, 6, 19. See also 1 John iii. 2.

with the earthly life of Jesus.   On this point two views are commonly held :

(*a*) The first, and more usual, marks the point of transition at the beginning of *v*. 11.   According to this view St. John begins to speak directly of the historic incarnation with the words " he came unto his own " (the verb is in the aorist), whereas before he had been speaking of the presence and activity of the Logos all through history from the creation.

(*b*) Others hold that the transition is not really made till *v*. 14 with the words " And the Word became flesh ".   According to this view St. John in the previous verses has been affirming not only that all down history the Word, as the true light that lighteth every man, was always coming into the world, not only that he was always in the world, though the world knew him not, but also that in the history of the chosen people (perhaps in other history too ?) he came into his own, and his own people received him not.   Even before the incarnation there were some who received him, and to them he gave power to become sons of God.   (Such language might be used of Old Testament saints.)   Then in *v*. 14 comes the climax.   At last in the fullness of time the Word became flesh, and then we beheld his glory.   What the Word had always been, and what he had always done, was at length revealed in outward fact.

(*c*) A third view, however, is possible, and, I think, convincing.   According to this we should mark the transition at the beginning of *v*. 4, with the words, " That which came to be in him was life."   This view, however, requires a punctuation and translation of *vv*. 3 to 5 different from that which we find in our English Bible.   I agree with Dr. J. O. F. Murray (*Jesus according to St. John*) that in *vv*. 3 and 4 St. John intends a contrast between " all things ", which came into being *through* the Word, and the one thing, " Life ", which has come into being *in* the Word.   I should translate *vv*. 3 to 5 as follows :

All things came into being *through* him, and without him nothing came to be.   That which hath come into being *in* him was Life, and the Life was the light of men.   And the light (still) shineth in the darkness ;   and the darkness did not overtake (or overcome, or come over) it.

In these verses St. John is asserting that in Jesus something was born into the world which was in a new relation to the eternal Word ;   it was not (like all created things) *through* him, but actually *in* him, or, as later theology put it, in hypostatic union with him.   This something was true eternal Life, and this Life, in the historic ministry of Jesus, was the light of men. And, though Jesus left the world to return to the Father, the light still goes on shining in the world's darkness, and the darkness did not come over it. (There is an allusion here to the synoptists' story of the darkness at the crucifixion, which St. John omits from his own narrative.) The next verses, 6 to 8, deal with the Baptist's relation to the life of Christ. (There is no awkwardness in the mention of the Baptist at this point, if *vv.* 4 and 5 are understood as I have just suggested.) Verses 9 to 13 amplify the meaning of what has been said about the same historic life. Verse 14 sums up what has gone before, and the " we " in this verse (" we beheld ") is to be understood of those disciples, John and others, who are referred to in *vv.* 12 and 13 as among those who had received Christ and been born again as God's children.

Thus understood, the Prologue most clearly relates the revelation of the communion between the Father and the Son, which the rest of the Gospel records, to the doctrine of the Logos, a doctrine which must have had some special importance, owing, probably, to misuse of it in the interests of gnosticism. St. John wishes to insist on the identification of the Logos with the Son who is eternally and personally God, whereas heretical gnostics, following Philo, probably made the Logos a sort of intermediate being, who could be regarded as the agent of creation precisely because he was not fully or purely divine. St. John carefully identifies the Logos, who was in the beginning with God and was God (i. 1), with God only-begotten, who is in the bosom of the Father (i. 18), If the interpretation of the Prologue given above is correct, St. John would express the fundamental mystery of the incarnation by saying that with the birth of Jesus true Life, which is *in* the Logos as his own nature, without ceasing to be in the Logos, nevertheless came into the created world, whereas all things that are simply created came into being through the agency of the Logos, but not *in* him.

CHAPTER XII

THE CHRISTOLOGY OF THE EPISTLE TO THE HEBREWS

No SURVEY of New Testament teaching on the incarnation would be complete without some mention of the Epistle to the Hebrews. The Epistle is of peculiar interest for the Christian theologian, because it shows how a quite unknown author, of very different temperament and training from either St. John or St. Paul, held the same essential faith as to our Lord's divine person and genuine humanity, and yet could give to that faith a quite distinct theological expression in the days before any definite standard of intellectual orthodoxy had been established.

1. THE AUTHOR'S TEMPERAMENT AND CHARACTER

In one very important sense the Epistle to the Hebrews is the most *religious* book in the New Testament, and indeed the only one which bears throughout the marks of a definitely *religious* motive.[1] In all the other books, though their central theme is the gospel of God in Christ Jesus, allusions to cultus and worship are scattered and incidental. This Epistle, on the other hand, is the work of a mind concentrated on worship, and on the ideas and practices associated with it. Its author is a man of austerely religious temper, with a large natural endowment of that reverential awe for God which is kindled and expressed by dignified and solemn ceremonial. He also shows a con-

---

[1] If this use of the word " religious " seems too paradoxical, I may perhaps express my point more clearly and accurately thus : Hebrews is marked out among all the books of the Bible by the interest which it shows in man's approach to God, whereas elsewhere the main emphasis is laid on God's approach to man.

siderable inclination to rigorism ; and in both respects his attitude of mind has a resemblance to that of the early Tractarians. He has great literary gifts ; but his art, while it shows many traces of a training in rhetoric, is modelled on severe and classical lines. Utterly unlike both St. Paul and St. John, he is careful to avoid the language of the emotions. The word ἀγάπη only occurs twice in the Epistle,[1] and the verb ἀγαπάω not at all, except in one quotation from the Old Testament. The only mention of God as Father is made in connexion with fatherly chastisement,[2] in a passage which suggests that the author's nationality was not Jewish. Yet at the same time no other writer in the New Testament dwells so movingly on the truth that it became the Son of God to share our common flesh and blood, and to become in all things, save in sin, like us, so that as the great high-priest of humanity he might be sympathetic to human sufferings and temptations.[3]

The general impression that the Epistle gives us of its author is that he was a man of strong human emotions rigidly disciplined both by religious awe and by a stern adherence to intellectual consistency. Just because intellectually as well as emotionally he so deeply appreciates the perfect fittingness of Christ's atonement as he apprehends it, he is uncompromisingly stern to those who having once believed become apostate. Just because God's offer of grace through the sacrifice of Christ is so perfect, there can, he feels, be no second chance for those who accept and then fall away. He pictures God as himself severely consistent both in his love and in his justice. On the one hand, the Epistle contains no hint of any divine wrath to be visited on those who have not heard or do not understand the gospel. On the other hand, it offers no hope to those " who have done despite to the spirit of grace " itself.[4]

The thought of the author to the Hebrews is like St. Paul's in that his primary interest is in the atonement rather than in the incarnation ; but there is as much con-

[1] Heb. vi. 10 ; x. 24.　　　　　[2] xii. 9–11.
[3] See ii. 10–18 ; iv. 15.　　　　[4] x. 29.

trast as resemblance. St. Paul, astonishingly acute and
powerful thinker as he is, expresses his feelings freely and
passionately, without any great regard either for literary
style or for logical consistency. At one moment he offers
us a picture of all humanity doomed to suffer the punishment of divine wrath, at another the picture of all humanity
redeemed by God's love in Christ. He does not hesitate
to suggest that it is God's love which delivers man from
his wrath. The author to the Hebrews does not use the
language of love and wrath in St. Paul's manner. His
emotion is much more restrained, and his thought more
unified by logic. He does not convey the same impression,
which St. Paul and St. John both convey each in his
different manner, that God himself has drawn near to man
in Jesus Christ. To him Christ is rather the perfect high-
priest who by his sacrifice of himself enables us to draw
near to God in perfect worship. He has a greater sense of
the abiding remoteness of God's holy and awful majesty,
even though he shares the common conviction of Christians
that God has in these last days spoken to us by his Son.

2. THE AUTHOR'S PLATONISM

Such being the author's habit of mind, it is not surprising
to find that the influence of Alexandrian Platonism, and
especially of Philo, is more apparent in this Epistle than
anywhere else in the New Testament. And this influence
causes the author's eschatology to approximate, at least
in appearance, rather to St. John's than to St. Paul's.
Jewish and Jewish-Christian apocalyptists envisaged the
relation between imperfect and perfect states of being
primarily in terms of time, distinguishing between this
age or world of imperfection and the perfect age or world
to come. But in general the language of Hebrews is true
to Platonism in distinguishing between the imperfect world
as a world of shadows or images, and the perfect world as
that of heavenly and spiritual realities. For this author
the present reality of the heavenly sphere, the sphere into
which Christ has passed, and to which we are *anchored* [1]

[1] vi. 19.

by hope, is the fundamentally important thing. It is evident that when Christian hope is likened to an anchor, it has lost much of the strictly temporal significance which it had for St. Paul.

However, in the intermingling of Gentile and Jewish ideas, which had been going on for some time before the Christian era, neither the Hellenizers nor the more strictly Hebraic thinkers could afford to be quite consistent. Even Jewish apocalyptists pictured a *true* Jerusalem already in the heavens, a conception to which St. Paul alludes in Galatians,[1] and which corresponds with that of " the city which hath foundations ", which is also " the city to come ", in Hebrews.[2] For his part the author of Hebrews looks forward quite unplatonically to a time when this imperfect world-order shall be abolished.[3] The essentially Hebraic expression " world to come " occurs more than once in his Epistle.[4] And one of the main points in his exhortation is to emphasize the need of the forward outlook by reference to the faith shown by the saints of the Old Testament. Moreover, even the word " shadow ", which sounds strictly platonic, has in his use of it a temporal reference which is really quite unplatonic, as it has in Campbell's line " coming events cast their shadows before ".[5] The author imperfectly reconciles a Hebraic or Pauline philosophy of history with a Platonism for which history is irrelevant.

On the whole, it seems true to say that his Platonism excludes any great interest in eschatological speculation; but, like other New Testament writers, he is so keenly aware of the conflict between Christianity and the life of this world that he is convinced that such acute tension cannot last very long. Thus, he writes of an imminent judgement, but only in quite general, though most solemn, terms.[6] He uses eschatological phrases mainly to suggest the absolute finality of the revelation in Christ.[7] There is

---

[1] Gal. iv. 26.   [2] xi. 10 ; xiii. 14.   [3] See xii. 26 ; vi. 5.
[4] ii. 5 ; vi. 5. But in the former passage the word translated " world " is not $\alpha\iota\omega\nu$ (age), but $o\iota\kappa o\upsilon\mu\acute{\epsilon}\nu\eta$ (lit. the inhabited earth).
[5] See x. 1. Cf. Col. ii. 17.   [6] See, e.g., x. 26–31.
[7] See, e.g., i. 2 ; ix. 26.

one quite explicit reference to the Second Coming.[1]   But
this reference hardly accords with his picture of Christ as
having once for all entered the heavenly sanctuary, or of
Christ as our forerunner and pioneer who has opened up
the way by which we are to follow him.[2]   The whole theme
of the Epistle is our pilgrimage to the heavenly city where
Christ reigns, and the expectation of Christ's return to
earth seems logically irrelevant to it.   The dominance of
this same theme accounts for the absence of any teaching
about Christ's *resurrection,* as distinct from his passage
through death into the heavenly world.   It is the resurrection which carries with it in St. Paul's mind the prophecy
of a future transformation of material nature and the final
redemption of the body.   But such ideas are much less
congenial to the Platonism of this Epistle than they are to
the more Hebraic thought of St. Paul and St. John.

3.   THE AUTHOR'S DOCTRINE OF THE INCARNATION

The Christology of Hebrews has more affinity to the
kenotic theories of modern theologians than any found
elsewhere in the New Testament.   On the one hand, the
author makes it quite clear that Jesus is the eternal Son,
the effulgence of God's glory and the very image of his
substance.[3]   Again, in comparing our Lord with Moses,
he writes that " Jesus hath been counted worthy of more
glory than Moses by so much as he that hath built the
house hath more honour than the house "[4]—a passage
which implies that, if we consider the difference between
creator and creature, Jesus must appear, as it were, on the
divine side of the differentiating line.   On the other hand,
no other book in the New Testament emphasizes so strongly
as does Hebrews the genuineness not merely of our Lord's
manhood but also of the limitations imposed on him by

---

[1] ix. 28.
[2] See vi. 20 ; ix. 12 ; ii. 10, where the word translated " cap-
tain " means rather " pioneer ".   In this discussion of the author's
eschatology and its relation to his Platonism I have derived help
especially from Narborough's commentary in the Clarendon Bible
Series.
[3] i. 2, 3.   [4] iii. 3.

the flesh. The author can actually write of Jesus, " who in the days in his flesh, having offered up prayers and supplications with strong crying and tears unto him that was able to save him from death, and having been heard for his godly fear, though he was Son, yet learned obedience by the things which he suffered ".[1]

How then are these contrary aspects of our Lord's person reconciled in the thought of this Epistle ? The key surely is in these words, " Having therefore, brethren, boldness to enter into the holy place by the blood of Jesus, by the way which he dedicated for us, a new and living way, through the veil, that is to say his flesh ",[2] etc. The author's thought starts with the assumption, consonant both with Platonism and with Judaism, that there is a veil between man and God, something which hides God from man, and hinders man from drawing near to God. This veil or barrier, which exists in spiritual reality, is symbolized outwardly or " shadowed " by the veil which separated the inner shrine of the Tabernacle, so that no one was allowed to enter it except the high priest on the annual day of atonement. The real veil is made impassable by sin ; and hence it is that in the world of outward symbol the high priest, before entering the shrine, must always offer sacrifice for the sins of the people and for his own. But the real veil does not consist only in sin, though it may be wholly its consequence.[3] In the natural material body the spirit dwells, as it were, encased by mortality ; the flesh, though not in itself evil or sinful, is still like a curtain which hides from man the true vision of spiritual and eternal realities. This curtain would still be there even if man were sinless, though it is sin which renders it altogether opaque, and perhaps, if man had never sinned, there would have been no mortal flesh to constitute a veil.

The essence of the Christological belief which we find in Hebrews is that through this real veil Jesus has opened and

---

[1] v. 7, 8. To insert either the definite or the indefinite article before the word " Son " misrepresents the Greek.

[2] x. 19.

[3] There is nothing to show whether the author regards the existence of the veil between man and God as a result of the Fall.

dedicated for man the one true way into the fullness of God's presence and eternal life. This finished work of Jesus presupposes two conditions. First, Jesus is himself God's Son. He came forth from the divine side, from beyond the veil. The work had to be initiated from God's side. Through Jesus as his Son God speaks and acts. But, secondly, although Jesus came forth from God, it is equally true that he really did come *forth* to the human side of the veil which separates man from God. The way to God which he has dedicated is a way which man has to follow, and it must be therefore one which man is capable of following in spite of the limitations of his now mortal nature. Therefore Jesus, in being born as man, accepted all the restrictions which belong of necessity to natural, fleshly, and mortal manhood. Sin is not among these, since the flesh, which constitutes the veil, is not in itself evil or sinful. Nevertheless, there was even for Jesus a veil of the flesh. He did not enjoy on earth that uninterrupted consciousness of full and open communion with the Father, which belongs to him as Son in heaven. Hence the extraordinarily bold statement which we have already quoted from the fifth chapter, and also the repeated insistence that Christ's work for man required that he should really share our flesh and blood and should sympathize with us in all things through entering into the experience of finite and mortal manhood.

How, then, was the living way opened and in what does it consist ? To these questions the Epistle gives a clear answer. The way was not found in any mystical union with Godhead in which the spirit seems to separate itself from the body. It was found in the complete surrender of the human will of Jesus to the will of God, the surrender of obedience consummated in the self-sacrifice of the perfect high-priest upon the cross. That sacrifice accomplished through death leads on to the life of the ascended Christ in heaven which now communicates itself to believers and enables them to follow in his steps. The blood of Jesus, which sprinkles our consciences,[1] means to the author of Hebrews, in accordance with Old Testament symbolism,

[1] ix. 13, 14.

his life which has passed through death. The complaint of some commentators, that the author gives no reason why the shedding of the blood should be necessary, is quite unjustified. The shedding is necessary, because death alone can exhibit and complete the perfect obedience of the life self-offered. And, for the sacrifice to be effective, the life thus offered must in all its purity and power be communicated to those whose consciences are stained with disobedience. Of this communication the author finds a parable or " shadow " in the sprinkling of the victim's blood on the people in the covenant-sacrifice of Exodus. So the sacrifice of Christ avails for Christians, because his offered life of obedience in all its heavenly and spiritual power is communicated to them from the unseen world in answer to their faith.

And thus a new light bursts upon God's whole ordering of the universe. Man, the author of Hebrews boldly maintains, is destined to be the highest of all God's creatures.[1] In the world to come man is to be higher even than the angels ; for does not the psalmist say that man is crowned with glory and worship, and that God has put all things in subjection under his feet ? How can this be true ? The answer is in Jesus. We do not yet see all things in subjection to man ; but we do behold Jesus, who for a little while was made lower than the angels, crowned with glory and worship because of the suffering of death. In other words, Jesus, in his manhood, is already above all, because he endured the cross. It is that supremacy of self-sacrifice and obedience which places him as man above all grades of angelic beings. And, in so far as he enables us to share that same obedience, we shall also share his glory, a glory brighter than that of spirits who have never known the meaning of bodily death. Thus Jesus has shown that the veil of mortal flesh which hides God from man may nevertheless be made the opportunity for an obedience which brings human nature through humiliation nearest to God's throne at last. This is the new and living way, not a way of ascetic separation from the flesh, but

[1] This and the following sentences are a paraphrase of Heb. ii. 5–9.

a way through the flesh, through obedient acceptance of its limitations and mortality, into the highest sanctuary of the heavenly world, which is the world to come. This is the way which Jesus has opened and dedicated for us.

If the foregoing exposition of his thought be accepted, it will be seen that the author of Hebrews, while sharing in all essentials with St. Paul and St. John the same faith in Jesus Christ as truly God and truly man, nevertheless has his own quite distinctive contribution to make to the theology of the incarnation. Because in his mind, as in St. Paul's, the atoning work of Jesus takes precedence of all else, he, like St. Paul, tends to regard the flesh in which Jesus lived on earth as a veil rather than as a direct means of revelation. But, because he regards the earthly life of Jesus as the perfect life of human obedience and trust in God, he adds a suggestion, which St. Paul never makes, that the flesh was in some sense actually a veil between Jesus, as he was on earth, and God, a veil through which Jesus himself had to penetrate by death. This suggestion, it seems, was made possible to the author of Hebrews by his sympathy with Alexandrian Platonism, which regarded material flesh as a barrier to the vision of spiritual realities ; and it is a suggestion of permanent importance in Christology. It seems natural to infer that the author of Hebrews was a Gentile, or at least a Hellenist, who had learned his Christianity, if not from St. Paul himself, at any rate in the Pauline school. The affinity of his thought with the characteristic features of St. John's is relatively superficial, and consists in little more than the disappearance of the Pauline emphasis on the last advent.

CHAPTER XIII

THE DEVELOPMENT OF CHRISTOLOGICAL
DOCTRINE IN THE CHURCH

IT HAS been truly said that all down the course of its
history Christian theology has suffered from the refusal
of the main body of the Jews to accept Jesus as their
Messiah. The original apostles were Jews, and the New
Testament is in the main Jewish literature. But from the
second century onwards the definition and development of
doctrine passed into Gentile hands, and Hebraic thought
ceased to make a fresh and living contribution to Christianity, although its influence through the New Testament
undoubtedly restrained and profoundly modified the
process of Hellenization. Thus the notion of the divine
οἰκονομία, which is so prominent in the Greek Fathers,
is clearly the result of an effort to combine a belief, derived
from the Bible, in God's providence and providential
action with a Hellenic theology which did not think of
God as personally active in mundane affairs.[1]

1. CHRISTOLOGY UP TO CHALCEDON

To the Hellenic mind the most fundamental attribute
of the supreme Godhead was immutability, and from this
immutability the thought of God's impassibility was
immediately derived. From the metaphysical point of
view the doctrine of divine impassibility [2] means that
God is not in any sense subject to suffering or passion ;
for, being immutably perfect, he cannot in any way be
moved, nor can any effect be produced upon or within
him. Thus impassibility implies the exclusion of those

[1] On this subject, see G. L. Prestige, *God in Patristic Thought.*
[2] For a fuller discussion of the meaning of divine impassibility,
see Appendix, pp. 184 *sqq.*

mutual relations which hold between particular entities which act and react upon one another, and the exclusion also of any experience of conation or effort towards an end not yet realized. St. Thomas Aquinas afterwards expressed the same doctrine of the divine perfection by teaching that God is *actus purus*, pure actuality, the being in and for whom nothing is potential or unaccomplished.[1] It follows logically that, if God is in this way impassible, he cannot act in order to accomplish anything, although the eternal and changeless activity of his perfection may be the source and ground of action in his creatures.

The truth is that in Hellenic thought, as has often been pointed out, divine immutability meant not so much a moral stedfastness of will and purpose as the ontological unchangeableness which is contradicted if God from his side ever enters into a new or fresh relation with created beings. That God in Christ has entered into such a new relation is a fundamental presupposition of the New Testament ; and it was precisely at this point therefore that the Hellenizing theology of the Fathers could not do it full justice. The metaphysical dogma of divine impassibility stood in the way. The point at issue was not simply whether it is or is not tolerable to affirm that God suffered on the cross. To the metaphysical mind divine passibility is logically implied by the assertion that God was moved by man's sin to initiate the work of redemption through Jesus Christ. Thus, if we maintain that God is strictly impassible, it seems inconsistent to affirm that the incarnation is essentially God's act for man's salvation ; and the orthodox confession that Jesus Christ is both God and man becomes merely the statement of a problem which theology can do nothing to illuminate.

Of course orthodox Fathers did constantly affirm that the incarnation was God's act for man's salvation ; but they could never make the affirmation consistent with their philosophical conception of God's being and nature. And

---

[1] The above seems to be a fair statement at least of one aspect of St. Thomas's doctrine of the *actus purus*, viz., the Aristotelian aspect. See, e.g., *S.T.*, Pt. I, Q. 3, Arts. 1 and 2, and *S.C.G.*, Bk. I, C. XVI.

thus it was that during the early centuries one theory after another, which set out to make the incarnation more intelligible, ended by making it unreal. Either—and this was the constant danger of Alexandrian theology—the manhood turned out in the last resort to be a mere mask for the deity of Jesus Christ : or the incarnate person was represented as an intermediate being compounded, so to speak, of Godhead and manhood, but not fully God and man—the error of Arianism and, in a different form, of Apollinarianism also : or else, as in the Antiochene school and in some forms of Sabellianism, the reality of the human experience of Jesus was preserved by representing him as the perfect example of a man's communion with God, so that in the last analysis he appears only as the human revealer and servant of the divine being who remains impassible in heaven.

All these types of heresy the Church as a whole strenuously and successfully resisted. But what was the upshot ? The Chalcedonian formula and the Tome of Leo, in which it is declared that Jesus as the incarnate Son of God upon earth possessed in his single person the fullness of both natures, divine and human, with all the proper attributes of each, including the impassibility of the Godhead and the passibility of the manhood. No fresh attempt whatever is made to explain how this paradox could be true. It is, I am sure, a mistaken exegesis which would find in Leo's Tome a definite theory that the Saviour used his two natures, so to speak, as alternative and mutually exclusive organs, acting and speaking now as God and now as man. All that Leo is trying to insist upon is that the Saviour must really have been both God and man ; and he points to the miracles as obvious evidence of his Godhead, and to the sufferings as obvious evidence of his manhood. Thus heretical and subversive explanations are finally rejected, and Christian theology is thrown back upon the witness of the New Testament as the datum of faith.

So the original gospel was preserved ; and, so far as it goes, that was a triumph indeed. But we must not let it blind our eyes to the fact that the thing left uninter-

preted by the Chalcedonian formula is the saving act
of God in the human life of him, " who for us men and
for our salvation came down from heaven ". Each nature,
human and divine, is affirmed to have been present in the
Saviour, each in its completeness and unconfused with the
other. For a theologian who holds deity to be strictly
impassible and not subject to any limitation, it seems to
follow that Jesus Christ suffered and was subject to
limitation only as man, and that as God he himself remained unaffected by any of the human experiences
which involved suffering or limitation. Thus it becomes
impossible to conceive God as acting through and in the
manhood of Jesus at all, although this is clearly what
orthodoxy did affirm. Orthodox teachers saved their
logic by asserting that the incarnate Son suffered and
was limited *only* in his human nature. But this solution
suggests both a separability of the human nature from
the divine and a separability of the divine person from
his divine nature, which are hardly reconcilable with the
fundamental gospel of the incarnation. The truth is that
Hellenic theology cannot, without self-contradiction, go
further towards a doctrine of the incarnation than to say
that the historical life of Jesus symbolizes the perfect
goodness of the Godhead more truly than any other human
and passible life. It cannot say that in Jesus it is God
who acted ; for if he acted, he also " suffered ". Thus
the epoch of theological history which closed with Chalce-
don affords a striking illustration of the truth of White-
head's dictum that, whereas Buddhism is an example of
a metaphysic generating a religion, Christianity has always
been a religion in search of a metaphysic.[1] Leo's Tome
proved that the search must continue.

2.   SCHOLASTICISM

Scholasticism made the proof still plainer. For by
St. Thomas Aquinas the full implications of the doctrine
of divine impassibility are drawn out, and are seen to

---

[1] *Religion in the Making*, pp. 39 *sq.*

preclude any mutuality of relation between the creator and the creature.

> Every relation [he writes] [1] which we consider between God and the creature is really in the creature, by whose change the relation is brought into being, whereas it is not really in God, but only in our way of thinking, since it does not arise from any change in God.

He illustrates the possibility of such a one-sided relation by the way in which sensible and intelligible objects remain unaffected by our perception and knowledge of them, and also by the relation of " being on the right or on the left ", which comes to be between a column and an animal, not by any change in the column, but solely by the movement of the animal. St. Thomas concludes that " the union of the two natures in Christ is not really in God, except only in our way of thinking; but in the human nature, which is a creature, it is really ". Strictly speaking, therefore, even in Christ there can be no real entry of God into manhood, nor any self-adaptation or self-limitation of the divine nature in the human which is its organ. Yet, according to St. Thomas, Jesus Christ was personally God; and therefore throughout the period of the incarnation, even in the Virgin's womb, he must have possessed the fullness of free will, conscious vision of the divine essence, and omniscience. The Saviour therefore can hardly be said to have felt, thought, or acted as a man at all: the humanity is but a mask.

This manner of conceiving the incarnation is all the stranger, because the theories of the atonement which held the field in St. Thomas's time belonged to the type of St. Anselm's satisfaction-theory, the logic of which forces us to regard the Saviour primarily and principally as man. Indeed, so far as devotional interests were concerned—and devotion centred on the atoning sacrifice of the cross and of the mass—the whole emphasis of medieval Christianity was on the reality of our Lord's suffering manhood, as the contemporary type of crucifix

[1] The passages referred to are in *S.T.*, Pt. I, Q. 13, Art. 7, and Pt. III, Q. 2, Art. 7.

is witness.   Thus, while in the medieval doctrine of the
incarnation Jesus Christ remains God, in the medieval
doctrine of the atonement he remains man.[1]   But the
reconciling thought that the divine person really acted
through the reality of the historical manhood is made
impossible to theology by the terms in which the divine
nature is conceived.

3.   FROM LUTHER TO THE MODERNS

With Luther Christology makes a fresh start, and most
modern theories on the subject may trace their origin to
him.   The main value of Luther's doctrine lies in his
refusal to allow preconceived doctrines of the nature of
deity, whencesoever derived, either to modify the witness
borne by the New Testament to the Saviour's manhood
or to suggest (as did Calvinists) that the divine nature of
Christ remained external to the incarnation.   Very modern
his language sometimes sounds.

> The Scriptures begin very gently and lead us on to Christ as
> to a man, and then to one who is Lord over all creatures, and
> after that to one who is God.   So do I enter delightfully, and
> learn to know God.   But the philosophers and doctors have
> insisted on beginning from above ; and so they have become
> fools.   We must begin from below and after that come up-
> wards.[2]

Brunner remarks [3] that no one after Irenaeus had taken
the *vere homo* so seriously as Luther.

Luther spoke quite openly about our Lord's childhood, about
his gradual growth and development, even in the spiritual
sphere, pointing out that, so far as his humanity was concerned, " Like any other holy man he did not always think,
speak, will everything, like an almighty being, which some

---

[1] This criticism of medieval Catholicism was made by Ritschl,
The Christian Doctrine of Justification and Reconciliation, pp.
389–91.

[2] Quoted by Mackintosh, *Person of Jesus Christ*, p. 232.

[3] *The Mediator*, pp. 328 *sq.*, footnote, from which the following
quotations are taken.

would fain make him out to be, thus mingling unwisely the two natures and their work ; for indeed he did not always see all clearly, but was led and aided by God."

Again Luther writes : " He endured good and evil things like anyone else, so that there was no difference between him and anyone else, save only in this, that he was God and had no sin." At the same time Luther returns uncompromisingly to the scriptural and primitive emphasis on the reality of God's victorious act through Jesus, which involves the truth that Jesus himself is God.

For to conquer the sin of the world, death, the curse and the wrath of God in his own person (*in semet ipso*) is not the work of a creature but of the Almighty. Out of this there necessarily results that he who personally (*in semet ipso*) conquered is truly and by nature God. . . . Because the Scripture ascribes all this to Christ, therefore is he himself life, righteousness, and blessing, which is the nature and substance of God. . . . Therefore when we teach the people that they are justified through Christ, that Christ is the conqueror of sin, death and the eternal curse, we bear witness at the same time that in his nature he is God.[1]

In other words, God's nature consists not only in what he unchangeably is but also in what he triumphantly does. Luther will allow no separation between God's nature and his work, or between divine nature and divine person. He who does God's work in person (*in semet ipso*) is thereby shown to be both by nature and personally God.

Since the Reformation, Christological theory in the Roman Catholic Church has remained practically at a standstill. Further developments have been confined to the reformed Communions. In general, the common characteristic of modern theories has been that they have followed Luther in starting from the reality of the Saviour's manhood, and even of his human limitations, as a datum, and in proceeding from that starting-point to determine more clearly the meaning of his divinity. In Luther's epoch-making phrase, they have begun from below and after that come upwards. The most typical of these

---

[1] Quoted by Brunner, *op. cit.*, p. 239.

modern Christologies fall into two main classes, the first being that generally associated with Liberal Protestantism, and the second being the work of those more conservative theologians who have developed the doctrine of the kenosis.

4. LIBERAL PROTESTANT CHRISTOLOGY

The Christology of Liberal Protestantism starts from the thought contained in a passage just quoted from Luther, that Jesus was a man like other men save for his supreme goodness which shows him to be divine. It argues that in and by his goodness Jesus reveals in a unique way the very nature and character of God. Jesus is not only the true teacher about God ; his very character as man symbolizes and reflects God's nature. We may therefore affirm that " God is like Jesus ", or that the quality of the manhood of Jesus is divine, in such a way that we are committed to the assertion that Jesus himself has the value of God. On that ground, it is maintained, Christians are justified in worshipping Jesus Christ as their Lord, in praying to God through him, and in declaring their faith in him in the language of the historic creeds of the Church, though modern Christians may and should interpret this language in a symbolic sense.

Liberal Protestantism was founded by the German theologian, Albrecht Ritschl. Before the war it won a large following in Germany and also in England, where its influence has been more lasting. In spite of the Unitarian tendency of much of their thought, which is especially evident in Harnack's well-known book, *What is Christianity ?*, the Ritschlians strongly maintained the divinity of Jesus Christ. But having rejected as falsely metaphysical the doctrine of the Catholic Church that Jesus is personally identical with the eternal and pre-existent Son of God, and being determined to think of him as the human subject of those value-judgements of faith which truly ascribe to him divinity, they found themselves obliged to justify the altogether unique position which Jesus holds in the Christian religion by actually

D.C.   K exaggerating his uniqueness as the one human revealer of the true God.   This exaggeration is already evident in W. Herrmann's striking and attractive book, *The Communion of the Christian with God*.   In England, Professor Bethune-Baker carried it to even greater lengths by asserting, " I know almost nothing of God's character apart from Jesus ",[1] and again that " of Christian theology the centre is not God but Jesus ".[2] Dr. T. R. Glover is equally emphatic : " For us, apart from Jesus, God is little better than an abstract noun." [3]

A much more balanced and persuasive statement of a Christology which still belongs to the Liberal Protestant type is to be found in Dr. Streeter's book *Reality*.   Here Jesus is represented as the ideal man whose every word and deed is intellectually, æsthetically and morally the right reaction to the actual circumstances.   On the ground of this human perfection it is argued that the personality of Jesus also reflects and embodies a universal principle, creative love, which is the ultimate explanation of the world-order and the essence of God's nature.   The man Jesus, therefore, in all he said and did and suffered, is " the mirror of the Infinite ".   In other words, he is the perfect human symbol of Godhead.

Dr. Streeter does not himself apply the term " symbol " to the life of Jesus, nor, in all probability, would he have accepted it as adequate.   For he explicitly rejects any inference that it does not vitally matter whether the gospel-story be actual fact or only " a true myth ".   Yet the reason he gives for the rejection is significant.

It is the actual death of Jesus [he writes] coming as the climax of the actual life he lived, which gives its meaning to the story.   Pose the question, How far is this story, if con-

---

[1] Article in *The Modern Churchman* for Sept. 1921, p. 301.
[2] *The Faith of the Apostles' Creed*, p. 42.
[3] *Jesus in the Experience of Men*, p. 16.   The truth for which Bethune-Baker and Glover seem to be really contending is that Jesus in his exaltation has received the *name* of God, only because God in his condescension has accepted the *name* of Jesus.   In other words, Jesus is known as God, only because God is known in Jesus.   As a positive statement this is both true and important.

sidered as a representation of Ultimate Reality in its qualita-
tive aspect, an adequate expression of the quality actually
inherent therein ?—and at once the factual character of its
historic core is seen to be essential. The quality of Reality
may be expressed in a construction of the imagination ; but
in what has in fact happened we have confidence that the
expression is authentic.[1]

In other words, the fact is necessary, because otherwise
men could not be *assured* that the symbol of Jesus living
and dying is a true symbol or expression of ultimate
reality. If the story were but myth, there would be no
reason in principle why the ultimate reality of God's love
should not be exactly the same as if the story were fact,
but we could not have the same certainty. Thus Streeter
seems to take us back to Christian Platonism.

The truth is that this whole type of Christology misses
something which is essential to the biblical and primitive
gospel, viz., its message that God is not only truly revealed
in Jesus, but that he has decisively and finally acted.
More than one modern theologian has made this criticism
of Liberal Protestantism. Thus Father Thornton writes,
" If we regard Christ as a human individual in the organic
series, in whom there is a unique manifestation of the
eternal order, then we have no ground for supposing that
Christianity has the final character which Christians have
ever found in it." [2] Brunner makes essentially the same
point. He would say that such a view as Streeter's
ignores the *einmaligkeit* (the " once-for-allness ") of the
Christian revelation. For if Jesus be merely the perfect
human manifestation of a divine goodness which remains
changelessly the same behind all symbols, there is nothing
in principle absolutely unique, decisive, and unrepeatable
about the revelation which he gave. But to Christianity
" revelation means the unique historical event which *by
its very nature* must either take place once or not at all ".
" A final event *can* only happen once." [3]

I should prefer to state the same argument in a way
which seems to me simpler. No *revelation*, considered

[1] *Reality*, p. 54.   [2] *The Incarnate Lord*, p. 259.
[3] See *The Mediator*, Chap. I. The quotations are from p. 26.

as such, can ever be final, in the sense of unrepeatable ; for an enduring reality once revealed may always be revealed as perfectly again. But with an *act* it is different. For what has once been done cannot be done again, except in so far as the same situation as that in which it was done recurs. And if the act in question be such as absolutely to prevent the same situation recurring, then that act is necessarily unrepeatable. If, therefore, Christ has really conquered death and sin, made atonement for man and opened the way to God, then the same situation which existed before his coming can never be repeated, and neither can his victorious act. The finality (*einmaligkeit*) of the Christian revelation is based on the finality of what Christ *did*. The fundamental defect of Liberal Protestantism is that it thinks of Christ *only* as revealer. Therefore it misses the point of the gospel of *the new age*.

5. KENOTIC CHRISTOLOGY

The second type of modern Christological theory is that which, while seeking to safeguard the genuinely human experience of Jesus with its necessary limitations, has nevertheless followed Luther also in sticking to the fundamental doctrine that Jesus is proved to be God by the victory and redemption which he wrought. This line of thought has led to the so-called " kenotic " theories, those, namely, which are based on the passage in the second chapter of Philippians which we have already discussed. This type of theory was originated by theologians of the Lutheran and Reformed Churches in Germany in the early part of the last century. Its first exponents tried to discriminate too exactly and academically between those attributes of the Godhead which the Son gave up in his incarnation and those which he retained. The original form of the theory therefore did not survive criticism. Nevertheless, its central principle, that the eternal Son or Word in his incarnation by a voluntary act limited himself to a historical human consciousness and human faculties of knowledge and action, has, I believe, proved itself to be the most important fresh contribution to Christology which has been made since the time of Irenæus. The principle is thus stated by Bishop Gore.

I see no help so great as is supplied by two phrases in which St. Paul characterizes the act of the Son of God in taking our manhood—" he beggared himself " (or " made himself poor "), and " he emptied himself " or " annulled himself ". St. Paul, in using these words, is not thinking of any particular aspect of the human life of Jesus, such as the limitation of his knowledge ; but he regards the incarnation in itself as having involved in some sense the abandonment of " riches " which belonged to the previous divine state of the Son. It is when we look at the facts in the Gospel that we are led to welcome St. Paul's words as giving us the clue to what we see there. The divine Son in becoming man must, we conclude, have accepted, voluntarily and deliberately, the limitations involved in really living as man—even as sinless and perfect man—in feeling as a man, thinking as a man, striving as a man, being anxious and tried as a man. . . . This was no failure of power. God is love, and love is sympathy and self-sacrifice. The incarnation is the supreme act of self-sacrificing sympathy, by which one, whose nature is divine, was enabled to enter into human experience. He emptied himself of divine prerogatives so far as was involved in really becoming man, and growing, feeling, thinking and suffering as man.[1]

---

[1] *Belief in Christ*, pp. 225 *sq.* The Chalcedonian Definition, as interpreted by Leo's Tome, seems to commit orthodoxy to accepting a kenosis, in so far as it affirms that the Son of God in his human nature subjected himself to human limitations. The essence of " the kenotic theory " is that it postulates a self-limitation *of the Godhead* in the incarnation. This is what Gore's language implies (see *ibid.*, pp. 226–28). Some modern theologians following the Reformed (Calvinist) tradition seek to justify language about the Son of God's *descent* by supposing that, although *he* descended and became limited as man on earth, his divine *nature* or deity remained external to the incarnation and did not as such enter the sphere of history at all. To Brunner (*The Mediator*, p. 343 n.) it seems that Biblical criticism has made this view the only possible one. To me the suggestion that God, *but not deity*, became incarnate is unintelligible. Still, though Brunner rejects " the kenotic theory ", it may be said that his Christology, like that of others influenced by Kierkegaard, is in a more general sense kenotic, in that it emphasizes the human limitations of Jesus Christ and attributes them to the descent of the Son of God.

The general aim of kenotic theories is sufficiently plain. They regard the earthly life of Jesus as one moment or constituent part in a whole divine act which has its beginning and end in heaven, an act which begins with a supreme condescension and ends in an exaltation of that humanity into which God himself has condescended to enter. These theories then make a fresh attempt to do real justice to that clause of the Creed which affirms that the Son of God " for us men and for our salvation came down from heaven " ; they interpret that clause, not in terms of physical fact, as though heaven were above earth in space, but of spiritual reality, in which descent means a voluntary self-humiliation and self-abnegation. Neither Thomistic orthodoxy nor the modernism of the Liberal Protestants can take such an interpretation seriously. For the latter understands by the divinity of Jesus only the quality or value of his manhood in revealing God ; whereas for the former the conception of the divine nature precludes the possibility that Godhead should ever enter into such a fresh relation with manhood as is postulated by a real, and not a merely formal or apparent, descent of God into a created nature. The kenotists would contend that the possibility of such a descent is proved, because to suppose that it took place is the only way to do justice to the content of the gospel. According to their doctrine Jesus on earth is really and fully God ; yet in his earthly condition the Godhead in him is really limited by the fact that he is also really and fully man. The Godhead is not really changed by this self-limitation ; for the self-limitation is itself the act of that absolute love, omnipotence, and wisdom, which constitute the divine nature. There is therefore no *conversio divinitatis in carne*. And yet that which is *directly* manifest in the earthly Jesus may be only manhood in its supreme perfection. That he is also truly God is indirectly manifest, when we account for all that Jesus accomplished and revealed by attributing it, as did St. Paul, to the act of a divine person in taking manhood upon himself in order through humiliation to exalt and save it.

6.   CRITICISMS OF KENOTIC CHRISTOLOGY

As we have already seen, upholders of the kenotic doctrine can make a fair reply to those who urge that to suppose that in Jesus, as he was on earth, the Godhead was in a real way limited by the manhood must contradict the truth that he was truly God.   Three other important objections, however, have been brought against the doctrine ; and we must consider them briefly in turn.

(a) The first is derived from its alleged inconsistency with the orthodoxy of the primitive Church.   Professor Creed points out that

this conception of the incarnate life is a wide departure from that which prevailed in the ancient Church.   Dr. Loofs has shown that no real precedent for this type of thought can be adduced from the patristic writers.   The nearest approach is to be found in the heresiarch, Apollinarius.[1]

The truth of these statements may be admitted.   But we have already seen why patristic theologians were prevented from working out the suggestions of a kenotic Christology to be found in St. Paul's Epistles.   They were committed from the start to a Hellenic conception of the divine nature.   Just for that reason, if a patristic theologian had seriously put forward a kenotic theory, he would almost certainly have laid himself open to the charges of making the deity passible, or of teaching that it was subject to variation ($\tau\rho\epsilon\pi\tau\delta\varsigma$), or that it was changed by becoming incarnate (*conversio divinitatis in carne*).   But if we conceive God's changelessness to consist simply in the absolute stedfastness of his perfect will of love, we can at once deny that the self-limitation of the eternal Son in the historical manhood of Jesus involves any real variableness in the deity ; since it is the consistency of God's love for man which is the very cause and ground of the self-limitation.   Moreover, Anglicans at any rate can hardly be accused of heresy for appealing to the Bible against a doctrine of the divine nature which, whatever its value, is certainly derived from extra-biblical sources.

[1] *Mysterium Christi* (edd. Bell and Deissmann), p. 133.

(b) A more substantial objection is raised by Dr. Temple, in criticism of Dr. Mackintosh.[1] In so far as Dr. Temple says that the kenotic theory has a mythological appearance, we may indeed not only agree with him, but go further in saying that it is inevitably expressed in terms of myth. For myth is the only language we can use about supramundane realities, in so far as we think and speak of them in the category of action. When we speak of the eternal nature and attributes of God, we make allowance for the imperfection of our human language and understanding by reminding ourselves that we are using our terms *analogically*. And if we speak of divine *actions* in the heavenly sphere, we must speak of them in the same analogical way, which means that we tell a myth about them. The myth is a true myth, if it serves to express a reality which we cannot express better in other ways. And the kenotist contends that the theologian, if he would express the truth about the incarnation as fully as he can, is bound to tell a myth in order to account for that element or moment in the incarnation which belongs definitely to the sphere of historical fact.

But Dr. Temple clearly means that he considers the kenotic theory to contain bad or false myth.

What was happening [he asks] to the rest of the universe during the period of our Lord's earthly life ? To say that the infant Jesus was from his cradle exercising providential care over it all is certainly monstrous ; but to deny this, and yet to say that the creative Word was so self-emptied as to have no being except in the infant Jesus is to assert that for a certain period of history the world was let loose from the control of the creative Word.

Now it seems to me that in this argument Dr. Temple is really pressing too far the mythology inherent in the kenotic theory. In the first place it is not necessary for its supporters strictly to affirm that the creative Word had no *being* except in the infant Jesus. What their theory demands is a limitation of consciousness rather than of

[1] *Christus Veritas*, pp. 142 *sq.*

actual being.[1]   The difference may be illustrated from the
cry of desolation uttered on the Cross.   That our Lord
underwent the consciousness of being forsaken by God we
may not doubt.   But it need not follow that he was in
very reality cast out from the Father's presence ;   indeed,
such a separation is unthinkable.   It must in a sense be
true that all through the period of the incarnation the
Son never really left the Father's side :   always he was
in the Father, and the Father in him :   it was the consciousness of the absolute unity and communion which in
varying manners and degrees was limited by the flesh.
And, if the critic proceeds to press the point that at least
the creative Word, while self-limited in the earthly Jesus,
was not consciously controlling the universe, the defender
of the theory has the alternatives of elaborating myth
still further [2] (which is no doubt precarious) or of remaining agnostic upon such a point.[3]   After all, in postulating
a supramundane act of the Deity we can only discern or
judge of its reality through our apprehension of its effects
in our world.   Of its direct conditions or results within
the supramundane or heavenly sphere itself we are necessarily ignorant ;   and it may well be that any precision of
logic based on the application of spatio-temporal categories
to the heavenly sphere will only lead conjecture astray.
The faith in the incarnation, which is based on the gospel
of the New Testament, leads us to believe that in the life
of Jesus the Godhead, by a wholly mysterious act of love,
both entered into a genuinely human experience, and, because it so entered, was made subject to the limitations of
a human consciousness.   And the kenotic theory, in its
essence, does but suggest that St. Paul in his hints about
a divine kenosis supplies us with a myth by means of
which the unimaginable reality may be least inadequately

[1] It must be admitted, however, that the particular distinction
here suggested is hardly in accordance with what Dr. Mackintosh
calls " the classic form " of the kenotic theory, op. cit., p. 267.

[2] Thus Godet suggests that during the period of our Lord's
earthly life the Father himself exercised directly the functions
which he normally exercises through the mediation of the Logos.
(See Mackintosh, op. cit., p. 268.)

[3] So Gore, Belief in Christ, p. 226.

expressed.   Of the application of the kenotic theory within the historical sphere of our Lord's earthly life more will be said later on.

Dr. Temple himself prefers to think that God the Word, without ceasing his creative and sustaining work, added this to it, that he became flesh and dwelt as in a tabernacle among us.   Such a doctrine may be, as Dr. Temple believes, more strictly Johannine.   But from the point of view from which Dr. Temple himself criticizes the kenotic theory, it would seem to involve the supposition that he who is at the same time both the creative Word and the infant in the cradle is at that time the subject of two distinct consciousnesses and experiences at once.   This may be the best way of thinking about the matter, provided we do not allow it to suggest to us that the Word was only partially incarnate ;   but it obliges us still to assume a kenosis, in so far as the consciousness of the Word made flesh is concerned.   Granted that the Word, without ceasing his creative and sustaining work, added something to it, what he added is precisely that experience in which his divine consciousness was limited and his divine state surrendered.   Thus the difference between Dr. Temple and the kenotists concerns only events in the supramundane sphere, about which no direct revelation has been given, and man's knowledge is necessarily but guess-work.

(c) A third objection to kenotic Christology is connected with the doctrine of the Trinity.   It may be urged that the theory involves a kind of distinction between the divine persons which brings us perilously near to tritheism.   Liberal Protestants who are accused of a Unitarian tendency, may not unnaturally feel inclined to use this counter-charge as a retort.   Nevertheless, I think that upholders of the kenotic theory again have a good defence, and that on two grounds.

(1) Historically the dogma of the Trinity arose out of the original necessity in which Christian thought found itself at once of distinguishing Jesus Christ from God and of identifying him with God.   This necessity in its turn arose out of the Christian experience itself, that is, out of

the impression which Jesus Christ in his life, death, and resurrection made upon the minds of his disciples. Theologically speaking, we might almost say that it was in order to make intelligible the experience of the incarnation and the atonement that the doctrine of the Trinity was formulated. Therefore we ought to test the truth and significance of our doctrine of the Trinity by our apprehension of the truth and significance of the incarnation, and not to limit the significance of the incarnation by the supposed demands of the doctrine of the Trinity.

(2) In speaking of the eternal relations within the Godhead itself we are again in the sphere of the inscrutable where the only truth for us is in the form of analogy or myth. But if we base our theology upon the New Testament, and especially upon St. John, we find the main positive significance of the doctrine of the Trinity to be that the God who revealed his love in Jesus is eternally the perfection of love in his own nature, and that therefore there must be within God the mutuality of perfect communion. It is into the perfect and eternal communion that manhood has been taken up through the incarnation of the person of the Son who is the head and representative of redeemed mankind. Therefore it cannot be the best expression of the unity of God to declare that God is a single person. Among New Testament writers it is St. John who insists most clearly and fully upon the eternal communion between the Father and the Son ; and in making this distinction between divine persons, he supplies a thought which becomes a support for the Pauline myth of the kenosis. If we thus base our teaching upon St. John and St. Paul, we can at least appeal to the New Testament against the theological judgement of any doctors of a later age.

7. SUMMARY AND CONCLUSION

It is time for us to sum up the results of our brief historical sketch of Christology, before we turn back again to apply them to the original facts of the life on which Christology is based.

One of our chief aims has been to show that the main differences in Christological doctrine are rooted in different conceptions of the nature of the Godhead. The difference of Christian theology from others is not adequately expressed by saying that its centre is not God but Jesus. Christology as such does not wholly determine the Christian's thought about God. On the contrary, it is a particular way of thinking about God, whether derived from Jesus himself or from another source, which is the determining consideration in Christology. If the Christology of the Fathers or of modern theologians is inadequate, it is because it does not do justice to that revelation of God with which Christianity both completes and corrects the imperfect ideas of Godhead derived from God's universal witness to himself.

Having thus set the thought of God at the centre of Christian theology, we have seen that all down the course of its history there are two principal ways in which the human and historical life of Jesus has been positively related to the Godhead in such a manner as to justify the affirmation that Jesus is himself divine.[1] In the first way, the earthly life of Jesus is regarded as the instrument of God's action ; in the second, it is regarded as the symbol of God's unchanging nature and character. The first way coheres with the Hebraic thought of God as the living sovereign Jehovah who works through historical events towards a future goal. The second way coheres with the Hellenic thought of God as the unchangeably perfect being who is the ground of all reality and value. Again, the first way leads us to value the earthly life of Jesus chiefly for its effects, which Christian faith has held to be the conquest of death and sin, the justification of believers, and the bringing in of the life of the new world. The second way leads us to value the life of Jesus chiefly

---

[1] The notion that the life of Jesus represents the perfect personal communion of a man with God cannot in itself justify the affirmation that Jesus is himself divine. Even that form of Liberal Protestantism which comes nearest to Unitarianism postulates a divine quality or value in the personal humanity of Jesus which makes him divine as being in himself the human revealer of Godhead.

for what it is in itself as the revelation of the eternal truth which has been from the beginning, is now and ever shall be.

Both lines of thought have their origins in the New Testament ; and there they are never separated, though we may find the first to be specially characteristic of St. Paul, and the second of St. John.   But in the history of the Church's theology the two lines have tended to diverge from one another.   What God has joined together in Christ, man's thought, to some extent inevitably, has set asunder.   And one main reason for the separation has been the fact that right up to the Reformation the Christian intellect was dominated by Hellenic ideas of God which made it impossible for theology to take quite seriously the notion of any act of God in history, and most of all that of a divine act of self-limitation and self-sacrifice.   The results of this great inhibition are seen most clearly in the orthodox theology of the Middle Ages, where on the one hand the doctrine of the incarnation is interpreted to mean that the manhood of Jesus was but a superficial mask hiding his deity, while on the other hand the atonement is represented as an act of sacrifice offered by Christ as man in reparation and satisfaction for man's sin.   It is the persistence of the Hellenic inhibition which has driven Liberal Protestantism to get rid of the medieval anomaly by subordinating the deity to the manhood of Jesus in its doctrine of the incarnation, as medievalism had subordinated the deity to the manhood in its doctrine of the atonement.   Thus for Liberal Protestantism the incarnate Lord becomes a man whose manhood has a divine significance or value.   On the other hand, the doctrine of Karl Barth, at least in some of its aspects, represents an irruption of Hebraism into Christian theology, which is the more violent because of its long exclusion.

The truest Christology is that which does most justice to the life of Jesus recorded in the New Testament, when we consider it as the ground and source of its results in the experience and faith of men.   True Christology must therefore enable us to hold together in unity, and yet perhaps always in mutual tension, the two ways of thought which

we have just distinguished. It must enable us to think
of Christ's life as one which by what it victoriously accomplished has made all the difference to the relation between
man and God, one which by God's action through it has
brought a new world into being. It must enable us also
to think of Christ's life as one which has made no difference
at all to the eternal truth about God and man which it
has revealed.

If we face the problem squarely and steadily, we shall,
I think, find ourselves constrained to build our Christology
on that fundamental conception of God's nature as eternal
agape, which we have already tried in some degree to make
clear. Our guiding idea must be that the historic life of
Jesus is the supremely characteristic action of God's love.
But we must give its full force to the word " characteristic ". Primarily it means that the action reveals God's
constant nature ; but, if God's nature is that of the love
which works to achieve its purpose in history, then its
supremely characteristic action will be not only revealing
but also directly effective. It will not be a mere *gesture,*
that is, an act the only purpose of which is to reveal or
signify what is. It will be an act which is in itself creative,
redemptive, victorious—only so will it fully reveal God.
With this thought in mind we can proceed to lay down
conditions which are criteria of truth and adequacy in
Christological doctrine.

(1) Such love as the New Testament attributes to God
can only be revealed to man in person and in act. No
mere message or oracle on the lips of a semi-divine mediator,
or of a man, however divinely inspired, could ever really
have conveyed it. That is the most fundamental reason
why we must affirm Jesus Christ to have been, and to be,
himself personally God. Yet at the same time no act
even of God could ever have conveyed such love, except
the act whereby God put himself at man's side to suffer
with him and for him in man's own condition. We cannot
be content to say that " the whole process of the universe
in evolution is incarnation : God is in the process indwelling : the whole universe is not merely the scene of
his operations, but a manifestation of him, in all the stages

of its evolution : the whole is incarnation ".[1] Such statements are at best the expression of a Christian Hellenism,
modified by modern doctrines of evolution. They ignore
the force of St. Thomas Aquinas's reply to the objection
that, since love makes us give ourselves to our friends as
much as we can, the Son of God ought therefore to have
assumed human nature in all human persons. " The
love of God to men," answers St. Thomas, abandoning
Aristotle, " is shown not merely in the assumption of
human nature, but especially in what he suffered in human
nature for other men." [2]   The Son of God's love, of whom
the Bible speaks, could only be incarnate in *one* man, who
suffered for all *others*.

(2) The Christian revelation of God is absolutely final,
because it is inseparable from the final victory which
Christ accomplished. The revelation is in the redemption ;
and God's redemption of manhood in Christ was either
achieved finally, or it was never achieved at all. And
if it was achieved, it was achieved through certain historical events. It follows that the essence of Christian
faith consists in the hearing and accepting of a gospel or
good news of fact, not in the conclusions of abstract
reasoning, nor in the mystical vision of an eternal reality
behind and apart from outward things or immanent in
all. That is the fundamental reason for the tremendous
emphasis on the word of the gospel, which is specially
characteristic of Pauline and Evangelical theology.

(3) At the same time, Christ's victorious and redemptive
life not only reveals God's love but also embodies in manhood man's own true ideal of human goodness. That is
the truth which Christian humanists from Abélard to the
Liberal Protestants have persistently vindicated, and
which Augustinians and modern Barthians too often reject. God created man's spirit to mirror his love, and
never has the glass been completely darkened even by
sin. These are necessary presuppositions of belief in the
incarnation. It was the human nature of Adam that the
Son of God took upon himself, and it is to all that is most

[1] Bethune-Baker, quoted by Creed, *Mysterium Christi*, p. 137.
[2] *S.T.*, Pt. III, Q. 4, Art. 5, ad. 2.

truly human in the sons of Adam that he makes his appeal
from Nazareth and Calvary and from heaven itself. As
therefore the life of Christ makes no change in God, so
also, in one sense, it makes no change in man. We must
beware of those evolutionary teachers who invite us to
compare the difference between Christ's manhood and
that of unredeemed mankind with the difference between
unredeemed manhood and any subhuman nature.
τὸ ἀπροσληπτὸν ἀθεράπευτόν. If it was but some superhumanity which the Son of God took upon himself, there
is no real redemption and no incarnation either. And we
must beware also of the " dialectical " theologians who
persuade us that the human nature was so completely an
incognito or disguise for the divine person, that his human
goodness can do nothing to reveal him as divine. The
manhood that was made in God's image, even though the
image is marred by sin, is still capable of recognizing
God through, not in spite of, his incarnation in the goodness of a man.

We may thus mark in outline the central truths of the
gospel which any adequate Christology must secure.
These truths, of course, are not in themselves sufficient
as a Christological theory ; they do but challenge the
efforts of the theologian and metaphysician to suggest
theories which will do them justice, and there is wide
room in such theorizing for differences of emphasis and for
diversities of philosophical and historical opinion. But
we can at least say that a theory of Christ's person which
is irreconcilable with any of these truths has missed an
essential element in the gospel of Christianity.

We will now conclude our general sketch of Christological
doctrine by suggesting the permanent significance of each
of the three great titles in which the Apostles' Creed
expresses the Christian faith about Jesus.

First, he is the Christ. That title presents him as the
one through whom God's promise and purpose in history
reach their victorious fulfilment. The promised victory
of the Christ himself has been won already, and in him
manhood has already entered the new world, the world to
come. This title therefore speaks to us especially of the

opus operatum, the accomplished work, which is the essential content of the gospel of deliverance and freedom. But it reminds us also of the glory of the Kingdom still to be revealed when all things have been subjected to Christ, and we shall see him even as he is.

Secondly, Jesus is our Lord. This title presents him as the present object of our personal devotion. It reminds us of the faith and loyalty which must be ours, if we would appropriate the benefits of the *opus operatum* which God through Christ has wrought.

Lastly, Jesus is the only Son of God. This title declares the mystery of the person of Jesus, which alone enables him truly to be both the Christ and our Lord. The promised victory and deliverance could in the end only be wrought by God himself. It was his own arm which brought salvation when man had utterly failed. And again, the worship and adoration of the heart are rightly due to God alone. To give to any being who is not God the place which Christian devotion gives to Jesus is to fall under St. Paul's condemnation of those who honour the creature more than the creator ; and it is to be deceived by that vainest of all human philosophies, which makes man the measure of all things and the spiritual centre of the universe.

Thus the three titles of the Apostles' Creed set forth what are to the Christian theologian the conditions of his problem, and to the believer the grounds of his glorying in Christ.

CHAPTER XIV

THE INCARNATION AND HISTORICAL CRITICISM

HAVING COMPLETED our survey of Christological doctrine, we turn back to the historical facts which are its foundation. What does it mean in relation to those historical facts themselves to say that the prophet of Nazareth whom Pontius Pilatus crucified was very God ? And, in the first place, is any such affirmation credible at all, if we allow its legitimate place and function to the critical and scientific study of the historical records concerning Jesus ?

1. THE DIFFERENT PRESUPPOSITIONS OF THE BELIEVER AND OF THE CRITIC

It may seem that some answer should have been attempted to these most searching questions, before we proceeded to any examination of the doctrines which have been built upon the alleged facts. We should have made sure, it may be said, of the historical foundation first ; for if the foundations be insecure, it is but waste of time to examine the comparative strength and suitability of various parts of the superstructure. Nevertheless, the order of treatment which we have followed has been deliberately chosen for a reason, the bearing of which upon the strictly historical problem I propose now to discuss. The facts concerning Jesus, strictly as facts, cannot be fairly studied or estimated solely by reference to the documents and oral tradition which are their original record, but only when they are considered also as the sufficient cause of the effects which they have subsequently produced in human thought and life. For that reason some study of the nature of those effects in the sphere of faith and doctrine is required in order to give us part of the evidence

146

on which we determine the nature of the original facts themselves.

I can imagine a historical critic objecting to this line of argument altogether, on the ground that it is but a thinly disguised attempt to import theological prejudice into a historical discussion. He may support his objection thus. "Historical conclusions are to be determined by purely historical considerations. This principle implies that the historical facts of the life of Jesus are to be established by exactly the same methods as we should use in the case of any other man. Now, if we are endeavouring to arrive at the original facts which made up the life, say, of Julius Cæsar, we do not first consider all the beliefs about Julius Cæsar which men have held in subsequent ages. We do not, for instance, regard Shakspere's tragedy as part of the historical evidence. Rather we are careful, so far as may be, to dismiss all later beliefs from our minds. Having thus freed ourselves from bias, we search out the most nearly contemporary records which are available, and by scientific comparison and criticism of their contents we reconstruct the most probable account of Cæsar's life. This account then becomes the criterion by which we judge the historical truth or error of subsequent beliefs about Julius Cæsar. The same method ought to be followed in the case of Jesus. In this case the early evidence consists almost entirely of the books of the New Testament ; for the references to be found in non-Christian authors of the same period are but scanty. This evidence then has to be sifted and criticized on the same principles as we should employ in any other case. And, having thus determined the most probable account of the original deeds and words and character of Jesus, and having carefully separated what may be regarded as reasonably certain from more or less doubtful hypothesis, we must judge all subsequent beliefs about him in the light of this account, dismissing as probably untrue or at least as doubtful any belief which rests on something not contained in the residuum of fact which the historical critic has certified."

All this sounds very plausible ; but there is a catch in it. That there must be a catch somewhere is shown by

Quick's reply to objection

real flaw in the objection

two facts.   First, if we agree to take as the residuum of reasonable certainty those facts on which competent critics are unanimous, we find that we have practically no information about Jesus at all, except that a religious agitator of that name was condemned to crucifixion by Pontius Pilate, the procurator of Judæa, about A.D. 30.   This seems a really absurd conclusion, when we compare the amount of nearly contemporary evidence we have about Jesus with the much smaller amount available in the case of other men about whom critical historians agree in giving us much more considerable knowledge.   It seems too paradoxical to say that we really know no more about him than we know about the man who was probably his namesake, Barabbas.   Secondly, we notice that in order to support *negative* conclusions as to what we know about the original life and teaching of Jesus, historical critics often allow themselves to search the whole doctrinal field opened by the comparative study of religions.   If historical conclusions are to be drawn from comparisons between Christian and non-Christian doctrines, it would seem after all to be part of the historian's function to study and understand the doctrines which he compares.

But what is the real flaw in the argument which we have put into our critic's mouth ?   It lies in the initial assumptions stated in its first two sentences.   How far must the historian really treat the life of Jesus like that of any other man ?   Scientific methods of historical criticism assume, and must assume, that in all events which have ever happened human and physical nature conform to a certain order, the laws of which are known.   If therefore any event is alleged to have happened, which demands for its explanation a causal agency transcending the possibilities of human or physical nature as known elsewhere, scientific criticism will tend to dismiss the allegation as untrue, and will at least require a much greater cogency of evidence in its favour than it would in other cases. Now there is no doubt that the earliest evidence which we possess for the life of Jesus assumes that, although he was a man, he was nevertheless a unique person in such a sense that what happened in his case was not restricted

by the limits of what would be possible for human and
physical nature in any other case.   It follows that historical
criticism, working on scientific lines, is strongly prejudiced
against this evidence.   Rather than accept the absolute
uniqueness of Jesus as the true explanation of any event,
it will exhaust every other possible way of reconstructing
the facts, and, if in the end it finds no alternative which
it can honestly pronounce to be satisfactory, it will content
itself with saying that no certain conclusion can be reached.
On the other hand the Christian believer, having reached
his faith, not by scientific examination of historical evidence but by the acceptance of religious teaching verified
in his own moral and spiritual experience, if he is asked
to examine the historical basis of his beliefs, will approach
the primitive records with a quite opposite presupposition.
He will have no antecedent objection whatever to the
hypothesis that certain things happened which were only
possible because Jesus was the unique person whom he
has always believed him to be.   And if this hypothesis
seems to be the most obvious and natural way of accounting for the evidence, he will not trouble himself about
alternatives, even though he cannot show them to be in
themselves incredible.

Let us try to make clearer the fundamental difference
between these two points of view by considering the cruciai
instance of the resurrection.   Every writer in the New
Testament believes the resurrection of Jesus to be a fact.
One main purpose of the earliest Christianity of which we
have any record was to bear witness to that fact, and even
our written records go back to a time about twenty years
after the alleged event.   Now the historical critic, rightly
from his point of view, regards all this evidence with the
gravest suspicion.   If he is true to his scientific principles,
he will certainly not dismiss it off-hand, but he will demand
from it almost absolute cogency, and he will prefer any
other possible explanation of the evidence to the supposition of its truth.   But suppose (though the hypothesis
is most improbable) that in the end he is convinced, as a
scientific historian, that the resurrection did happen.   He
will then believe it on the ground that no fair-minded

critic could reject such weight of evidence for the resurrection of anyone, and ever afterwards he will approach stories of other resurrections with presuppositions less hostile to their truth.   On the other hand, the Christian believer will be predisposed to accept the New Testament evidence for the resurrection.   He will not refuse to test the evidence critically ; but he will not demand from it any proof that science or the law courts would call cogent. And if (as in all probability he will) he finds the evidence sufficient, he will accept it, precisely not on the ground that such evidence would establish the resurrection of *anyone*, but on the ground that it is the uniqueness of Jesus which makes it credible.   Just because, therefore, he believes in the resurrection of Jesus, he will approach stories of other resurrections with presuppositions *more* hostile to their truth, since their truth would seem prima facie to conflict with his belief in the uniqueness of Jesus. Thus the historical critic and the Christian believer, if they were both to accept the fact that Jesus rose again from the dead, would not really agree with one another any more than they do while the one rejects the fact and the other accepts it.   The difference in presuppositions is radical and decisive ; and yet neither point of view seems to be in itself unreasonable.

2.   SCIENTIFIC IMPARTIALITY IMPOSSIBLE

At this point we may imagine our historical critic to make a large concession, which indeed many critics would have been entirely ready to make at the start.   " I agree," he says, " that we cannot really settle the facts of the life of Jesus, without taking some account of the faith which was their consequence.   The ultimate question which every student of Christian origins has to answer is this : the Christian faith being what it is, is it on the whole more reasonable to suppose that it came into the world in some such way as the New Testament alleges, or in some different way ?   I grant that the existence of the faith must be adequately accounted for somehow, and we cannot account for it, if we do not consider what it *is*.

Doctrinal considerations therefore are not wholly irrelevant to the historical inquiry. But still, if we are to reach the historical facts, we must divest our minds of all presuppositions as to the value or truth of the Christian faith. Any such presupposition is really a vicious prejudice. I will abandon the parallel of Julius Cæsar, for it is obvious that the life of Cæsar gave rise to no new faith for which the historian has to account. But my essential point will remain the same and be more clearly indisputable, if I substitute for Julius Cæsar the founder of some other great religion, let us say, Sakya Muni or Mahomet."

Yet even this fair-minded concession is one which as Christians we cannot accept. We are obliged once more to dispute the parallel and the conclusions based upon it. Buddhism and Islam invite faith in the *teaching* of Sakya Muni and of Mahomet. And, since the recorded teaching remains the same whatever be its historical origin, we are not necessarily passing any judgement on the essential value of Buddhism or Islam as a religious faith by any conclusion we may reach as to the facts of its founder's life, although no doubt certain conclusions might cause grave scandal to the orthodox Buddhist or Mohammedan. In the same way certain conclusions of historical critics about the life of Moses have caused scandal both to Jews and Christians ; but they cannot be said in themselves to involve a denial of the divine authority of the Mosaic Law, since that Law remains what it is and may be equally inspired, whether its origin were a gradual growth or a single oracular pronouncement. But Christianity does not invite faith simply in the teaching of Jesus. Christian faith is faith in the living Lord who died and rose again to bring to men the eternal life which is the goal of history. According to Christianity therefore the life of Jesus stands in a unique relation to history as a whole, and the truth of that relation is of the essence of its faith. Therefore to suppose either that the main facts alleged by Christianity concerning Jesus are not historical facts at all, or that they are simply historical facts to be judged like any others, is necessarily to judge that the Christian faith is false, or at any rate that its truth is something essentially different

from what the main tradition of Christianity has supposed
it to be. It is strictly impossible to give any account of
the historical origins of Christianity, which is impartial
in the sense of being wholly detached from any particular
estimate of its truth and value.

The same point may be expressed, perhaps more simply,
thus. If the meaning of the Christian faith, involving
certain beliefs about the historical life of Jesus, seems to
us to be such as to make it of absolutely unique value for
human life and thought, our treatment of the historical
evidence concerning the life of Jesus will inevitably and
rightly be different from what it would be, if we saw no
such value in the Christian faith at all.   If the resurrection
of Jesus means to us the redemption of mankind, so that
it transforms our whole understanding of the universe, it
will rightly seem to us ludicrous to suppose that belief in
it originated from a natural mistake of some overwrought
women as to the tomb in which their Rabbi's body had
been laid. But this same explanation may as rightly
seem to us perfectly adequate, if the whole gospel of
redemption, based on the resurrection, seems to us to
be in any case no better than a fantasy. Moreover, to
maintain a strict impartiality as to any value, good or bad,
in the resurrection-gospel is simply to deprive ourselves
of the means of reaching any reasonable judgement whatever upon the facts. The truth is that Christianity is a
faith so unique in its connexion with history, so universal
in its implications, and so searching in its claims, that we
must make some answer to its challenge in the present
before we can judge at all of its origins in the past.

3.   THE SIGNIFICANCE OF HISTORICAL CRITICISM FOR
CHRISTIAN FAITH

Christians therefore should be quite candid in saying
that they do not and cannot reach their conclusions as to
what is historically true in the gospel-narrative in a spirit
of scientific impartiality. They do not deny the duty,
or prejudge the results, of critical investigation. They
must always be prepared to admit the force of evidence

which shows their beliefs to be mistaken. But their minds are prepared to accept narratives about Jesus as statements of fact on evidence which the non-Christian critic cannot regard as adequate. For Christians will always think it reasonable to suppose that their wonderful and mysterious faith had its origin in a wonderful and mysterious person.

But does it follow that the Christian, while he remains a Christian, is either entitled or obliged to refuse consideration to the conclusions of all critics who do not share his faith ? May he assume either (*a*) that the Gospels contain an inerrant record of fact, or (*b*) that the original facts must have been such as to vindicate everything that orthodox Christians have subsequently taught and believed about them ? If, after what has been said already, we are to answer these questions in the negative, we must clearly give precise reasons for our denial.

(*a*) The object of the Christian's faith is the person of Jesus Christ whose historical life and work the New Testament records ; it is not the documents of the New Testament themselves. The New Testament warns the Christian that he must not believe in its letter, as the orthodox Jew believed in the letter of the Mosaic Law. Exactly because as Christians we believe, partly through the evidence of the New Testament, that Christ lives to enable us to know and to have faith in him by his Spirit, we are obliged to judge the New Testament by the apprehended perfection of Christ rather than Christ himself by the supposed inerrancy of the New Testament. If we believe that perfection is in Christ *only*, we cannot escape the duty of criticizing, in some measure, the documents in which imperfect men have recorded their impressions of him. The words which, according to St. John, Jesus addressed to the Jews might well have been addressed also to some more modern " fundamentalists ", in reference to the New Testament as well as to the Old. " Ye search the Scriptures, because in them ye think that ye have eternal life ; and they it is which testify of *me* ; and ye will not come to *me* that ye may have life." [1]

[1] John v. 39 *sq.*

(*b*) The fundamental doctrine and mystery of the Christian faith is the historical incarnation, the fact that the eternal Son of God was made man. But, as we have already seen, from early times Christians have differed considerably from one another in what they have thought to be the demands of their faith in respect of the nature of the incarnate Lord's experience and powers upon earth. Here then we are faced by differences of doctrinal presupposition among Christians themselves, which inevitably affect their historical judgements. Thus orthodox teachers who believe that our Lord's deity made him omniscient are obliged to reject or explain away the Marcan saying in which our Lord acknowledges a certain ignorance of the future,[1] just as others, who emphasize in a particular way the reality of our Lord's manhood, reject or explain away some stories of miracles contained in the Gospels. It is inevitable and reasonable that the logical process by which the Christian arrives at his historical conclusions should be, to some extent, circular. He bases his doctrine of the Lord's person mainly upon the general record of the New Testament, and then uses his doctrine to test and criticize certain details of the record.

For our own part we have already suggested that the particular doctrine about the incarnation, which best fits the whole mystery of our faith, postulates a real kenosis and self-limitation on the part of the Son of God in taking our manhood upon himself. In going back therefore to consider the historical life and personality of the incarnate Lord, we shall assume as a hypothesis that he was really limited by all the restrictions necessary to make his experience that of a man living at a particular time and place. Just in so far as we believe that Jesus shared such restrictions with all other men, we shall be ready to use and acknowledge the value of the method of the critical historian, whether Christian or not. For it is the essence of that method to assume that Jesus was a man like other men. On the other hand, just in so far as we acknowledge the uniquely divine and supernatural element in Jesus operating in and through his humanity, we shall not think

[1] Mark xiii. 32.

the critical method adequate to give us the whole even of the historical truth. We shall not, for instance, assume, as the historical critic does assume, that, provided there is no cogent proof to the contrary, any manifestation of that supernatural element in the record concerning Jesus must be due to a later tradition of the Church, and cannot have been part of the original facts. In other words, while we fully acknowledge the value of the critical method in helping us towards the truth, we cannot allow it to dictate to us, or strictly to limit, all our historical conclusions. It is, we shall say, a good servant but a bad master.

To the ultimate challenge, that by making such a claim to a relative independence of historical criticism we are only reserving the right of doctrinal prejudice to falsify history, we can make a perfectly straightforward and rational reply. The defence of the Christian's convictions about the historical origins of his faith will always rest mainly upon the principle that effects must have an adequate cause. And the judgement as to the adequacy of an alleged cause must always depend on a judgement as to the value of the given effect. Therefore our judgement as to the value of the Christian faith must necessarily affect our judgement as to the historical causes which are adequate to account for it. Men do not gather grapes from thorns or figs from thistles; nor is the Christian gospel likely to be the product of credulity and deceit. The story of Jesus, as the New Testament presents it, cannot, whatever critics may say, have been in its essential characteristics the fabrication of an ecclesiastical tradition. If it were, reason might as well put up the shutters. But of course, if a critic sees no peculiar value in the record concerning Jesus, his conclusions as to its historical origin will rightly be different from ours. What reasonable man could believe in " the resurrection of one Jesus who was dead and whom Paul ", and some other obviously unbalanced and neurotic enthusiasts, " affirmed to be alive " ?

CHAPTER XV

THE VIRGIN BIRTH

W E HAVE already said enough to show that belief in Christ's resurrection is an integral and essential element in the Christian faith, and to indicate in a general way the grounds on which Christians regard the evidence sufficient to justify their belief in it as a historical fact. Further consideration of the meaning of the resurrection will be deferred until we discuss it in connexion with the Christian doctrine of salvation and of " the last things ". The miracle of the Virgin Birth is, however, more exclusively linked with the doctrine of the incarnation, and we must at this point say something further as to its place in the Christian gospel, considered both from a doctrinal and from a historical point of view.

1. THE DETERMINING CONSIDERATIONS ARE DOCTRINAL

We here enter a region of acute and most perplexing controversy. But there is one proposition on which all parties ought to be able to agree, namely, that doctrinal considerations must be the determining factor in our belief upon the subject. The strictly historical evidence is (and in the nature of the case it could hardly be otherwise) quite insufficient to satisfy anyone that the Virgin Birth is a fact, who is not already at least strongly inclined to believe in the truth of the incarnation. On the other hand, there seems to be no warrant for denying that the historical evidence must be regarded as considerable by one who approaches it with a really open mind.

2. THE HISTORICAL EVIDENCE

The historical evidence is in fact of a puzzling and ambiguous nature. However dubious it may appear to the critical historian, it certainly is not negligible. Let us briefly sum up the position, stating first the grounds for scepticism.

The positive scriptural evidence is found almost entirely in the first chapters of the first and third Gospels. There is nothing to show that either St. Mark or St. Paul was aware of any tradition that our Lord was born of a virgin ; and it is somewhat strange that St. Paul, if he knew and accepted such a tradition, should have made no use of it in his Christological teaching. Again, the special sources of St. Matthew, which are responsible for the form of the tradition found in his Gospel, obviously contain a good deal of material which looks mythological and is of little weight as evidence for historical fact. As to St. Luke, there is considerable doubt whether the birth-narrative belonged to the earliest edition of his Gospel.

On the other hand, the two traditions, embodied severally in the first and third Gospels, show no trace of dependence on each other ; and this fact points to an early origin for the belief in the Virgin Birth. Again, it is an important fact that, whereas reverence for virginity belonged to Gentile rather than to Jewish religion, is absent from the Old Testament, and played no part in prophecy or expectation about the Messiah's birth, nevertheless the birth-narratives both of St. Matthew and St. Luke show a distinctly Jewish and Palestinian colouring. The prophecy of the Virgin Birth cited by St. Matthew from Isaiah [1] is not in the original a prophecy of a virgin birth at all, and was not so understood by the Jews. Finally, and most important of all, it seems almost impossible to argue that these early traditions about our Lord's birth were invented in the interests of Christological doctrine, for the simple reason that no doctrinal use whatever is made of them in the New Testament, save for one doubtful exception in two verses of the Prologue to St. John's Gospel.[2] All the evangelists mention our Lord's brothers ; yet none affirms, or uses any language which implies, the perpetual virginity of his mother. And St. Matthew's assertion of the Virgin Birth certainly seems to weaken

[1] Isa. vii. 14 ; Matt. i. 22 *sq.*   [2] See below, p. 160.

the force of the genealogy whereby he shows the Davidic descent of Jesus the Messiah through Joseph. The first Christian apologists certainly had a doctrinal interest in maintaining the Davidic descent of Jesus, but apparently none in maintaining his birth of a virgin mother.

Any full estimate of the historical evidence would of course require a much longer discussion and the mention of many points of detail which have been here ignored. But enough has been said to indicate the main considerations which have to be taken into account on both sides.

3. DOCTRINAL CONSIDERATIONS

The historical evidence being inconclusive, it is theology which must determine our belief whether or not the Virgin Birth is a historical fact. If the Virgin Birth seems to us to be an integral part of the Christian gospel, and in particular of the doctrine of the incarnation, we shall naturally and reasonably affirm it. If we doubt whether belief in the Virgin Birth belongs to the essence of the Christian faith, we shall naturally and reasonably doubt also whether it happened. But again this doctrinal or theological issue, though confident assertions are to be heard on both sides, is by no means easy to decide. In favour of dogmatic affirmation four arguments are of primary importance :

(*a*) There is the almost unbroken and universal tradition of the Church from the second century down to modern times that the Virgin Birth is an integral part of the faith.

(*b*) There is the particular fact that the Creed of most truly Catholic authority definitely states that the Saviour was incarnate by the Holy Ghost of the Virgin Mary.

(*c*) Many Christians feel that the Virgin Birth is so peculiarly appropriate a sign and expression of the new creation of manhood by divine act in the person of Jesus Christ, that belief in it is practically inseparable from a genuine and full belief in the incarnation.

(*d*) There is the importance that reverence for the Blessed Virgin has for Christian devotion. Her perpetual virginity is recognized as an article of faith by the main body of the Catholic Church ; and to the piety of many,

perhaps of most, devout Christians it seems quite intolerable to permit it to be questioned. Any Christian must
allow great weight to a consideration of this kind.

On the other hand, there are strong arguments in favour
of the opinion that belief in the Virgin Birth is at least
not among the primary essentials of the Christian faith.

(a) No attempt is made in the New Testament to show
any connexion between belief in the Virgin Birth and saving
faith in Christ. Thus the very fact which strengthens
the case for belief in the Virgin Birth on historical grounds,
to some extent weakens it on doctrinal grounds. The
contrast between the place in the Christian faith which
the New Testament assigns to the resurrection, and the
place which it assigns (if it can be said to assign any place
at all) to the Virgin Birth, is so conspicuous that it can
hardly be without significance. For those therefore who
do not allow to tradition an authority independent of
scripture, there are grave difficulties in affirming as " necessary to salvation " belief in a fact of which St. Paul does
not seem to have been aware, and of which the New
Testament makes virtually no doctrinal use at all.

(b) While it is agreed that the fact of the Virgin Birth
was universally believed from the second century onwards,
the express mention of it in the text of Creeds was probably
due in the first instance to the need of affirming that the
Son of God was really born of a human mother, rather
than to the direct intention to affirm that he was not born
of a human father. Hence the latter belief is assumed
rather than actually asserted in the Creeds.

(c) There are some modern believers in the incarnation,
and among them some who are not in the least influenced
by any Unitarian tendency, to whom the Virgin Birth
appears to constitute a difficulty, rather than a help, in
Christology. It seems to them more consonant with the
whole character and content of the Christian revelation,
that, when the Son of God took our manhood upon himself, his birth should have been completely natural in its
physical circumstances and conditions. Even so strong
a supernaturalist as Brunner can describe the Virgin Birth
as an idea with which the amazingly glorious message of

the incarnation has been burdened and its central meaning obscured.[1]

(d) Apart from the perpetual virginity of our Lady, the Virgin Birth loses its devotional significance ; and it is precisely as the condition of the further doctrin f the perpetual virginity that the Virgin Birth itself i hiefly valued by Christian piety. Yet for the perpetual v inity there is no positive evidence in the New Testament at all. To make this doctrine therefore an article of faith is to make necessary to salvation a belief which has no scriptural support.

4. CONCLUSIONS

I have tried to summarize the main arguments on both sides as impartially as I can. The chief result to my mind is to suggest that on the subject of the Virgin Birth we ought to be especially tender and sympathetic towards the convictions of those who differ from ourselves. But, if we want to grasp the real meaning of the Virgin Birth in relation to the incarnation, we can hardly do better than ponder carefully the text of St. John's Prologue, to which reference has already been made. " But as many as received him, to them gave he power to become children of God, even to them that believe on his name ; who were born not of blood, nor of the will of the flesh, nor of the will of a man, but of God." [2] There is evidence of a very early variant in the text which substitutes the singular for the plural in the last clause (" who *was* born ", etc.), thus making the words refer to our Lord himself. I do not think that this variant represents what St. John originally wrote ; but it seems at least highly probable that, as he wrote, he had the tradition of the Virgin Birth in mind. St. John means that the true eternal life of every Christian, into which he is born again of water and the Spirit, is a life which has its cause, not in human heredity, nor in sexual desire, nor in a man's will, but in the gift of God's Son. And of Jesus, who was himself the Son or Word made flesh, it is true in a unique way that the life, in which

---

[1] *The Mediator*, p. 322.   [2] John i. 12 *sq.*

he was really born as man on earth, was not produced by
the operation of natural causes or of human volition, but
by the fresh creative act of God refashioning human nature
according to his love. So far all Christians may agree.
Those who accept the Virgin Birth as historical will believe
that this fresh creative act had its appropriate physical
and outward sign of newness in the fact that Jesus had no
human father. Others may prefer to think that, inasmuch
as the manhood of Jesus was no superhumanity but our
own human nature spiritually fashioned anew by an amaz-
ing act of divine condescension, the physical conditions of
its conception and birth did not vary from those which
nature ordinarily requires. In view of what has already
been said as to the inconclusiveness of the scriptural evidence both in the historical and in the doctrinal sphere,
I think we must hesitate to say that this latter opinion is
inconsistent with the essentials of saving faith in Jesus
Christ. On the other hand, when we consider the evidence
for the Virgin Birth which the New Testament does contain, the constant tradition of the Church, and the value
of all the devotion which has been centred upon the perpetual virginity of the Lord's mother, it seems very hard
for a Christian to believe that all these things, so intimately
connected with faith in the historical incarnation, have
their origin, nevertheless, not in the truth of historical fact
but in a pious myth.

CHAPTER XVI

OUR LORD'S KNOWLEDGE IN HIS EARTHLY LIFE

1. TWO ELEMENTS IN KNOWLEDGE

TWO ELEMENTS are distinguishable in the object of knowledge, the general and the particular, the law and the fact. Knowledge of particular facts is only possible because there is some kind of pattern or system in events which is expressible in terms of general laws. In knowing an event or fact the mind is at the same time aware of its relation to other events or facts in a system. There can be no knowledge of particulars without some knowledge of universals.

Generally speaking, intellectual excellence consists in a special capacity to detect patterns or laws determining wide ranges of events, or to detect them through the observation and analysis of relatively few events. Those intellects which are rightly called great have a deeper knowledge than others of the laws according to which events cohere ; and, because of this, they are better able to arrive by inference at particular facts which are beyond the reach of immediate observation whether through remoteness in time or space or for any other reason. Hence, on the one hand, it is true that men of outstanding intellect do, in one sense and up to a certain point, know more facts than do others. Indeed, it is impossible to carry an unusually large number of facts in the memory without some unusual power of arranging facts according to some kind of system, although for mnemonic purposes the system may be quite subjective, like that invented by Kennedy for remembering the genders of Latin nouns. On the other hand, the special excellence of men who have real knowledge, as distinct from mere learning, consists essentially in the knowing of pattern, system, or law, rather than in the ability to cite large quantities of particular facts or events.

Again, there is discoverable in the universe an infinite number of distinct patterns, systems or laws. All these fall into two broad classes, (*a*) those which manifest orders of *de facto* occurrence, and (*b*) those which manifest orders of value or goodness. Thus the playing of a piece of music illustrates both (*a*) laws of acoustics and (*b*) laws of beauty in sound. Each set of laws belongs to a different principle of order. If the music is played badly, the laws of acoustics are equally well illustrated, but the laws of beauty are illustrated only by the spoiling of the beauty through bad playing. The whole theory of knowledge is confused by the common assumption that the mental activity whereby we discern orders of value and their embodiment in fact is somehow less really knowledge than that whereby we discern orders of merely *de facto* occurrence. If I judge conscientiously that a certain action is right, that judgement is just as much a matter of knowledge as a judgement of sense-perception that there is a fire in my room, or a judgement based on logical inference that the angles at the base of an isosceles triangle must be equal to one another. All these judgements are equally both matters of knowledge and, in reference to their application, fallible.

Finally, the patterns, systems or laws, of which we have been speaking, enfold one another *ad infinitum* ; but, if the universe be real at all, there must be one principle of order which is all-inclusive ; and, if Christianity be true, this all-inclusive principle of order must be a principle of spiritual value. Therefore it is knowledge of *that* principle of order and of its operation in facts and events, which, according to Christian belief, must be the deepest and most precious knowledge that there is.

2. DIVINE KNOWLEDGE

The nature of God's knowledge is necessarily a mystery which man's mind cannot penetrate, nor ever will. But it would seem that we conceive divine omniscience most truly and intelligibly, when we think of God's knowledge, not as an immediate vision of the total number of all particular events actual and possible, but as a perfect understanding of, and insight into, the order and law by which all events are determined towards their end. We must not of course exclude the cognition of particular facts from God's knowledge, still less the most intimate insight into the being of every one of his creatures. God's knowledge transcends altogether that process of abstraction which produces, in human knowing, the antithesis between particulars and universals. Still, when we speak of omniscience, we mean first and foremost, not that God is immediately aware of everything that has or might have happened and that will or may happen, but rather that he knows infallibly the order, plan and purpose, the origin and end, of all things. And we may add that the divinest element in that knowledge is the insight into that order of goodness whereby all that happens is controlled or overruled according to God's will to the fulfilment of his unfailing purpose for his creatures. It follows that a right knowledge of values, which includes knowledge of what matters most and is most important, is always a deeper and diviner knowledge than a knowledge of mere facts, however extensive. It is of course true that for certain purposes the knowledge which matters most is precisely the knowledge of bare facts and of the uniformities according to which they happen. But this is only so, because considerations of value, i.e., the consideration of what is really worth doing, rightly lead men, for a particular and limited purpose, to ignore the value of the facts which they study in order to discover simply what they are. Ultimately the Christian at least is bound to hold that the order of absolute value or goodness, which gives things positive worth, does control the order of mere fact, according to which one thing, whether good or bad, is bound, whether for good or evil, to produce another. So for the Christian the knowledge which is most characteristically divine must always be that which consists of insight into the good and holds the key to its mysterious and ultimately triumphant operation. " Ye shall be as God, knowing good and evil."

3. THE EVIDENCE OF THE GOSPELS

We come to the historical evidence about our Lord's knowledge. Nothing is more strikingly characteristic of his mind, as it stands revealed in the record, than his unwavering belief in, and insight into, the unity of that fundamental order of value whereby God works all things together for good.

A. evidence. 1.

(a) Consider what is implied in our Lord's use of parable and proverb. The *general* lesson of most of the parables is that the natural order *as such* illustrates the supernatural, and can be shown to illustrate it by one who knows the mind of the one creator. We do the parables grievous wrong when we mar their truth at the natural level in order to make them fit our sermons. The father of the prodigal is at least not less genuinely human and natural a character than the worldly employer of a dishonest steward, or the woman who sweeps her house for a lost coin. The father, the employer, the steward, the housewife and many others, are all ordinary people, who all in their various manners and degrees, all more or less unconsciously and some even against their will, bear witness to the law of their creator's goodness. The proverbs again (" Seek and ye shall find ", " To him that hath it shall be given ", etc.) all represent enormously far-reaching laws of spiritual reality disguised under a paradox or an apparent platitude.

(b) A similar conviction as to the spiritual ordering of the world underlies the seemingly prudential character of some of our Lord's ethical teaching and exhortation. 2. He makes a demand for absolute self-sacrifice ; but he insists at the same time that God's service is really worth while and cannot fail of its reward. The discussion of the problem thus raised really belongs to the subject of Christian ethics. But it is at least clear that such petitions as those of the familiar prayer that " we may give and not count the cost " and " toil and not ask for any reward ", are quite alien from our Lord's method of expression, however truly they may interpret his inward unselfishness. And in truth to suppose that the ethical value of self-sacrifice is enhanced when the cost is not counted, is impossible for any moralist who takes his own language quite seriously. Self-sacrifice is not more unselfish when it is unreflecting and not deliberate ; and, if it is deliberate, it must be undertaken to achieve an end which is believed to be very much worth while. Jesus gave his own life, because he was sure that God would make the life thus given " a ransom for many ". His assurance was either a delusion or the profoundest insight into the spiritual order of God's world.

(c) Again, our Lord's habit of seeking to elicit truth from his hearers' own minds by question or parable, rather than to insert it by imparting direct information, has often attracted the attention of commentators. In this characteristic our Lord's method of teaching shows a marked affinity with that of Socrates. But in his case the characteristic is especially noticeable in matters that concern his own person and work. Again and again our Lord replies to searching questions concerning himself in this indirect and superficially unsatisfactory way. And yet he gives no impression of uncertainty in his own mind as to the nature and scope of his authority. It is difficult not to conclude that our Lord knew, though probably he could not have formulated the truth in that way, that the Church's creed concerning him must be the Church's own work and could not be delivered ready-made by his own lips ; for man cannot make the deepest truth his own except through the travail of his own mind and soul in expressing it. It seems not at all fanciful to conclude that our Lord's reticence was the fruit of some such profound understanding, and is as sure a witness to his knowledge as any speech. In any case his whole method in teaching reveals a quite astonishing confidence that man can and must see what is true and right for himself, and act accordingly. A faith in man so stedfast even in its indignation, and so far removed alike from Augustinian pessimism and from the cheerful superficialities of the

Pelagian and the humanist, certainly gives the impression that its source is an understanding as profound as it is mysterious.

(*d*) But how did our Lord meet man's apparently complete and final failure to justify his faith in manhood ? The answer to that question is clearly given by St. Mark. " And he began to teach them that the Son of Man must suffer many things and be rejected by the elders and the chief priests and the scribes, and be killed, and after three days rise again. . . . And he called the multitude with his disciples, and said unto them, If any man will come after me, let him deny himself and take up his cross and follow me. For whosoever will save his life shall lose it ; but whosoever shall lose his life for my sake and the gospel's shall save it." [1] No doubt the exact form in which these utterances are set down by the evangelist shows traces here and there of the influence of a faith which the Church came to hold after the resurrection. But to suppose that St. Mark substantially misrepresents what our Lord said at the crisis of his ministry is simply to make the whole gospel-story unintelligible. And if the record is substantially a true one, we can only conclude that our Lord, in the very moment of realizing that facts are inexorably refuting the very trust in man's response which had been the inspiration of his ministry, realizes at the same time no less clearly the profoundest of all the spiritual laws of God's universe, that the salvation of man can only be achieved by the absolute self-sacrifice of the one for the many. The Son of Man must suffer. That is the law of love. And in that knowledge he starts towards Jerusalem for the last time.

So far we have dealt in very summary fashion with the evidence as to the kind of knowledge which the incarnate Lord did possess. We must now as briefly estimate the evidence as to the knowledge which he lacked.

(*a*) There is considerable reason for thinking that he expected the end of the world to follow closely in time upon the temporal event of his own death, although St. Mark records a saying in which he professed ignorance

[1] Mark viii. 31 and 34.

as to the interval which must elapse before the final day.[1]
But it is impossible to reach any definite conclusion as to
our Lord's knowledge, or lack of it, upon this subject.
Such sayings as the reply to St. James' and St. John's
request for chief seats in the Kingdom, as well as many
parables, indicate clearly enough that our Lord apprehended God's Kingdom as a reality of the spiritual order,
entry into which depended upon spiritual conditions. It
is also evident that he thought of the Kingdom as the final
goal of history. But the question of the historical or
temporal relation which the divinely appointed goal of
history bears to the historical process, is a problem so
perplexing in its own inherent nature, that it is impossible
to estimate degrees of nescience or error where no one
knows the truth. Granted that our Lord did teach the
imminence in time of the final coming of the Kingdom,
it may still be the case that such teaching represents a truth
which could not have been better expressed otherwise,
even although history endures for countless centuries
after the teaching was given.[2] And how far our Lord
in his own mind interpreted literally (whatever the word
" literally " means in this connexion) the eschatological
symbols which he used, must be a matter of conjecture.

(b) Again, there is much evidence that our Lord accepted,
and no evidence that he did not accept, the general beliefs
of his time in the matters of demon-possession and the
authorship of the Old Testament. It is of course possible
that he consciously accommodated his language to ideas
which he did not himself share, in order to make his
teaching intelligible and to avoid distracting attention
from the main point of his spiritual teaching. Such an
explanation may have its legitimate place in accounting
for some utterances recorded in the Gospels; but it is
obviously too artificial to furnish a solution of the whole
problem. On the evidence which the Gospels provide, it
certainly seems more straightforward to admit that in
matters of human science and scholarship our Lord's
information did not extend beyond what a man, born
and educated as he was, might naturally have acquired.

[1] Mark xiii. 32.   [2] See below, pp. 244–51.

4. CONCLUSIONS

What then are our conclusions ? To say that the knowledge proper to Godhead was altogether excluded from our Lord's consciousness in the days of his flesh would be a serious mistake. It is indeed precisely the divinest kind of knowledge which he seems most fully to have possessed. On the other hand, it is at least probable that, as regards facts or events occurring in space and time, his knowledge did not transcend the limits imposed upon it by the particular time and place at which he lived as a man. He probably did not know any particular facts, past, future or contemporary, which were outside the range of a human mind living at that particular time and in those particular circumstances of education and environment. But this assertion may be qualified by adding the words : except in so far as his divine insight into universal order and values affected even the knowledge of particular facts present to his human consciousness.

According to this line of thought we leave abundant room for a genuinely human growth and development in the mind of the incarnate Lord and for a human faith and disappointment in regard to the actual course of particular events ; while at the same time divinity reveals itself in the depth, simplicity and certainty of his apprehension of God's will of holiness and love, which orders all. Thus, while remaining faithful to the historical evidence of the Gospels, we may begin to picture to ourselves, however inadequately, the historical reality of what is at once divine knowledge in a human mind, and a human learning and nescience in the mind of the incarnate God.

Let us remind ourselves once more in conclusion how constantly Jesus emphasized as the most important knowledge, knowledge of real values, a right sense of proportion in all things. Such is the main point, for instance, in his frequent use of the figure of *treasure*. All is well with a man whose treasure is in the right place, whose value-judgements are sound and true ; his heart is even now in heaven. The very Kingdom of heaven itself is the one true treasure even upon earth. Therefore Pharisaic for-

malism and the sentimental piety of the man in the street
are alike abhorrent, because each represents a perverted
sense of proportion, a value-judgement which is fundamentally wrong. St. Paul teaches the same general lesson
in a quite different way.[1] The supreme achievement of his
Christ-inspired wisdom is his discernment of the relative
values of spiritual gifts, culminating in the perception
that faith, hope and love are what abide, and that the
greatest of these is love. It is by the same kind of standard
that the Christian must judge the divinity of the knowledge
revealed in the incarnate Christ. Is it too much to say
that, the more closely the standard is applied, the more
divinely wonderful that knowledge is seen to be ? Once
we have pondered the insight into ultimate reality which
turned the steps of Jesus towards Jerusalem for the last
time, it is impossible to deal with the problem of his
knowledge as though the issue hung on a question whether
he was unaware that David did not write a particular
psalm,[2] or conceivably forgot that Ahimelech was high-
priest when David ate the shew-bread,[3] or supernaturally
read the thoughts of Nathanael under the fig-tree.[4] Surely
we have seen greater things than these.

[1] 1 Cor. xii., xiii.   [2] Mark xii. 35.
[3] Mark ii. 26.   [4] John i. 48–50.

CHAPTER XVII

THE MORAL PERFECTION OF JESUS

IT IS a postulate of the truth of the incarnation that Jesus can never have thought, said, or done anything that was either unfitting for God in the state of condescension into manhood, or unworthy of man as raised into union with the Godhead. We have already tried to show that the limitations belonging to earthly manhood were not unfitting for the incarnate God. But we must now consider more closely the problems suggested by the second half of our postulate.

1. " AUT DEUS AUT HOMO NON BONUS ? "

If our Lord's thoughts, words and acts were really not unworthy of man as raised to union with God, we are obliged to reject at once certain interpretations of the celebrated dilemma, aut deus aut homo non bonus. On the strength of this dilemma it is sometimes urged that, because our Lord is God, his conduct is not subject to judgement by any standard of human morality. Thus an easy way of escape is found from any awkward question raised about the moral perfection of Jesus ; for it may be pleaded that men are simply not qualified to pass any moral judgement at all upon the conduct of one who is God. This plea of course makes it impossible to use the human goodness of Jesus as evidence for his divinity, and invalidates altogether the witness of the natural conscience to the truth of the gospel. For these reasons we cannot accept the plea. And therefore difficulties felt about the moral perfection of Jesus are for us real difficulties which have to be carefully considered, and may not be simply swept aside.

2.   THE BIBLICAL POINT OF VIEW

At the outset, however, it must be recognized that as a distinct and definite concept the idea of moral perfection is not present in the Bible.   The Bible does not speak the language of moral philosophy, and even in its portrait of Jesus Christ it sets before us no ideal of human goodness *as such*.   In the Bible perfect holiness and righteousness are simply identified with the nature and character of God ; perfection for man consists in obedience to God's revealed will ; and, since all duty is regarded as something which man owes to God, moral obligation is never clearly distinguished from religious.   When we come to the New Testament, it is evident that the perfect holiness and sinlessness of Jesus are treated as axiomatic.   But it is equally evident that we are not here invited, as we are by some modern theologians, to infer the unique relation of Jesus to God from the moral perfection which his human character manifests.   Rather, according to the thought of the New Testament, the unique holiness of Jesus is manifest through and in the fact that he is revealed as the agent of God's love and righteousness and power for the final redemption of his people from bondage to sin and death.   The thought of the moral perfection of Jesus, as distinct from the thought of God's salvation manifested through him, is for the writers of the New Testament impossible.

3.   THE PHILOSOPHICAL PROBLEM

When we reflect on the idea of moral perfection from a philosophical point of view, we find ourselves confronted with difficulties which the thought of the New Testament avoids.   In one sense at least, the realization of perfection in a single personality is impossible.   For the ideal of moral life is inherently social ; its realization consists in a communion and fellowship of spirits, wherein each enriches the others by the free and unselfish communication of whatever good is its own, and where the special contribution of each is necessary to the perfection of the whole.

Such a community can be made actual only in the final Kingdom of God, where all are free and all are one in his love. A real truth therefore is expressed by the contention, often heard on the lips of social reformers, that it is impossible for any man, however pure in heart, to be morally a perfect Christian when he is obliged to live as a member of a very unchristian society. In so far as this contention is true, it would seem that Jesus, as a man on earth, cannot have attained to the moral ideal of Christianity.

On the other hand, it may be argued, with exactly equal force, that, in so far as the moral ideal consists in absolute self-sacrifice at painful cost to the self, it can be realized only in an imperfect and even sinful society which affords the opportunity for moral heroism. Strictly moral perfection, it may reasonably be said, is more nearly approached by a life which sufferings, unselfishly endured for a perverse and thankless generation, have isolated, than by one which finds fruition in the complete responsiveness of its fellows. The cross is the crown of the moral perfection of Jesus. In the perfect society morality is left behind.

4.   THE SOLUTION OF CHRISTIAN THEOLOGY

There is only one satisfactory way of removing the apparent contradiction. We must return to the biblical or theological point of view. We assume, and cannot here give reasons for the assumption, that moral perfection can only be realized in life according to the spirit of love. Now perfect love, according to the New Testament, is in God alone ; indeed, it is the supreme characteristic of his nature as revealed in Christ. But it is communicated to man by a double revelation, the two necessary stages of which correspond with the first and second advents of Christ, the incarnation and the final reign of God. In this sinful world love is supremely revealed in forgiveness and in the self-sacrifice of the cross, which represents the cost of forgiveness to the forgiver. In the world to come love is revealed as the eternal bond of the glorious triumphant

society of the forgiven and redeemed. In both revelations
the love is the same, deriving its identity from the fact
that it belongs to the changeless nature of the eternal
God. But in each the love is revealed under different
conditions and in a different mode. In the first it is
revealed in act towards the achievement of an end not yet
realized. In the second it is revealed in fulfilment and
completed victory. Each stage of the revelation has its
own characteristic perfection, the first on the lonely cross
of Calvary, the second in the unimaginable beatitude
pictured for us in the apocalyptic vision of the great
multitude which no man can number. The perfection of
the first belongs to Jesus Christ alone, the perfection of
the second belongs also to all whom Christ has made his
own. But neither perfection could be itself apart from
the other. The cross would not be the symbol of the
perfect self-sacrifice, if it were not also the real means of
redemption. Nor would the life of heaven be the fulfilment
of redemption, if it did not consist in the thankful worship
of the divine sufferer by those whom his suffering has
won, and who have been enabled in some measure also to
share it. No such perfection is possible in this world :
nevertheless, in the communion and fellowship of the
Church, which is Christ's body, the life of the world to
come begins to be present already. Thus from one point
of view the fellowship of the Church on earth goes beyond
the perfection realized in the solitary life of Jesus, though
from another point of view it is infinitely inferior to it.

5. HOW JESUS WAS MORALLY PERFECT

How then are we to judge of the moral perfection of
Jesus ? It belongs to the whole thought of Christianity
about God, the world and man, that no strictly absolute
ideal of manhood is realizable in this world. All moral
perfection here below is inherently instrumental ; it is
relative to a work and end to be accomplished, the final
state of accomplishment belonging, not to this world, but
to the world to come. In Jesus we see manhood raised
to fulfil its highest capacities on earth in becoming the

instrument and organ of God's great act of love for man's
salvation. But, just because the human perfection of
Jesus upon earth is relative to the accomplishment of God's
work through his manhood, and that work is unique, the
life of Jesus cannot present an absolute example for the
imitation of all other men. None other may or can do
what Christ did for all. God's will for each man is to do
with him something different from what he did through
Jesus ; and in his particular task of obedience each realizes
his own particular perfection. But, inasmuch as what
God wills to do in and with every man is a work of that
same love which redeemed mankind through Jesus Christ,
and no man's conscience is so far destroyed by sin as to be
quite incapable of response to that love, each man may and
ought to recognize in Jesus a truly human goodness made
worthy, by God's condescension into it, to be the instrument of that saving work which God accomplished through
Jesus alone.

It follows that our broad judgement of the moral perfection of Jesus will be based, not upon a minute examination of particular acts and sayings in reference to some
generally accepted rule of human conduct, but rather
upon our recognition of the fitness of his whole life to be
the human instrument of the divine love for that purpose
of salvation which is revealed in it.

Nevertheless, even so, certain acts and sayings of Jesus
recorded in the Gospels present serious difficulties which
have to be faced. Some of them may be fairly disposed
of by the historical criticism which teaches us to distinguish,
and to allow for, the particular doctrinal interest and
method of composition which are characteristic of each
evangelist. For instance, we may very reasonably suppose that the occurrence of the saying " There shall be
weeping and gnashing of teeth " in certain contexts of St.
Matthew's Gospel is due to St. Matthew's own editorial
work. And if we admit that St. John makes our Lord's
revelation of the reality of his own divine person and
mission more direct and explicit throughout his ministry
than at that time it was, we can hardly refrain from
inferring also that some verbal controversies between

Jesus and the Jews, which the Fourth Gospel contains, have value as showing the religious and theological issues at stake rather than as recording actual conversations. In other cases we may rightly feel that difficulties as to words used by our Lord would disappear, if we possessed a fuller knowledge of the circumstances in which they were spoken. And in others again difficulty may be removed, if we remember the necessary limitations of thought and activity to which the Son of God made himself subject in the flesh. For instance, the apparent harshness of the saying to the Syro-Phœnician woman is surely to be attributed, not to the racial prejudice of the Jew, but to the inward struggle of the love which is compelled to restrict its immediate activity lest it fail of its widest aim. In the flesh Christ was straitened indeed. His particular words and acts are to be judged in the light of that coherent plan which determined his whole ministry. And that plan reveals its full moral significance only when it is regarded as God's way of perfecting a universal fellowship through the limitations and the self-sacrifice of one who could not suffer himself to be a popular hero.

Perhaps the most serious of the difficulties of which we are now speaking arises from our Lord's occasionally extreme severity in denunciation. Do we not sometimes catch an echo of a self-regarding and vengeful animosity against his most obstinate opponents ? A study of the whole character and teaching of Jesus, as the Gospels record them, justifies a negative answer. It is perhaps hardly too much to say that, in the eyes of that love which was our Lord's supreme motive, the one temper which is intrinsically damnable is that which is content to consign others to damnation. In denunciation of such unforgiving hardness or callous indifference the language of Jesus is quite unsparing ; but it is for that temper that his extreme invective is reserved. The one sure way to incur God's ultimate condemnation, he teaches, is to invoke that doom upon others. It is precisely here that supreme moral goodness affirms a doctrine of relativity which upsets the apparently absolute standards of conventional ethics. One man is not absolutely better than another because he has more closely observed the rules of a moral code, however admirable.   The surest way for a man to know how the eternal goodness judges him is to consider how he himself judges his fellows.   That great principle of relativity lies at the root of our Lord's ethical teaching.   And to recognize that fact fully will not diminish our reverent acknowledgement of the divine and human goodness of the teacher.

CHAPTER XVIII

THE PERSON OF THE INCARNATE

Was JESUS a human person? The question raises an ancient difficulty, which may be stated as a dilemma. If we affirm that Jesus was a human person, we are driven either into an impossible conception of a double personality in the incarnate Son of God, or else into the Christology of Liberal Protestantism which we have found to be inadequate. If we deny that Jesus was a human person, we deny by implication the completeness of his manhood and stand convicted of Apollinarianism. Dr. Raven argues [1] that most of those whom the Catholic tradition has honoured as doctors of orthodoxy were in fact Apollinarians, though they condemned Apollinarius.

1. MYSTERIUM CHRISTI

From the point of view of the kenotic Christology, which we have provisionally adopted, what are we to say in answer to this dilemma? We are bound to hold, as historical orthodoxy has always held, that Jesus Christ in the fundamental principle of his being was not man but God. He was not a man who was made or became God, nor one who was divine merely in the quality of his manhood. He was the Son of God who was made or became man. On the other hand, we cannot be content to say that in Jesus Christ the Son of God took on himself a human nature without becoming a human person; nor do we make the proposition any more acceptable by suggesting that in taking the human nature he put off the divine. Such separations between nature and person are really unmeaning. They are but devices of logicians who seek to avoid formal self-contradiction by imagining im-

[1] See his book, *Apollinarianism*.

possibilities. Jesus Christ on earth was a divine-human
person who combined two natures in himself. *He* was God
and *he* was man ; yet he was one person. That is to say
that the Son of God by an act of divine power and self-
limitation really identified himself with the created man
born of Mary. But that does not mean that the man was
created first, and that the Son of God afterwards identified
himself with him. Such a hypothesis would imply that
the human being Jesus, like all others, was created by God
through the eternal Word, so that Jesus would at first
have had that same relative externality to the Godhead
which belongs to all other created souls. But, as St. John
according to our interpretation suggests,[1] the human being
Jesus was created *in* the eternal Word, so that the created
human being was from his very beginning altogether
enfolded in the creative divine being, as the divine being
was at the same time self-limited in the human. This is
the ultimate mystery of the incarnation, the γένεσις Ζωῆς
in the created world.

All human personality is a finite image of the divine
which is its source ; and assuredly our human personality
mirrors the divine not least in its capacity to restrict
voluntarily its own range of activity in order to sympathize
with, and put itself in the place of, others which have not
yet attained to its own measure of spiritual stature. At
the moment of the incarnation, then, we suppose that by
a quite unimaginable act of divine sympathy the Son of
God took upon himself both the human fullness and the
human limitations of a created personality which, through
his self-identification with it, became the personal expression of himself as man. The experience of Jesus was
the experience of the Son of God as limited by a personal
and individual manhood, and it was also the experience of
a man so created wholly *in* the eternal Son that in the
inmost reality of his being he was one person with him.[2]

---

[1] See above, pp. 110 *sqq.*
[2] Commenting on some lines in Browning's " Easter Day ",
Mr. F. H. Brabant writes : " It might be pointed out that Beauty
here is spiritual, not because it is divorced from matter but because
it dominates and organizes the material ; Music is spiritual, not

2. THE CONSCIOUSNESS OF THE INCARNATE PERSON

It cannot be too strongly emphasized that the dogma of
the incarnation is primarily a doctrine concerning Christ's
person, not his consciousness. It answers the questions,
who and what was he ? not, how did he think or feel concerning God, the world, and himself ? The answer to the
latter question is inevitably a matter of conjecture from
the data which the New Testament provides, and it is a
matter on which there must probably always be some
divergence of opinion among Christians. In any case we
can hardly expect to penetrate far into the consciousness
of the incarnate. Nevertheless, because he was the incarnate, we must make the attempt to enter even there,
if we would know, as fully as we may, the truth of what
God has revealed of himself in manhood. And, when we
make that attempt, it is obvious that our conclusions will
rightly affect, and be affected by, our interpretation of the
Church's doctrine concerning Christ's person.

Starting therefore from the doctrinal interpretations we
have already reached, we may proceed very tentatively to
conjecture as follows. There was in Jesus what we should
call a human ego. He thought of himself, and thought
truly, as being the man Jesus, the son of Mary. And,
being thus conscious of himself as a human being, he could
not be fully conscious of himself as the eternal Son and
Word of God. The divine person and nature were indeed
fully present in the human, as the human were assumed
into the divine ; but they were not fully present to the
consciousness of the incarnate. Nevertheless, they were
not wholly hidden from that consciousness. If this line

when the notes are faintly audible but when they perfectly express
the emotion ; it was Pater who said that all arts aspire to be like
Music (i.e., in the complete penetration of their material). So
we might perhaps venture to say that Jesus is divine, not because
his divine person or nature is divorced from the human, but
because his human person and nature are dominated and organized
by the divine. Because in him the divine is self-limited by the
human, in him also the penetration of the human by the divine
is complete." (See Brabant, *Time and Eternity in Christian
Thought*, p. 181 n.)

of thought guides us in any way towards the truth, we should conjecture that in the mind of Jesus there must always have been a certain tension between the limitations inherent in his humanity and the transcendence belonging to the deity which was the inmost reality of his being. He would have been in a limited yet growing degree conscious that, though he was a man, he was yet more than man, that his humanity was the earthly vessel through which the divine love, which he knew to be *his own*, was accomplishing its redemptive work.

Is not this the kind of conjecture which the gospel-portrait of Jesus, especially that given by the synoptists, most naturally suggests ? Clearly it would seem that our Lord not only felt and thought and spoke, but also actually prayed, as a man, and so far did not identify himself with God. But it is also clear that what impressed his disciples and others was the unique way in which he spoke of God as his Father, and assumed, in spite of his humility, a certain absolute authority in dealing with the things of God, which was different in kind even from the prophetic, though prophet men acknowledged him to be. Again, we have to take into account our Lord's identification of himself both with the Messiah and with the Son of Man. It would appear that he spoke of himself as Son of Man in the third person, especially when he referred to the redemptive work which he was to accomplish through suffering. The figures of the Messiah and of the Son of Man were intimately connected each with one form or aspect of that hope of the final Kingdom of God which was a principal constituent of Jewish religion. Jesus deepened, spiritualized, and transformed the current conceptions of the Kingdom. If, then, the Kingdom of God was in his mind such as the Lord's Prayer and the parables present it, and if he believed himself to be, as Messiah and Son of Man, God's representative in the heralding and establishment of *that* Kingdom, what must have been his own thought about himself ? Historical critics exhaust their learning and ingenuity in order to explain away the evidence of the Gospels for any such unique element in our Lord's personal consciousness and power as we have tried to account for on the hypothesis that the evidence stands. But historical critics, as we have argued, have their own presuppositions. And it may still be that to accept the evidence brings us nearer to the truth of the historical facts than to explain it away.

3. THE JESUS OF HISTORY AS RELATED TO GOD AND MAN

In conclusion we may try to sum up in non-technical language the truth about the Jesus of history to which we have been trying to give such measure of precision as the subject allows. He learned, we suggest, about the world and about God as a man learns through human faculties of body and mind. He was tempted through those faculties, as a man is tempted, though the thought of sin in connexion with him is impossible. He guided his life, not by a divine vision altogether beyond man's scope, but by a prayer and trust in his heavenly Father which were genuinely human. At the same time his human sense of sonship towards God was rooted in the reality of a sonship which belonged to him alone as the eternal Son. How clearly or constantly that reality was present to his consciousness we cannot know ; and our uncertainty is increased by the fact that the titles, Messiah, Son of Man, and even Son of God, did not, according to Hebrew thought, necessarily imply the divinity of the person to whom they belonged. But that our Lord was conscious of *some* unique relation in himself to God the Father cannot fairly be doubted. And we may say that his consciousness of a human sonship towards God merged in, while it limited, the consciousness of the divine sonship and did not altogether exclude it, because the relation in which man naturally stands to God, in so far as man's nature is unmarred by sin, is itself an image and reflexion in the creature of the relation in which he who is begotten but uncreated stands eternally to the Father of all.

However that may be, Jesus, by the use he made of naturally growing human faculties, trod man's path to God, knew God, and knew himself as God's own appointed representative on earth, all with an undeviating sureness and insight such as no mere man could have displayed. In all he did he was through human faculties taking up manhood to a new level of life whither no mere man, but God only, could have raised it.   Just as our own human mind in the body, limited by the body, and using bodily means, can train and enable the body to perform new feats and acquire new habits, so the Son of God in our personal humanity, limited by it and using it, was raising it to new and glorious capabilities.   He showed what can be done with common manhood, when God himself " takes hold of the seed of Abraham ".   And what Christ did with common manhood he enables believers in him to do also.   The most essential difference between Jesus and the greatest of his saints lies in this, that, what they attain of union with God, they attain in that fellowship which God's only Son established through the loneliness of his self-sacrifice. Jesus remains the divine and solitary pioneer of their salvation.

DIVINE IMPASSIBILITY IN RELATION TO CREATION AND INCARNATION

In view of what has been said as to the influence of the Hellenic doctrine of divine impassibility on Christian theology, some separate discussion of the whole notion of passibility and impassibility seems to be required. Three kinds of passibility are to be distinguished, (1) external, (2) internal, (3) sensational.

(1) " External " passibility refers to the relations of a being towards that which is beyond or outside itself. In this sense passibility means the capacity to be acted upon by something from without, or, in a word, the capacity for passivity. Aristotle maintained the strict impassibility of God in this sense. For him God is the perfect being eternally enjoying his own perfection, and entirely unaffected by the movement towards his perfection which causes the restlessness of the imperfect world. St. Thomas Aquinas keeps as close to his philosophical master as he can, but cannot follow him the whole way, since he is obliged to maintain that God of his own will created the world and therefore is not unaware of its existence. St. Thomas saves the external impassibility of God by the exceedingly difficult doctrine that, though the world was created by God, it does not in any way exist outside of, or over against, or in addition to, him. The bringing into existence of created beings adds nothing to reality, since God already from eternity comprehends in himself all the plenitude of the perfection of all being.[1] Thus, properly speaking, there can be no external or even reciprocal relation between God and his creatures. Creatures are really related to God ; but God is not related to them, except in our way of thinking.[2] This doctrine comes dangerously near to making nonsense of the Jewish-Christian conception of creation. That which is of value in it seems to be sufficiently conserved, if we suppose that, in creating free agents other than himself, God voluntarily limited himself so

[1] *S.T.*, Pt. I, Q. 9, Art. 1.
[2] *Ibid.*, Q. 13, Art. 7, and elsewhere.

184

as to allow them really to act of their own motion, and even to rebel against his will, if they would. In this way therefore God makes himself " externally " passible by creating. But we can still maintain that God is never acted upon by anything which he did not himself voluntarily create and does not himself always control by his over-ruling power. God is therefore never *subject to* the action of any other being. As far, then, as " external " passibility is concerned, we may say that God is *absolutely* or *ultimately* impassible, though he becomes *relatively* passible by his own act of creation.

(2) " Internal " passibility refers to relations within a conscious being or personality. The human being is conscious within himself of emotions and instincts which move him powerfully this way and that. He calls these " passions ", because it seems to him, when he reflects, that he is acted upon by them " in spite of himself ", i.e., in spite of the rational will and deliberate purpose with which his true self is identified. Thus St. Augustine actually defines the term *passio* (translating the Greek πάθος) as meaning a movement of the mind contrary to reason, although he goes on to say that passions such as anger and sadness can be turned to purposes of righteousness.[1] In this sense it is that the Anglican Article declares God to be " without passions " ; and we need not hesitate to assent. If we use about God terms like " anger " and " pity ", we must remember that they do not denote *passiones* or πάθη in the proper sense. The divine will and reason are not passive to changing emotions as are the will and reason of man. God's nature, as St. Thomas Aquinas puts it, is immutable, because it is simple. There is no cause of division or disturbance in the divine mind, similar or analogous to that opposition between rational will and non-rational feelings and desires which is so commonly the cause of mental conflict in ourselves. In this connexion, then, the doctrine of divine impassibility signifies the absolute stedfastness of the will in which is " no variableness nor shadow caused by turning ", while at the same time it provides a safeguard against anthropomorphism.

(3) " Sensational " passibility is intermediate between " external " and " internal ". It denotes liability to those feelings of pleasure and pain, and more especially those of pain, which are caused within a conscious being by the action of some other being upon it. In the past the main tradition of Christian orthodoxy has certainly denied the " sensational " passibility

---

[1] See J. K. Mozley, *Impassibility*, p. 104.

of God, while on the other hand it has never drawn the apparently logical inference that God is insensitive to human sin or virtue, or unsympathetic with the sufferings of his creatures. In modern times many theologians outside the Roman Communion, who could hardly be called either eccentric or heretical, have maintained that, since God loves his creatures, he must be said to suffer pain or sorrow on account of their unhappiness and sin. At the same time these theologians would probably desire to add that, what in God may be called pain or sorrow, is assuredly not *mere* suffering, but is part of the victorious activity whereby he ultimately subdues all things to himself. Thus, according to this view, the truth of God's " sensational " passibility is always limited and qualified by the truth that his " external " passibility, which is the cause of the " sensational ", is strictly relative and self-imposed.

If the awareness and sympathy of God on the one hand, and his victorious and all-controlling power on the other, are fully agreed upon, I am not sure that the Christian theologian need greatly concern himself about any further unanimity. But a few words must be added to show how the Christian doctrines of creation and incarnation are affected by such an admission of divine passibility as we have found ourselves obliged to make.

Creation, we have said, involves divine self-limitation. Through this self-limitation both the time-process and created beings become real to God, so that God becomes relatively passible. God's acceptance of this passibility is the negative aspect of that which, in its positive aspect, we call the original act of creation. By the same act there is set up a relation of interaction between God and his creatures ; and it is thus that God's activity in and for his creation becomes *purposive*. The fulfilment of the divine purpose is finally attained when the creation becomes fully and wholly the *expression* of God's love in created being. In that fulfilment the relation of interaction between God and his creatures ceases, since God cannot be thought of as in any way passible towards that which is fully and wholly the expression of himself. The relation of interaction having ceased, the time-process, at least as we now experience it, comes to an end also, since if there is no further, and as yet unrealized, object for which to act, the metaphysical cause and ground of what we know as *time* no longer exist. Nevertheless, when creation has reached its goal, temporal events will still be real as past, though not as present or as future. For the final perfection could not be what it is, unless it had been brought about by the divine self-limitation which caused the temporal world, and by the purpose which directed it to its end. In this sense time itself may be said to have an eternal value or reality.

The relation between the truth of the divine impassibility and that of the historical incarnation seems to be more complex than is sometimes supposed. The created manhood of Jesus in the days of his flesh is the perfect self-expression of Godhead within this world of history and space-time. Since that self-expression is in one way perfect, it follows that in the incarnate person, Jesus Christ, the Godhead is not (externally) passible towards the manhood ; for in Christ's person there is no sort of external relation between man and God. Because the manhood of Jesus is created without any external relation to the deity,[1] it is from its beginning a new creation—a truth which has been safeguarded by the tradition of the Virgin Birth. Neither divine nor human nature, considered *in se*, is changed by the incarnation, but a new relation between them is established by divine act.

Nevertheless, in so far as the manhood of Jesus is the self-expression of Godhead *within this world*, it is not the absolutely or finally perfect expression, since it is also the *instrument* of that redemption and salvation wherein finality will hereafter be attained. In this world the manhood of Jesus is the effective instrument of salvation, because, in expressing himself in it, God enters upon a further passibility than that which was involved in the first creation. This further passibility has a double aspect, in respect (*a*) of internal and (*b*) of sensational passibility. For (*a*) the divine-human person becomes the subject of human emotional experience and temptation (he becomes a man " of like passions " with us) ; and (*b*) he endures everything which the world's sin can inflict upon the sinless one, while he renounces the immediate divine consciousness of triumph over all evil, which constitutes the blessedness of God in heaven. It is by *thus* expressing in manhood his love for man that God wins the victory the fruit of which is final redemption.

[1] See the Note on St. John's Prologue, pp. 110 *sqq.*

PART III

THE CHRISTIAN DOCTRINE OF SALVATION

INTRODUCTION

THERE ARE two points of view from which the whole body of truth concerning Jesus Christ can be approached and interpreted. As we have already suggested, the beginning of the distinction between them is to be observed even in the New Testament, in the different emphases which are characteristic respectively of St. John and of St. Paul. From the first or Johannine point of view, the truth that is in Jesus is primarily the self-revelation of God. From the second or Pauline, that truth is primarily the way of salvation for man. From the first point of view the doctrine of the incarnation is the centre and starting-point of Christian theology. The atonement is derivative from it, and the eschatological doctrines concerning the ultimate destiny of the human soul tend to appear, as it were, on the circumference of Christian theology, since they are concerned with those elements in the revelation which are most remote from our present experience. But from the second point of view the main doctrines of Christian theology are seen in a different perspective. The atonement, as God's redeeming act for man's salvation, now becomes the centre and starting-point. The incarnation is seen as the method of the atonement ; and the end, of which the incarnation is the means, is found in the fulfilment of God's saving work in the life of the world to come.

Thus, from the second point of view the problems of eschatology appear as more immediately urgent than they do from the first. For, as long as we are thinking strictly of God's *self-revelation* in Christ, it is no doubt reasonable and right to say that, while we know by faith what has been revealed, we must be content to leave in God's hands what will be revealed in the unknown future. " It doth not yet appear what we shall be." But, when we are thinking of God's *saving act* in Christ, the future end and fulfilment of that act is of primary importance for our theology, and we need some more definite assurance concerning what is not yet, but will be. That is why St. Paul's teaching on eschatology, with all its perplexing varieties, is more definite and explicit than St. John's.

If therefore we take the doctrine of the atonement to be in its essence the theological exposition of God's redeeming action in Jesus Christ, we find that it must inevitably lead into some doctrine of those " last things " in which God's action towards man reaches its ultimate goal. For myself I cannot but feel that Christian theology has on the whole failed to do justice to this logical connexion, and that some classical treatises on the doctrine of the atonement are gravely incomplete, because they do not face the eschatological issues which are raised by the very nature of the doctrine itself. No doubt we do well to emphasize passages in the New Testament which warn us that there is much we cannot know about the ultimate destiny of man, and much that lies hid in the counsels of God. But, just because the gospel of atonement and redemption is so central in the New Testament as a whole, there are truths about that ultimate destiny which it insists on affirming with the voice of divine authority ; and what it teaches as to the terrors of divine judgement is but one aspect or element in that final universal triumph of God which is the very issue of salvation.

In any exposition of the Christian doctrine of the atonement it seems natural, and perhaps inevitable, to start from what I have called the Pauline point of view, rather than from the Johannine. Accordingly I propose at this point, not to consider by itself that clause of the creed which speaks of Christ's sufferings and death for man, but to join with it those clauses which speak of resurrection, judgement, and the life of the world to come. We shall therefore view the doctrine of the atonement as one element in the whole Christian doctrine of salvation, which includes the consideration of the evil from which man needs to be delivered, of the means of that deliverance, of the life which is its final issue, and of the possibility and consequences of rejecting it.

CHAPTER XIX

THE PROBLEM OF SALVATION AND ITS CONDITIONS

THE IDEA of salvation implies that of deliverance ; and deliverance means deliverance from something. Salvation is salvation from evil, and the doctrine of salvation is closely connected with what we are accustomed to call " the problem of evil ".

1. THE RELATION OF EVIL TO SALVATION

We rightly speak of the problem of evil as the greatest obstacle to Christian belief in God. But we must not forget the complementary truth that, if there were no problem of evil, there would be no need of salvation, and no doctrine of a redeeming God at all. Berdyaev's words on this subject are worth quoting.

In the historical development of the human consciousness faith in the divine arose just because men experienced great sufferings and felt the need of freeing themselves from the power of evil. The existence of evil is not only the obstacle to our faith in God, for it is equally a proof of the existence of God, and the proof that this world is not the only nor ultimate one. The experience of evil directs man's attention towards another world by arousing in him a discontent with this. It is pessimism and not optimism which lies at the bottom of religious experience and the religious consciousness. Our natural world is apparently in the victorious grip of the inane ; for it is dominated by corruptibility and death, animosity and hatred, egoism and discord. Man is overwhelmed by the meaningless evil of the whole of life. In religion and in faith he turns towards the world of meaning, and receives strength from that world where love triumphs over hatred, union over division, and eternal life over death.[1]

---

[1] *Freedom and the Spirit*, pp. 158 *sq.*

It would, I think, be equally true to put Berdyaev's point the other way round, and say that the problem of evil only exists in relation to the conceivability of some sort of salvation. If no thought of a world wholly better than this ever arose to kindle immortal longing in man's heart, evil would cease to be a problem, and man would be a purely natural animal, content on the whole, like other animals, to accept the conditions of life as he finds them. When all apologists have said their say, it remains true that man's fundamental discontent is God's most universal witness; and discontent implies some sort of effort after some kind of salvation.

But neither of the two terms, " evil " and " salvation ", represents a quite simple idea, the concrete meaning of which is the same for all. There are manifestly different conceptions of salvation in the religions of the world; and the differences between them are largely determined by different conceptions of the fundamental evil from which deliverance is sought. Among primitive peoples, no doubt, evil is largely, though perhaps never wholly, identified with physical discomforts. In that case good hunting, good crops, and victory in war constitute the essence of salvation, even if the giver of salvation be thought of as a divine and spiritual being. Throughout the Old Testament Jehovah's salvation or redemption is closely connected with the thought of deliverance in war from human enemies and oppressors. Spiritual and intellectual development brings deeper insight into the real nature of evil. Civilized and philosophical man has to face the perplexing question : what is the fundamental evil from which I must pray to be delivered ? According to his answer to this question his conception of salvation is determined.

Experience and reflexion seem to show that there are four possible answers to it : (1) death, i.e., the negation or destruction of life ; (2) pain, i.e., uncomfortable living, the evil of feeling ; (3) ignorance or error, the evil of the intellect ; (4) sin or moral wrong, the evil of the will. Generally it may be agreed that all four of these are genuinely evils, and that a complete salvation, if such were

D.C.   O

possible, would deliver us from all. But the history of thought and belief shows wide differences of opinion as to which is the fundamental form of evil, on deliverance from which man's main endeavour is to be concentrated ; and from these differences the characteristic contents of the various doctrines of salvation are in great measure derived.

In endeavouring to answer the great question about evil, the Hellenic world on the whole wavered between the first and the third of the answers given above. At the beginning of the Christian era the more popular Gentile religions of the Empire undoubtedly regarded death as the chief of evils, and correspondingly identified salvation with the attainment of immortality. Corinthian converts needed St. Paul's reminders that " the sting of death is sin ", and that " the *last* enemy that shall be destroyed is death ".[1] Nevertheless, the philosophy of the Platonic tradition has always inclined to make ignorance or error rather than death the devil of its creed. Plato, and even Aristotle with certain reservations, taught that moral delinquency is caused by lack of knowledge or intelligence. The pain of life, they suggested, only seems unendurable to the ignorant or unphilosophic ; and even death could be treated as an event of little moment by one who had trained himself to intellectual communion with eternal verities. According to the Platonic gospel salvation essentially consists in the philosopher's vision of the unchanging perfection behind and beyond the ceaseless movement of phenomena. This general conception of salvation has lived on in much modern idealism, and it has exercised a powerful influence on the theology of the Catholic Church.

Buddhism, on the other hand, has fastened on pain as the fundamental evil in the world. Pain, it teaches, is caused by unsatisfied desire ; and, since the basic desires of human nature are incapable of any final satisfaction, salvation must consist in the systematic eradication of desire from the soul. The preoccupation with the problem of pain forms a link between Buddhism and much of the more popular philosophy of the modern West.

Meanwhile Judaism and Christianity, receiving at this

_____
[1] 1 Cor. xv. 56, 26. Cf. also Heb. ii. 15.

point some support from Stoicism, have steadily insisted that sin or moral wrong is the true fount of all evil, the one enemy to be fought without compromise or truce, in deliverance from which all salvation is to be achieved even through the willing acceptance of pain and death. In its doctrine of deliverance from sin through Christ Christianity stands unique, and the essential characteristic of its soteriology is expressed in the simple and profound affirmation of the Apostles' Creed, " I believe in the for-giveness of sins ". Thus the Christian doctrines of the atonement, judgement, heaven and hell, are all alike unintelligible except in relation to the presupposition that the radical evil in the world is sin. Our next task there-fore must be to explain and justify this presupposition.

2.   EVIL AS PAIN AND AS WRONG

As we have seen, the Christian conception of the funda-mental nature and source of evil places Christianity at once in opposition both to the philosophies of Plato and Aris-totle and to the religion of Buddha. Of its opposition to Plato and Aristotle little need be said at this point. The whole tendency of our time is anti-intellectualist, and the doctrine of salvation by knowledge or pure reason finds few disciples. It is sufficient to notice that, from the strictly Platonic and Aristotelian point of view, no divine act of atonement is either necessary or possible as a means of salvation. To Plato and Aristotle what is required for salvation is not the forgiveness of sin, but the dissipation of error ; and, even if salvation were to come from God, it must take the form, not of an atoning incarnation, but of a theophany.

The case is different in regard to Buddhism. For in the humanitarian culture of the late nineteenth and early twentieth centuries the view that pain or suffering is the essential and radical evil has become ever more widely prevalent. And this fact gives a more direct relevance to some general remarks upon the Buddhist conception of salvation.

According to Buddhism, in its apparently most original

and authentic form, the pain from which salvation is sought is essentially the fruit of those unsatisfiable desires which are inherent in human nature.   Life in this world consists in the ceaseless activity of cravings for which the universe affords no final satisfaction.   Therefore, concludes the Buddhist, the way of salvation must be found in the extirpation of these cravings, which involves the disappearance of the distinct personal life of the individual.   Belief in *Karma* prevents the Buddhist from suggesting suicide as a way of escape.   The suicide's unhappiness would be only continued and intensified in a further life on earth. Desire can only really be overcome by a long-continued moral and spiritual discipline.   By this discipline the soul gradually realizes that all men's valuations of earthly things as good and evil are alike illusory, and it finally enters into a state of complete calm and detachment which henceforth nothing can disturb.   The true way of escape from suffering, and the nature of the goal, the Buddha himself realized after long search in a moment of illumination as he sat in meditation under the Bo-tree.   He might then and there have entered Nirvana never to return.   But we are told that he conquered this last temptation, and came back into the world, out of pity for the suffering multitudes who knew not the way of deliverance.   Thus he became an evangelist and founded a religion.

In the philosophy of authentic Buddhism moral and intellectual valuations are retained, and indeed emphasized, up to a point ; but in the end they are subordinated to the supreme value of release from pain.   A discipline of unselfishness is certainly enjoined, yet only so that in the end the self as subject of desire may be utterly extinguished. The final virtue to be retained is a love which seems to be more akin to compassion than to the Christian *agape*. Compassion simply recognizes the fact of suffering in others, and moves us to show them the way of escape, without taking the side of right against wrong.   Unlike *agape*, it involves no exercise of the will to make a better world, and no devotion to any person for his own sake. Again, Buddhism may commend the zeal for truth, in so far as " right belief " is part of its holy eightfold path, and all personal prejudice is to be rigorously excluded. Yet this zeal is only a stage in learning the complete detachment which sees even the strife between truth and falsehood as an illusion born of desire. Mr. Valiant-for-Truth could find no place in the Buddhist heaven.

There is an evident coherence in logic between the fundamental judgement that pain or suffering is the radical evil and the denial that the distinctions between right and wrong, true and false, are in any way absolute or ultimate. At both points the sophisticated and sceptical humanitarianism of the modern West, which at least in Britain and America still survives the new gospels of nationalism and communism, shows itself more akin to Buddhism than to Christianity. It shows a genuine zeal to alleviate the sufferings of humanity, and to provide the opportunity of a healthy and happy life for all, while at the same time it assumes that all our ideas of an absolute right and wrong in conduct, and of an absolute truth and falsehood in belief, are but illusory projections of our own desires, which tend on the whole to create suffering rather than to relieve it. At the same time the differences between Buddhism and modern humanitarianism are no less strongly marked. The Buddhist identifies suffering with the whole process of natural existence. " Birth is suffering ; death is suffering ; presence of the hated is suffering ; age is suffering ; sickness is suffering ; absence of the loved is suffering ; to wish and not to get is suffering ; briefly, the fivefold nature by which beings cling to existence is suffering." [1] Accordingly the Buddhist seeks salvation in escape from the unending cycle of birth and death and temporal becoming. The humanitarian, on the other hand, believes that suffering can be sufficiently eliminated, and the basic desires of humanity reasonably satisfied, by some scientifically directed process of social reform. He therefore looks for salvation in some Utopian society of the future. Nevertheless, for the humanitarian, as for the Buddhist, salvation is essentially salvation from pain, and it is to be achieved by purely human effort.

It is exactly on these points that Christianity joins

[1] The first of the Four Noble Truths delivered by the Buddha.

issue.   And, after all, there is grave difficulty in carrying
to its logical conclusion the doctrine that pain or suffering
as such is a greater or more radical evil than moral wrong.
Consider some of the events which are most apt to cause
men to form such a judgement.   An earthquake or a flood
spreads death and misery among a whole population ; or
a young life, on which hope is centred, is suddenly struck
down by accident or disease.   Let us notice first that the
problem of pain, rationally regarded, is certainly no more
acute in the former case than in the latter.   It is mere
confusion of thought to suppose that when a great many
cases of terrible pain occur together at one time and place,
the actual amount of pain caused is really greater than
in the same number of cases occurring singly and at inter-
vals.   The problem of pain is really no more, and no less,
perplexing in a Japanese earthquake or a Chinese flood,
than in all the other untimely and distressing deaths which
have occurred severally since the world began.   But what
is it that really shocks us in all events of this kind ?   We
say to ourselves not simply, " This thing is agonizingly
painful."   We say, " This thing is utterly cruel and sense-
less and unjust ; it shows that there can be no goodness
ordering the world at all."   In other words, what causes
our worst distress is precisely the fact that our moral sense
is outraged by such happenings.   When we are greatly
moved by any evil, it is as a moral evil that we instinctively
condemn it.   We are thus unwilling witnesses, even against
ourselves, that we regard the fundamental essence of evil
as moral.

That very modern writer, Mr. Walter Lippmann, sees
this truth clearly, and bases upon it an acute and logical
argument.[1]   All great disasters, he admits, lead us to pass a
moral judgement on the ordering of the universe, and such
judgements are accompanied by a sense of the absolute
character of moral evil.   Nevertheless, these judgements
and the sense of absolute moral evil which accompanies
them, are in his view entirely mistaken ; for the objectivity
claimed by moral valuation is only an illusion produced by
the projection of man's own desires.   Our moral condemna-

[1] *A Preface to Morals*, pp. 216 *sqq.*

tion of the universe is in reality only our way of expressing our disappointment at the discovery that things are not ordered as we should like. And once this acknowledgement is made, " the problem of evil " begins to disappear. For the whole difficulty arises because of our desire to impute to the universe itself, or to the god who rules it, purposes like our own. To get rid of this desire and of the illusion which it causes, as Mr. Lippmann proceeds to point out, alters radically the nature of evil itself. For, as we now see, " evil is not a quality of things as such ; it is a quality of our relation to them. A dissonance in music is unpleasant only to the musical ear." And a little later on Mr. Lippmann adds, unwarily as I think, the coping-stone and logical conclusion of his whole argument. " Evil exists only because we feel it to be painful." [1]

Be it so. Then the most obvious way to get rid of the crying evils of the universe, is to cease to take them to heart. Cease to feel them, and all will be well indeed. Why make such a fuss over a child mangled in a street-accident or born with a hopeless and incurable disease ? Enjoy all you can, cease to heed the rest ; you will have solved the problem of evil once for all, and find the world an admirable place. But is such the counsel which Mr. Lippmann really means to urge ? Of course not. He is an ardent social reformer with a moral zeal not only for getting rid of pain by the handiest means but also for helping his fellows to lead a really virtuous and honourable life. The truth is that Mr. Lippmann, like many of our modern sceptics, is at once far too good a man and too confused a thinker to accept the consequences of his own reasoning. He really intends his book to be a *preface* to morals, and not, as his own logic would suggest, their epitaph.

What, then, is the true conclusion to be drawn from our instinctive feelings of outrage and indignation at the terrible disasters of life ? Grant, for the sake of argument, that pain or unhappiness is the greatest of evils. It will

---

[1] Lippmann's doctrine of evil therefore appears to be essentially the same as that of Hobbes. But he ignores all the trouble taken by subsequent philosophers to show that Hobbes was wrong.

still be found that the greatest unhappiness springs from the disappointment of our moral nature. It is not sheer pain which distresses us most, but the meaning of moral evil which we read into it. Therefore, fundamentally and on the whole, it is truer to say that the world is painful and distressing to us, because it appears to be immoral, than to say that it appears to us to be immoral, because it is painful and distressing. And there are only two remedies conceivable for the distress. Either we must stifle altogether the demands of our moral nature ; or else we must persevere in the faith that the universe is such as somehow in the end to provide satisfaction for those moral demands of which it has itself somehow been the cause. It is precisely because Utopias, whether classical, humanitarian, or communist, seem to offer some promise of such satisfaction that they seem to be worth striving for. Consider merely the question whether they will be sufficiently pleasant, and their attractiveness begins to wane. After all, as Aldous Huxley has convincingly shown, there are few things more distressing than the spiritual boredom, called by medievalists acedia, which no brave new world can exorcize.

3. NO PURELY MORAL SALVATION

Hitherto we have tried to give some justification for the Christian view that evil has a moral root, and that salvation must mean fundamentally salvation from wrong, and not merely from suffering or pain. This proposition holds good whether salvation is to be salvation of the world itself, or rather salvation of human souls out of the world. But it does not of course follow that a full acceptance of the truth thus stated is of itself sufficient to bring salvation ; and we have now to argue that it is not. Acknowledgement of the nature and authority of right is not enough to deliver us from wrong. There is no hope of salvation in mere moral philosophy.

Our moral consciousness assures us of two fundamental truths : first, that the world of our present experience does not satisfy our moral demands or fulfil our moral

ideals ; secondly, that part of its unsatisfactoriness is due
to the moral defects of the human will and the wrong
actions of men.   What hope then can the pure moralist
provide to be the object and motive of our moral endeavour ?   Two kinds of answer to this question have
been attempted, which we may distinguish as (1) the
stoical, and (2) the utilitarian.[1]

(1) The former assumes that we must not look for any
" new world ", however achieved, in which the conditions
of life will be radically different from what they are now.
It is utterly uncertain whether the future will fulfil any
hope of this kind ; and in any case the right should be
done purely for its own sake, and not for any good consequences to the world at large which may be supposed to
follow from the doing of it.   The only hope of salvation,
therefore, to which we may rightly cling, is the satisfaction
of our own moral nature in the act of doing our duty for
its own sake.   The harmony of our will with the moral
law is its own reward.

Obviously this is a disappointing gospel to the benevo-
lent ; but it is also open to two further objections which
from a strictly moral point of view are more serious :

(a) It simply cuts the root of what most men to-day
would take to be the noblest form of heroism.   It is impossible for a man to sacrifice himself wholly in a great
cause, unless he believes that the sacrifice will not be in
vain, that it will really promote the end for which it is
made.   The really unselfish man is less interested in doing
his own duty than in furthering the cause for which he is
content to give his life.   And if that cause has a large or
possibly a universal range—as for instance the good of
humanity as a whole—self-sacrifice in it demands some
faith that the universe is such as to respond in the end to
that effort of which self-sacrifice is the supreme expression.
In giving his life as a ransom for many, Jesus believed
that God would provide that the life so given was not
thrown away.   Take away all such faith from human

---

[1] I use both these terms in a loose and popular sense, merely
as convenient labels.   What I mean by them will I hope be made
sufficiently clear in the following paragraphs.

endeavour after a better world, teach that the only sure
hope for the good man is the satisfaction he must find in
doing his duty whatever the issue, and inevitably the finest
heroism is robbed of its motive. The moral ideal of
stoicism in all its forms, noble as it may be, is inherently
self-centred.

(*b*) Secondly, the general doctrine which we have described as stoical is evidently defective as a gospel of
salvation, in that it offers no hope to the man whose past
failures or inherited weaknesses have so oppressed his
mind or impaired his will, that he is in practice powerless
to do what his conscience tells him that he ought. This
ancient problem of morality is one which the medical
psychologists of to-day still find it impossible to solve
without the help of religion. The ethics of stoicism ignore
it.

(2) The other attempt to offer salvation in terms of
moral philosophy is that which we have described as
utilitarian. Utilitarianism (in so far as it promises " salvation " at all) assumes that moral effort will be rewarded
in the end by the bringing into existence of some better
world or state of life in the future. This is the hope which
has inspired both the evolutionary philosophy of such
thinkers as Herbert Spencer and the dialectical materialism
of the Marxists. The salvation which such philosophies
offer is of course a hope only for human society ; they do
not suggest that individuals now alive can reach the
promised land. But there is no doubt about their power
to elicit heroic devotion from individuals in the service of
humanity ; and in this respect they have some advantage
over the more " stoical " doctrine already considered.

Nevertheless this kind of hope turns out on examination
to be profoundly unsatisfactory—and that apart altogether from the well-founded suspicion that it can never
be realized. It is morally unsatisfying. For in proportion
as the conditions of the future Utopia fulfil all that is
demanded of them as the goal of effort, it seems that under
those conditions the heroism needed to bring them into
existence will be unnecessary, and will be succeeded by a
natural happiness which, whatever its attractions, is alto-

gether inferior in moral value. The devotion of Marx himself seems to be worth far more than the life of that classless society which he thought was its goal. Is the heroism of the ages to produce nothing better than an age in which men are content to improve and elaborate the happiness they enjoy, until they also pass into the unknown ?

It must be added that a similar objection applies with equal force to certain conceptions of " heaven " which have discredited the Christian faith in the eyes of many who were not far from the Kingdom of God. Unless our eschatology be a good deal more profoundly Christian than that of Paley, our doctrine of heavenly salvation may lay itself open to the charge of seeking to reward virtue with a happiness which is intrinsically of less value than itself. That difficulty is one which the stoic at least escapes. It constitutes a problem for theology to which we shall return. But, apart from the Christian revelation, the problem of salvation confronts the moral philosopher with an insoluble dilemma—either a hope which spoils unselfishness, or no hope which can inspire it.

CHAPTER XX

THE GENERAL SIGNIFICANCE OF THE ATONEMENT

IT IS precisely at the point we have now reached that the relevance of the Christian doctrine concerning evil and salvation begins to declare itself. According to Christianity moral good and evil, as states of *will*, are of infinitely greater importance in themselves than any pleasure or pain, happiness or unhappiness, which are states of *feeling*. And yet the supreme good in the universe is not the virtue of a being who either fulfils or requires the fulfilment of the law of duty recognized by conscience, but rather the love which spontaneously gives itself for the good of others, and finds its fruition in the complete communion of spirit with spirit. The dogma of the Trinity teaches that the absolute perfection of that communion is in the eternal God alone. But God created man " in his own image ", in order that man the creature, by reflecting in himself the creator's love, might enter into the joy of eternal communion in God and with God. Therefore according to Christianity the fundamental evil in man, though it is moral in quality, is not the transgression of any sovereign law considered as such, but rather the selfishness, the pride, the πλεονεξία, which by rejecting love rejects also eternal life.

1. THE CHRISTIAN CONCEPTION OF MAN'S END

By these considerations all Christian teaching about evil and salvation are determined. Man's personality is indeed a tiny finite image of the infinite Godhead. It is capable of loving *freely*. The statement implies that man's personality consists in a relatively independent mind and will, which can pass their own judgement as to what is

true and false, good and evil, select and devise means to
the attainment of the chosen end, and, as they do so,
influence and direct both the minds and wills of other
men and also beings of a lower order which they become
able to dominate more completely.   Man's is a personality
which can experience and understand the meaning of
parenthood and ownership, and so exercise purposive
control, rightly or wrongly, over what belongs to it.

And therein precisely lies man's danger and temptation.
For after all there is but one absolutely independent mind
and will, only one father and owner of all, whose love is
truth and goodness, and whose purpose in the end all
things must serve.   Therefore the creation of man involves
a self-limitation on the part of God.   Man as creature is
absolutely dependent upon God ; yet as bearer of the
creator's image he is relatively independent of him.[1]
Whether it be by a fall or a rise, he is as God knowing
good and evil, as God in exercising control over his own
for a consciously apprehended and chosen end.   But this
relative independence is not God's *end* for man.   It involves a condition of tension, and of various possibilities
arising out of the tension, which cannot be an end at all.
The end is that God should be all in all, that his self-
limitation should cease, when man has *freely* surrendered
himself and all he has to the God who has not only loved
him but allowed him to share his love.   Man's independence, therefore, in so far as it is real, exists to be
given up.   His true freedom is the freedom of his self-
surrender.   And in the free surrender of all and every
independence he enters at last into the glorious liberty of
God's children.

The accomplishment of that self-surrender in spiritual
creatures is the final cause of the creation, and of the age-
long process of finite life through time.   Therefore the
world bears fruit of itself, first the plant and the animal,
then man.   And therefore man himself lives and grows
and learns the meaning of truth and goodness, of father-

[1] To be like God is to be independent of God.   This is an impossible situation.   In that fact lies the whole paradox of the Christian doctrine of the creation of man.

hood, ownership and creative power. He becomes as it were a limited god himself, so that in the really God-like freedom of love he may surrender himself and his petty divinity to the one God who gave them. " When the fruit is ripe, straightway he putteth forth the sickle because the harvest is now come." That is why all things in this world are transient. They must be cut off, in order that fruit, which has been grown in time, may be garnered in eternity. In the moment that the created spirit of man comes to its perfection, then birth and death, growth and decay, progress and decadence, the whole rhythm of this world, the rhythm which *is* this world, are no more. The end is neither annihilation nor endless living, but eternal life.

2. SIN

But, because man is a self-determining yet finite creature, he *may* spoil his own growth and change the harvest into a bonfire of rubbish. He is initially endowed with a self-conscious separateness both from God and from nature ; and therein lies the opportunity both for his free self-giving and for his selfishness. And selfishness is sin.

The essence of sin therefore is much more closely connected with the new emergence of human self-consciousness than with any survival of animal instincts in man. The mere animal, just because it is not conscious of itself as a separate being over against God and the world of nature, is as incapable of selfishness as of self-sacrifice. We can of course observe in animals the germs of both, as their behaviour seems to be directed now to the gratification of the individual's appetite, and now to securing the survival of the species at the individual's expense. But what is peculiar to man is his consciousness of himself as a separate personal entity choosing his own ends and directing conduct towards their realization. At once the gratification of desire becomes *self*-gratification, just as its opposite becomes *self*-repression. More and more as he develops in civilization, man is desperately aware of himself as influencing all he knows and all he seeks, and

most of all when he tries his hardest to take objective
views and to act impartially.   The very speech in which
he expresses truth remains obstinately full of personal
pronouns, however many words, or substitutes for words,
modern logicians may utter in an unknown tongue.

It is in the conscious self-reference of all man's thought
and action, rather than in the animal basis of his appetite,
that the occasion of sin and selfishness resides.   Natural
creatures, like the lily and the raven, are natural just
because they are not self-conscious.   Man, because he is
so self-conscious, can never be just natural.   He must
either rise to the unselfishness which is supernatural, or
else sink into an artificiality, a hypocrisy or a self-indulgence, of which nature at least is innocent.   Every artistic
monstrosity with which man has defaced God's earth is
witness to the fact that man is called to rise above nature,
and that, if he will not rise above, he must inevitably fall
below it.   It is the pretentiousness and fundamental
insincerity of bad art which is its universal condemnation.
The ancient and modern forms of the philosophical doctrine
of Protagoras, that man is the measure of all things, have
the same mark of the parvenu who is pretentious because
he is uneasily doubtful of his own status.   And the
exaggerated humility of our logical analysts as to man's
capacity for reaching truth seems to have a not very
different origin.   To use the now popular language of
psychology, it looks like a " defence-mechanism " hiding
the " inferiority-complex " which self-conscious man feels
when he is called to a knowledge too excellent and wonderful for any natural creature to attain to.

The truth is that in human nature, as we know it apart
from Christ, the personal self-consciousness of which we
have been speaking is inseparable from some degree of
personal selfishness.   That fact constitutes the real strength
of the Buddhist doctrine that salvation is to be found only
in Nirvana.   But it is that fact also which the Church
seeks to account for in its doctrine of original sin.   From
the beginning of his history man has failed to treat his
godlikeness as a gift from God to be used and developed
in God's service and finally surrendered in the spirit of

the love which gave. On the contrary man, because of his godlike capacity, has " snatched at equality with God ".[1] He has sought to be himself the measure of all things, the standard of all values, and to gain and keep for himself everything which ambition leads him to desire. Or else, realizing the empty folly of such pride and covetousness, he has tried to deny his high calling altogether and to seek contentment in a purely natural happiness which the creator will not suffer him to find. Therefore God's world and the laws of nature have become in large measure hostile to him. To the soul tainted with selfishness goodness itself appears as an imposed law of duty, hard, irksome and obscure. Physical death takes on an altogether new aspect of horror. All the pain and disappointment, of which man's experience is full, are seen, at best, as incentives to his own effort to overcome them, or as vindictive penalties for his failure to do right. At worst they are taken as a proof that God's goodness is a delusion, and morality but a yoke of man-made custom. The uncertainties of our temporal lot become occasions for self-centred anxieties about the future, from which, it seems, we can only escape by cultivating a stoical apathy to all that happens. And, since selfishness darkens the mental eye no less than it corrupts the will, no intellectual revelation could have availed to make man see the truth. At best the greatest of non-Christian saints and thinkers have been enabled dimly to guess and hint at the true meaning and end of human life. For God has never left himself without witness, nor man wholly without grace.

3. THE RELEVANCE OF THE ATONEMENT

But the Christian gospel of the atonement meets man's need with the one really relevant message of deliverance and salvation. Not only does it declare that the ultimate truth is the truth of God's love. Such a declaration by itself could never have carried conviction, in either sense of that word, to fallen mankind. The Christian gospel

[1] See the comments previously made on Phil. ii. 6, p. 81 *sq.*

presents, as evidence of the truth, the fact that by a supreme act of love God in Christ has put himself at man's side to suffer with him and for him in his sinful condition, and so to win from him the free response of penitence which is the first condition of salvation through forgiveness. By that same act God in man, and man in God, has vanquished the powers of evil and exalted human nature to God's throne by the complete self-sacrifice. In Christ first the purpose of the original creation has been accomplished, and the life of the world to come has been made not only a future hope but also a present reality.

The gospel of the atonement is so simple in its total effect that its essence can be grasped by the least theologically minded of Christians ; yet at the same time its doctrinal implications are so many-sided that libraries of exposition cannot do justice to its inexhaustible meaning. At the present stage we must try to make clear some of the main aspects in which the doctrine of the atonement shows us the life and work of Jesus Christ as the true and sufficient remedy for the evil of the world, when, by the light of Christ, we see that evil in its true colours.

(1) The atonement primarily consists in a divine act of loving and gracious condescension. Whereas man has sinned by self-assertion, self-exaltation, " snatching at equality with God ", God in Christ redeems man by " self-emptying ", self-humiliation, putting himself on an equality with man. There can be no Christian doctrine of the atonement apart from the Christian doctrine of the incarnation. Some of the early Fathers taught that the incarnation was itself the atonement. The main tradition of theology regards the atonement rather as the effect of the incarnation accomplished through the cross. In any case the incarnation and the atonement together make clear the tremendous paradox of Christianity that the true path of ascension begins with an immeasurable descent ; and God alone, who " came down from heaven " and " descended into hell ", could reveal and open up that way.

(2) In its relation to sin the atonement recognizes the fundamentally moral nature of evil, and at the same time

provides a more than moral way of salvation, because it expresses God's love in a message of free forgiveness, which brings good even out of the evil of sin itself. Strict morality condemns the wrongdoer, and justifies the doer of right. But in strict morality, as both St. Paul and Kant in their very different ways have made plain, there is no gospel for the sinner. Morality may indeed provide a rough and ready way of purging an offence by undergoing punishment. But forgiveness, strictly speaking, is not a moral conception at all. If an offence be not fully purged, morality requires further penalty; if an offence be fully purged, there is nothing left to be forgiven. The law may temper justice with mercy; but it knows nothing of free and absolute forgiveness. To this day the law of England, which is severely moral in its theoretical foundations, reserves the expression " free pardon " for the one case where it is obviously a fiction, viz., the case of an innocent man found to have been convicted by mistake, who thereupon receives a " free pardon " from the Crown.

But the gospel of the atonement puts the whole problem of right and wrong in a new light. Wrongdoing is seen not merely as a breach of law, but also, and more fundamentally, as a rejection of God's love. Now, if a man realizes his wrongdoing to be essentially an offence against another's love, he knows at once two things: first, that no punishment by itself can ever purge its guilt; secondly, that he is penitent for what he has done. For he cannot realize what it means to have offended against love, unless the awakening response of love within him reveals it; and that is penitence. But, if what he has offended against is the perfect love of God, his penitence is met by free forgiveness. And this forgiveness does something different from, and better than, merely abolishing his guilt; it does something more even than restore him to that fellowship with God which he had forfeited. It converts the repented and forgiven sin into an actual stepping-stone by which he has been raised, and can be raised further, into a recognition of God's goodness which could never have been his apart from the sin. The greatest of all

the triumphs revealed through the cross—and apart from
this greatest triumph no full doctrine of salvation is
possible—is to overrule sin itself for some good end, to
produce out of it some good which could not otherwise
have been.   " O felix culpa quae tantum et talem meruit
habere redemptorem." Certainly the truth in that cry
of gratitude transcends morality altogether. Yet those
who think it wrong to utter it have not understood the
fullness of the gospel.

(3) In relation to the problem of pain also the atonement has its characteristic message. It need hardly be
said that, apart from the Christian revelation altogether,
positive value must be assigned to much of the pain
which we experience. Biologically regarded, pain is
nature's warning against danger, and a constant incentive
to effort and progress. Sensitiveness to pain is the condition of advance in evolution. Again, morally regarded,
pain has a value, both as retributive and as deterrent,
which few would altogether dispute ; and it is an essential
element in the conditions which train us for the more heroic
virtues. Nevertheless it is evident that the values thus
generally and legitimately found for pain fail altogether to
justify the place which it holds in the order of this world.
Theodicies conceived on the level of justice, which try to
represent this world merely as a hard school of righteousness, are notoriously impotent.

But the Christian theodicy, though it affirms the value
of justice, does not stop short at it. God, it declares, has
prepared for man some better thing than the reward of
hard-won virtue and the punishment of vice. Man is to
realize that victory of love through self-sacrifice which
for the finite creature is eternal life. The presence of
selfishness in human nature makes the self-sacrifice inevitably painful ; and the sympathy, which in the end
is the way of redemption, begins by causing extension of
the pain. But the revealing act of Christ's atonement
makes it clear that all the manifold sorrows and disasters
of life, even those which seem at first sight most evidently
to contradict belief in God's goodness, at least afford some
opportunity to the Christian to be made like his Saviour

in suffering, and thereby to be made partaker in that whole redemptive activity whereby self-sacrifice avails to redeem mankind and lift it up to God. Here below love displays itself at its greatest and highest in willingly accepted suffering even unto death. Christ the incarnate showed that once for all. It is for the fullness of such a revelation that all the evils of this present world provide the opportunity. And therefore it is not unreasonable to suppose that a world-order, in which pain and death are universal, and are more acutely felt in proportion as true progress is made, may be the order fitted to be that through which love wins its universal victory, and from which it rises again in glory. Thus, while the world-order which we know with all its miseries can never be made to satisfy mere justice, the greater paradox may still be true, that through the atonement it may be found in the end to have proceeded from God's love.

(4) To complete our general and preliminary survey of the relevance of the atonement to the evils of this world, we must say a few words in conclusion about its relation to death. The atonement of the cross would not be complete apart from the resurrection. For not only is the resurrection the guarantee that Christ's living presence and power are with his followers for ever; it is also the sign that in him God's love, in man and for man, has won the final victory over death and through death. The victory is not merely over death, but also through death; for it is the victory of self-sacrifice, and self-sacrifice could not be complete apart from the death which seals it. Moreover our Lord's victorious self-sacrifice was not achieved in order to make our own unnecessary, but to make it possible. Because in the nature of things the full triumph of self-sacrifice can only be won through death, therefore, and for no other reason, the Christian is obliged to believe in the reality of the world beyond the grave, in the life of the world to come.

It is vital to perceive that the really Christian belief in a future heaven is based simply on faith in the fulfilment of the atonement, Christ's work of love. It does not concern itself primarily with the reward of virtue, nor even

with the obligation of a righteous God to fulfil his promise
to his chosen. It does not postulate an imaginary heaven
in order to provide some redress for the real injustices of
earth. And its motive is as far as possible removed from
that self-assertive rebellion against death to which Matthew
Arnold attributed the hope of immortality when he wrote
of the

> Stern law of every mortal lot,
>   Which man, proud man, finds hard to bear,
> And builds himself I know not what
>   Of second life, I know not where.[1]

No, the question for the Christian is simply this : is the
atoning work of Christ *really* victorious, or is it not ?
It is belief in the resurrection, following on the sacrifice
completed in death, which enables him to answer Yes.
And, so answering, he submits himself to the law of the
cross. No final or perfect good is attainable in this world
at all. For only by the sacrifice which death seals can
the work of love be brought to finality. No doubt St.
Paul taught that even on this side of physical death the
Christian dies spiritually and rises again to newness of life
in Christ. Since the resurrection and exaltation of Christ
the life of the world to come has begun to be really present
and active already. But St. Paul would also have said
that the spirit is not the whole man, and the present
spiritual resurrection, still imperfect while the spirit is
hampered by the mortal and sin-stained flesh of this world,
can only give a dim foreshadowing or foretaste of the
future glory.

And thus it is that Christianity, alone among the religions
and philosophies of the world, succeeds in eliciting from
death, i.e., from the actuality of dying, a unique value,
so that it is found to make a positive and necessary contribution to the perfection of created life. Other philosophies
of immortality suggest either that death is in some way
unreal, or that it constitutes merely a release for the spirit
through the dropping off of the material body. Not so
Christianity. To it dying is an essential part or moment
in that act through which love accomplishes the self-

[1] *Grist's Grave.*

sacrifice which issues in eternal life. And thus physical death, in all its terrible universality, becomes for the Christian a sacrament of the spiritual truth that, because it is love which saves, life must be lost before it can be fully won.

So, finally, the Christian " heaven " is not the world of Utopian or Elysian fantasy which mocks the hopes of the utilitarian moralist, and provokes the righteous scorn of the stoic. It is not a sphere of being where the labours and sorrows of earth find a questionable compensation in perpetual ease. Neither must the painful process of self-sacrifice accomplishing itself through death be thought of like a ladder, which, having enabled us to scale the heights, may forthwith be kicked away. The Lord's risen body, as we are told in a symbol, bears for ever the marks of his cross. Heaven is the unimaginable state of being where souls made perfect in the sacrifice of love find their eternal fruition in the communion of Christ's Body. There, it is truly said, pain and death " are no more ". Yet we may also say that they have not been simply annihilated. They are no longer imposed or endured ; but, having been once for all accepted and passed through, they remain for ever, as it were, present in the memory of eternal life as elements which contribute to its essential joy. As for sin, its exclusion from heaven is of course absolute ; yet even so, were it forgotten or in process of being forgotten, the deepest note of thanksgiving would be excluded also.

The Christian, therefore, who believes in salvation through Christ's atonement has a much deeper and fuller hope than that of any future state of bliss in which the evils of our present life will recede into an ever dimmer and more distant past. It is indeed impossible for us adequately or completely to relate eternal life to that which is temporal. But we do well to think of " heaven " simply as the final accomplishment of the work of Christ's love, the hope of which quickens us to sacrifice, rather than as the reward of our loyalty, the hope of which taints our sacrifice with selfishness. It is thus that Christian faith transcends the moralist's dilemma—either a hope which spoils unselfish-ness, or no hope which can inspire it. St. Paul, in driving home the lesson of Christ's resurrection to his Corinthian converts, speaks not at all of the *reward* of our labour, but only of its *fruit*. " Be ye therefore stedfast, un-movable, always abounding in the work of the Lord ; forasmuch as ye know that your labour is *not in vain* in the Lord."

CHAPTER XXI

THEORIES OF THE ATONEMENT

W E HAVE now to consider more closely what we are to say of that historical doctrine of the atonement which in varying forms has, together with that of the incarnation, made up the very substance of the Christian's creed. But the doctrine itself cannot be rightly understood without some appreciation of the preparation for it which we find in the religion of the Old Testament.

1. THE OLD TESTAMENT PREPARATION FOR THE ATONEMENT

Nowadays many scholars maintain that the Old Testament records not so much the development of one religion as the story of the conflict between two, the prophetic religion and the priestly. The two religions, they would say, are irreconcilable in principle, though the deuteronomic writers and the later prophets effected an unsatisfactory compromise between them. I think these scholars are probably wrong if they assert that the great pre-exilic prophets actually intended to condemn all sacrifice as such, and to allow it no legitimate place at all in the worship of Jehovah. Whether the prophets would have done so, if they had followed out all the implications of their own revolutionary theology, is another question. From the point of view of logical analysis rather than strictly historical description, the opposition between priest and prophet amounts almost to a conflict between two religions.

The two religions, it is to be noticed, are differentiated from one another by their treatment of sin, no less than by their estimate of sacrifice. The prophetic religion rejects

sacrifice as a remedy for sin altogether. Nothing can
avail but a changed way of life. The priestly religion,
on the other hand, especially as it expresses itself in the
post-exilic parts of the Pentateuch, sets forth an elaborate
code of ritual sacrifice, the chief aim of which is to expiate
the sins both of individuals and of the nation as a whole.

Many modern theologians have been inclined to see in
the prophetic religion alone the Holy Spirit's preparation
for the coming of Christ. They regard the sacrificial
slaughter of animals as nothing but a degrading superstition and a relic of heathenism. Yet such a judgement
is surely one-sided. In denying all value to the priestly
religion, it ignores at the same time the characteristic
defect in the prophetic.

It is a noteworthy fact that the theology of the prophets,
though in one respect it is predestinarian and Augustinian,
in that it tends to refer all events alike to God's will as
their cause, is in another respect distinctly libertarian and
Pelagian, in insisting that the chosen people, and the
individuals which compose it, can always obey God and
be righteous, if they will. All the sinner has to do, say
the prophets, is to change his manner of life ; and they
assume without question that he can, if only he will make
the effort. That is why sacrifice is so unnecessary, and
may be so wrong. It is either a superfluous addition, or
else a substitute, for the obedience which God demands
and man is quite able to give. " What doth God require
of thee, but to do justly, and to love mercy, and to walk
humbly with thy God ? " [1] Micah almost speaks as if it
were an easy task. " God," so runs the prophetic message, " is quite ready to forgive the past, if you will now
forsake your sins and do right. The sins of the fathers
will not be visited on the children if only the children
will not follow their father's bad example." But there is
no message of any divine power to change the heart or
reform the will. " Come, and let us reason together, saith
the Lord. Though your sins be as scarlet, they shall be
as white as snow. If ye be willing and obedient, ye shall
eat the good of the land." That is all the gospel Isaiah

[1] Micah vi. 8.

knows. Jeremiah and Ezekiel certainly look forward to a dim and distant future, when God will at length give his rebellious people a new heart. Meanwhile they only proclaim that God's people can do right, if they will ; and continued disobedience is met only by deterrent threats of doom. The prophets know nothing of original sin. And their implied doctrine of free will does not do justice to the facts.

On the other hand, the priestly religion, which produced the sacrificial code in the Pentateuch, treats sin less as a matter of personal choice and responsibility than as a taint or defilement with which the sinner is, as it were, infected. The taint of sin inevitably cuts a man off from God's favour ; but sacrifice has been appointed by God's own merciful ordinance for the removal of the taint and the restoration of the sinner. Hence from one point of view the priest may be said to have regarded sin as more deeply ingrained than did the prophet, inasmuch as he acknowledged that the individual could not by any personal act of will get rid of it. Yet on the other hand the priest provided the more readily accessible remedy, since it is easier for sinners to offer sacrifice than to reform their lives. No doubt the whole sacrificial system was inseparable from superstition and unworthy ideas of God. The denunciations of the prophet and the criticisms of the moralist are not unjustified. And yet in three ways the priestly religion pointed towards profound truths which the prophets ignored.

Defect of the priestly religion

(*a*) Sin is not merely a matter of personal choice, nor does it end with merely personal guilt. To use the clear and convenient terms of Latin theology, there is an element of *vitium* and of *macula*, as well as of *reatus*, in sin. There is about it something analogous to a taint, disease, or infection, which weakens the will and impairs its power to do right, and which blinds the conscience so that it does not see what it is right to do. A further remedy is needed than exhortations to do right combined with the promise that God will forgive the past if the sinner will now mend his ways. There is in the sacrificial system an indication of that truth which the prophet in spite, and partly because, of his clearer vision of God's righteousness could not perceive.

(b) The priestly religion did not represent God as simply waiting for man to reform himself, before he could deliver him from the consequences of his sin. Imperfect, crude, and superstitious as the doctrine of sacrificial expiation necessarily was, still the Pentateuch presents such expiation as a means ordained by God to reconcile sinners with himself, which required only such simple action as the sinner was really able to perform. It is true that we cannot but notice in the ritual code of Leviticus a falling away from the spiritual heights which are reached in the prophetic books. And yet in Leviticus there is a note of pastoral care and tenderness for erring souls, which is absent from the great prophets.

(c) *Corruptio optimi pessima.* It may be that the whole blood-stained history of sacrifice represents the corruption of an indestructible instinct of the human spirit, which impels man to believe that he cannot have perfect communion with God except through the offering of life in death. The Christian fulfilment of that instinct lies in the revelation that the response to God's love in the creature which bears his image must consummate itself in the completeness of voluntary self-sacrifice. Nothing of course could be further from the moral and spiritual height of such a doctrine than most of the beliefs associated with sacrifice in pre-Christian religion. Yet sacrifice may still have been a blind and degraded testimony to the truth that what God ultimately requires from man is more even than righteous conduct according to his laws, it is the absolute devotion of man's self. The moral meaning of the term " self-sacrifice " may seem to have as little connexion with the ritual sacrifices of antiquity as it has with the jargon of modern commerce which speaks of " goods offered at a sacrifice ". And yet the use of the same word in all cases is not a pure equivocation or a mere accident of speech. Everywhere " sacrifice " expresses the notion of gain through loss, of the best won through the surrender of the good, or of life attained through death—it is the characteristic term of that " dialectic " which lies at the heart of the moral and spiritual experience of mankind.

The pious Jew knew well that to see God's face is the ultimate fulfilment of man's blessedness, and yet that in this world man cannot see God and live. The problem thus presented penetrates to the depths and heights of man's religious consciousness. The Christian answer to it is that he who believes on the incarnate Son has both seen God and died to himself in order to live anew in Christ. But even before Christ came there was a dim prophecy of that revelation, a prophecy which the prophets themselves never uttered, in the pathetic attempts of the priest to use a life, which had been made to pass through death on the offerer's behalf, as a means of removing sin and establishing communion between man and God. Later on we shall have occasion to notice in greater detail how it was that the characteristically Jewish conception of sacrifice constituted a true *praeparatio evangelica*.

2.   THE FACT OF THE ATONEMENT IN THE NEW TESTAMENT

We pass from the Old Testament to the New. Doubtless there are in the New Testament diversities and developments of theological interpretation. Traces may be found, especially in St. Luke and Acts, of a primitive Christianity which had not yet begun to understand Christ's death as the sacrifice for human sin. But one conviction is universal, and apart from it no Christian document could have been written. Through the coming of Jesus the Christ, God, by an act of forgiving and redeeming love, has touched man's heart in a new way. A new communion between God and man has been established, a new Israel has been born. Through Christ both the defect of the prophetic religion has been made good, and the need for priestly sacrifices done away. For now Christians are delivered from the powers of evil, and set in a perfect relation to God as their Father. In Christ both the *vitium* and the *reatus* of sin are overcome. The atonement is a fact. The danger which besets the early

converts is lest they should exaggerate, or rather mis-
interpret, the finality of what has been already achieved,
so as to suppose that Christians can no longer really sin or
really have to die. They have to be warned that there
is a conflict still to be waged and a victory to be won,
although in Christ they have that fellowship with God
which makes the issue certain.

3. FOUR TYPES OF ATONEMENT THEORY

The various theological theories, in which the Church's
teaching on the atonement has expressed itself, are simply
attempts to answer the great question : How has Christ
wrought this great change in man's relation to God, of
which Christian life and faith are themselves the evidence ?
Why and how has the coming of Christ made all this
difference ? We will begin by distinguishing in a quite
general way four main types of answer which have been
given.

(a) Some have said, " It is because Christ brought
God's message of forgiveness, and his human life revealed
God's fatherly love in a way which has stirred man's heart
to fresh repentance." This answer leads to what we may
call the " subjective " or " moral " theory of the atonement.

(b) Some have said, " It is because God in Christ has
won the victory over all the forces of evil, sin, and death,
and has broken the power of the devil over man." This
answer leads to what we may call (using Bishop Aulén's
terms) the " classic " or " dramatic " theory.

(c) Some have said, " It is because Christ as man has
borne the penalty for sin in man's behalf, and thus made
it possible for God to forgive man freely." This answer
leads to what we may call the " juridical " theory.

(d) Some have said, " It is because Christ, the Son of
God who is also the sinless man, has offered through death
that life of perfect human obedience and self-surrender,
which, having died, becomes the universal expiation and
cleansing power for sin-stained souls." This answer leads
to what we may call the " sacrificial " theory.

Of course, elements which belong to more than one of the

types of theory which I have distinguished have often
been combined with one another ; and the classification is
to some extent arbitrary.   On the other hand, theological
controversy has intensified the opposition between different
types, so that they are often represented as quite antag-
onistic to one another.   Nevertheless, if we start from
the fundamental and cardinal thought of God's act of love
in Jesus Christ, and then follow the lines of the classification
just suggested, I think we can reach a reconciling point
of view, from which each type of theory is seen to make its
essential contribution to the truth, although no one theory,
nor any number of theories, can be sufficient to express its
fullness.

revelation of G's love.   *insufficient.*
                                             (a) not act.
4.   THE SUBJECTIVE THEORY   *(b) relation t sin ques*

X's human life
reveals G's fatherly   A sharp dividing-line is often drawn between the first
love + brings forgive- type of theory, the subjective, and all the others, which
ness.   are called " objective " in opposition to it.   The ground
of the opposition may be stated thus.   According to the
subjective theory the life and death of Jesus Christ in
themselves effect nothing except the clear declaration of
something which has always been true, viz., the fatherly
and forgiving love of God for man.   Thus the effect of
the atonement, and the change wrought by it, begin only
when human souls perceive through the life and death of
Jesus Christ the truth of God's love, and are moved thereby to repentance.   In contrast with this doctrine the other
theories maintain that the life and death of Jesus Christ
in themselves brought into being some new relation,
which did not previously exist, between man and God, and
that of this newly established relation Christians by faith
receive the benefit.

The line of division seems clear enough ; but further
reflexion will tend to blur it.   We will begin by echoing
Rashdall's praise of Abélard, the classic exponent of the
subjective theory.

At last we have found a theory of the atonement which
thoroughly appeals to reason and to conscience.   There is of
course nothing absolutely original in the idea.   St. Paul is full

of the thought.   It is set forth in its simplest and purest form
in the Johannine writings.   It occurs over and over again in
the fathers.   Whatever else they teach about the death of
Christ, they all with one consent teach this—that it was a
revelation of the love of God, intended to call forth answering
love in man.   The theory of Abélard does but isolate and
emphasize the element in the preaching of the atonement to
which in all ages it has owed its moving and saving power.
Whatever were men's theories about the grounds on which the
death of Christ became necessary, it was the love exhibited by
Christ in submitting to that death which has really moved the
heart, touched the conscience, and regenerated the life of
believers. . . .   " Greater love hath no man than this, that a
man lay down his life for his friends."   And, if he who so lays
down his life is taken as representing and revealing the character of God, then no other way of ending the earthly life of
him in whom God made this supreme self-revelation could so
fully embody and symbolize the fundamental thought of Christianity that God is love, nor is any event in the history of the
world so calculated to awaken and stimulate that repentance
for sin upon which the possibility of forgiveness depends.[1]

The eulogy is true, and finely expressed.   But let us
grant that the essence of the atoning value of Christ's life
and death lies in the fact that they are a declaration or
demonstration of God's love for man.   Still we must press
the question, _how was God's love demonstrated by that
life and death_ ?   And then we begin to see that the subjective theory is by itself insufficient, on its own premises,
as an account of the atonement.   Two lines of criticism
suggest themselves.

(a) If Christ's life and death are in themselves _merely_ a
revelation or display of God's love, they cannot reveal or
display that love which Christian thought has at its highest
attributed to God.   The love of the living and redeeming
God can only be fully revealed and displayed in a divine
act.   If all we can say of Christ's human life and death is
that they _symbolize_ God's constant love, and _not_ that they
are God's own act, then the love which they symbolize
is after all something different from what the highest
Christian faith has held God's love to be.   But if, on the

---

[1] _The Idea of the Atonement_, pp. 360 _sq._

other hand, the life and death of Christ symbolize God's love because they truly are God's act, we cannot think of that divine act as a mere gesture which effects nothing beyond the declaration of what was already true before it happened. A revealing gesture is something much less than an act of power.

② Sin cannot be met by a display of love.

(b) If the nature of sin and its effects in man are really such as we have taken them to be, a simple display of love, which is not an act effecting something of which man in his sinful condition can avail himself, could not have met man's need, and therefore would not have been a full demonstration of God's saving love. Doubtless, in so far as sinful man retains the ability to see and choose the good when it is shown to him, the revelation of love on the cross constitutes by itself the most powerful motive to impel him to do so. And it would be worse than folly to belittle the wonder of the conversions which the revelation of the cross has wrought in this way. Nevertheless, the trouble expressed in the seventh chapter of Romans and in the familiar tag, " *video meliora proboque, deteriora sequor* ", bears witness to a more subtle influence of sin which no mere revelation can dispel. As long as a theologian finds the prophetic conception of sin to be adequate, he may also be satisfied with the subjective theory of the atonement. But to one who understands the power of sin as St. Paul understood it, that theory can never express the reality of God's saving act in Jesus Christ.

element of truth in subj. theory, but sin is more subtle than merely hindering man from see & choosing good.

The truth is that to accept fully Abélard's affirmation that the cross is the supreme manifestation of God's love for man must, if we follow out its implications, carry us beyond Abélard's theory of the atonement.

victory of G over evil.   lacks precise in complete

5.   THE CLASSIC OR DRAMATIC THEORY

In what then does the objective element in the atonement consist ? How did the life and death of Christ in themselves establish a new relation between man and God, of which man by faith receives the benefits ? According to the so-called " classic " theory, God's love by the cross and resurrection of Christ has won a great and final victory

over all the powers of evil; these powers have been de-
prived of their dominion over man, and man by faith in
Christ is henceforth established in a new and triumphant
life of communion with God; even in this world "he
tastes the powers of the world to come".

Undoubtedly language and ideas of this sort have always
been familiar to Christian orthodoxy, although, as Bishop
Aulén [1] points out, from the Middle Ages onwards their
full meaning and value have been obscured. That the
language in question stands for some vital and central
truth, hardly any Christian perhaps would seriously deny.
But by itself it lacks precision. It has the great merits
of declaring that the atonement is throughout God's work,
and of safeguarding the truth that God was in Christ Jesus
reconciling the world to himself. But it is not easy to see
how and with what degree of exactness the notions of conflict and victory over an enemy are to be applied. On the
one hand, we may take quite seriously the personification
of the powers of evil which is at first sight suggested. But
if we suppose that such powers have held mankind in
bondage, and have now by Christ's death and resurrection
been utterly and finally defeated, it is hard to explain the
remarkable vigour which they still apparently display even
within the life of the redeemed community of believers.
On the other hand, we may take the victory of Christ to
mean simply the victory of perfect holiness over all temptation and tendency to sin, a victory which takes away
death's sting and makes death itself the gate of immortality.
In that case the enduring power of evil over those who
have not yet attained Christ's holiness is fully accounted
for; but the way in which Christ's victory benefits them
requires further explanation. If that victory is no more
than a demonstration of the fact that the perfect holiness
of love must always triumph over sin and death, it would
seem that it provides for us only a supreme example and
a moving appeal; and thus our theory of the atonement
becomes in principle "subjective" after all.

Our criticism therefore of the "classic" theory is not
at all to suggest that it is false, but rather to point out that,

[1] *Christus Victor.*

like the subjective theory, it is incomplete. We need to know more of what exactly Christ's victory was. The old forms of the classic theory, that the victory was won by means of a ransom paid to the devil to release mankind, or by deceiving the devil as with a baited hook, certainly supply the lacking precision ; but they have never commended themselves for long either to the reason or to the conscience of Christians.

6. THE JURIDICAL THEORY

We turn to the third type of atonement theory, that which suggests that Jesus Christ as man bore the penalty for human sin, or offered satisfaction for it, in our stead.[1]

There seems to be no reason in principle why Christ's vicarious suffering of the penalty for sin should not be regarded both as a demonstration of God's love for man, and as a means of his victory over sin and death. For, to quote Harnack's criticism of Abélard, " is not that love the highest which, by taking the penalty upon itself, reveals at the same time the greatness of the absolution and the greatness of the cancelled guilt ? " [2] And again, if Christ's bearing of the penalty is the divinely purposed ground of the exaltation of his manhood to God's throne and of our own deliverance from the power of evil, may we not truly say that it is the method of God's victory in Christ ? Indeed, it is only when they are thus interpreted that juridical theories of the atonement can have any legitimate place at all in Christian theology. Notoriously the weakest point in the doctrine of St. Anselm, who first stated the juridical theory in a precise form, is that its logic seems to attach too exclusive an importance to the part played by Christ's manhood in the atoning work. According to this doctrine it is as man that Christ bore the penalty and offered satisfaction for human sin. Thus the vital truth that the whole act of atonement proceeded from God's love

---

[1] For the purposes of this quite general discussion Anselm's careful distinction between *poena* and *satisfactio* need not concern us.

[2] I take the quotation from J. K. Mozley, *The Atonement*, p. 133.

is liable to be obscured, and the notion is suggested that Christ's sacrifice propitiated God in a way which is quite alien from the thought of the New Testament. Juridical theories must be interpreted in the light of the classic theory, if they are to be made acceptable.

St. Paul's language in several places [1] does undoubtedly indicate his belief that Christ on the cross bore the penalty for sin on our behalf. But, if he had been pressed on the point, he would not, I think, have hesitated to declare that it is God's love which in Christ has provided a way of deliverance from his own wrath. He would certainly have agreed that we must interpret all juridical language about the atonement in the light of the principle that both the cross and its effects are the work of God's own love.

Paul's views in juridical + work of God's love.

Granted then that we are to understand the juridical theory as expanding the classic, and not at all as contradicting it, we have still to ask the question : how far and in what way may we believe that Jesus Christ on the cross endured penal suffering in man's stead ?

We must not forget that the theory which we are now considering is in principle juridical rather than sacrificial. It was developed by the Latin theologians of the Middle Ages from the hints contained in St. Paul's Epistles. It is true of course that St. Paul does use sacrificial language about Christ's atoning death. But whenever he or any other New Testament writer suggests that Christ bore our sins or the penalty for them, the implied thought about the atonement is juridical, and is really irrelevant to religious ideas which underlay the sin-offerings of the Pentateuch. For there the victims *sacrificed* for sin were not regarded as *bearing* the sin, nor as receiving in death the penalty for sin in man's stead. On the contrary, they were held to be pure from sin, and therefore their blood availed in expiation. The only victim believed to *bear* the sins of the people was the scapegoat ; and exactly for that reason the scapegoat was not sacrificed, because as a sin-bearer it was accursed and could not be offered to God. The body hanged on a tree was certainly not sacrificed.[2]

What sacrifice really is.

---

[1] E.g., Gal. iii. 13 ; 2 Cor. v. 21.
[2] Gal. iii. 13 ; Deut. xxi. 23.

And even in Isaiah liii. there is no close or obvious connexion between the words, " the Lord hath laid on him the iniquity of us all ", and the later prophecy, " when thou shalt make his soul an offering for sin, he shall prolong his days ".[1] In considering therefore the doctrine that Christ bore our sins on the cross, we do well to dismiss all sacrificial notions and analogies from our minds.

Can we, then, at all apply the notion of penal substitution to Christ's atoning death ? Not if we understand the word " substitution " strictly ; and that for two reasons.

Penal Substitution sufferings (a) It is impossible to maintain that the sufferings which Christ voluntarily endured for man's sin were *the same* as those which sinners would have had to endure and must endure if they remain unforgiven, but which through faith in Christ they escape. In what could such suffering endured by Christ, and to be endured by the unrepentant sinner but not by the faithful Christian, consist ? It cannot be physical death, or the pain connected with it ; for these Christians still have to undergo. And as to any other and more terrible sufferings, to which we may believe that Christ submitted, it is impossible to equate these with any which we can suppose to fall on the guilty and the unrepentant. However we interpret the cry, " My God, why hast thou forsaken me ? " it can hardly be denied that the suffering here expressed is that of a love which feels itself deserted by God—and that is precisely the kind of suffering which the hardened sinner could never know.

substitution (b) Again, a substitute, strictly speaking, is one who acts or suffers in order that the person whose place he takes may be free to do what he would have done, had he not been under the obligation of which the substitute has relieved him. In other words, the person for whom the substitute acts or suffers is affected by the substitution only negatively, in so far as he is relieved of something which otherwise he would have had to do or undergo. Thus, in the old story of Genesis, the ram was sacrificed as a substitute for Isaac, simply so that Isaac need not be

[1] Isa. liii. 6 and 12.

sacrificed. Now I venture to affirm that no Christian has ever really believed that Christ on the cross bore the penalty for sin strictly in substitution for the sinner. In so far as there was any real substitution, the purpose of the crucifixion must have been that the sinner might be unaffected by the cross, except in so far as he would be released from enduring the penalty for sin. But no Christian can seriously affirm that the cross had any such purpose. On the contrary, Christ died in order to raise the sinner from the death of sin to the new life of repentance and fellowship with God.

We conclude therefore that we must not seek to interpret with any logical exactness language which speaks of Christ as having suffered *instead of* the sinner. Indeed, such a saying as " One died for all, therefore all died ",[1] excludes the idea of substitution strictly understood, and signifies rather representation. As we shall see, the notion of Christ's death as *representative* is best interpreted as belonging to the sacrificial theory of the atonement rather than to the juridical ; but it is probable that St. Paul never made any clear distinction in his own mind between the two. The language of substitution then is but an imperfect attempt to express the truth that in the crucifixion the divine love showed itself willing to endure to the uttermost for man the terrible consequences of sin which in justice should have fallen on the sinner. Christ, we may truly say, endured for us and on our behalf, though not strictly *instead of us*, what we could never have endured for ourselves.

This vicarious suffering of the divine love moves us to penitence as nothing else could ; and it also reconciles our conscience to the fact that the world is not ordered on the principle of the justice which demands that pain should fall on the sinner in proportion to his guilt, and happiness reward the righteous in proportion to his merit. It may even be true that, if we reckon in terms of quantity of pain endured, the innocent and the penitent always suffer more because of sin than the guilty and the hardened. Who shall measure the suffering which evil inflicts on one who

[1] 2 Cor. v. 14.

loves much, against the suffering of an unrepentant sinner punished for his crime ?   Which suffered more, St. Peter when he went out and wept bitterly, or Judas when he went away and hanged himself ?   Pains, like pleasures, differ in quality, and a merely quantitative comparison is fallacious.   That is why the justice of rewards and punishments is never really satisfactory.   But he who through the atonement understands the law of vicarious suffering, will know why it is that justice, at least in this world, seems so incomplete.   It is in order that love by self-sacrifice may win its greatest triumph of redemption.

Nevertheless, in the light of the atonement the law of justice still stands unshaken as a moral principle ; and it is the main purpose and value of the juridical theory to emphasize this truth.   It is only when the sinner acknowledges that the sufferings which another bears for him were justly his own due, that he can know the penitence which brings salvation.   Christ's atonement therefore does not make the law of none effect.   It establishes the law, even while it goes beyond it and exposes its imperfection. Because Christ on the cross suffers what the sinner cannot suffer and yet what it is just that the sinner should suffer, therefore the cross becomes the ground and cause of the penitence which enables the sinner to be forgiven and restored.   Justice is satisfied, because the penitent sinner at last recognizes the righteous authority of its law.   Love triumphs over justice, because the sinner is delivered from doom.   What he has to suffer henceforth is transformed from mere punishment into a discipline gladly accepted because by it he is made one with Christ.

The elaboration of the juridical theory, which brings out this aspect of the atonement, is appropriately the work of Latin-speaking theologians.   The mind trained under Roman influences realizes that the impersonal and impartial law of justice must somehow be vindicated.   Traces of this conception of the majesty of justice are to be found in St. Paul, especially in Romans ; but it is certainly not characteristically Jewish.   To the Jew justice was not an abstract and impartial law.   Rather it meant the concrete vindication and deliverance of one person, and the concrete condemnation and overthrow of another.   The Jew realized all values only in concrete and personal terms.   It was his supreme and unique achievement to make religion the establishment of a personal relation to a personal God. But the terms in which he thought were apt to be too narrowly personal.   In his triumphs he was constantly guilty of what the Greeks called ἐπιχαιρεκακία,[1] in adversity he was always apt to become " a man with a grievance ".   It was left to the Latin mind, in its theology of the atonement, both to vindicate the full majesty of God's justice and also to utter the cry in which justice is forgotten, " O felix culpa."

Yet it seems that the juridical theory of the atonement, as we have sought to expound it, remains by itself incomplete.   For, according to the only interpretation of it which we have been able to accept, it is still in principle a " subjective " theory.   For the atonement is represented as producing its redemptive effect only by stirring man to penitence through his recognition of what Christ has suffered for him.   In itself therefore the cross remains only a manifestation or demonstration of God's love ; in itself it leaves unchanged the relation between sinful man and God.   The actual change in that relation begins only with man's penitence which the revelation of the cross produces. St. Paul gave objectivity to his doctrine of the atonement by combining elements of the sacrificial theory with those which belong properly to the juridical.   Later theologians have found a strictly objective element within the juridical theory by suggesting that Christ, by bearing the penalty for human sin, actually turned away God's righteous wrath and so changed God's attitude to man.   But this doctrine is not only theologically intolerable, it is also quite alien from the thought of the New Testament.   In the New Testament Christ's life and death are said to reconcile man to God, but never God to man.   It remains for us therefore to consider what is the distinctive contribution of the fourth type of atonement theory, the sacrificial.

[1] I.e., literally, " rejoicing over the evils of another ".   The " taunt-songs " of the prophets and psalmists would have shocked Plato.

7. THE SACRIFICIAL THEORY

Unlike the others, the sacrificial theory finds a systematic and coherent exposition in the New Testament itself, viz., in Hebrews. But two circumstances have combined to prevent this Epistle from taking the place which is its due in the theology of the atonement.

(*a*) The first is the persistent mistake of supposing that sin-offerings must somehow have been intended to propitiate God by the killing of a victim in the offerer's stead, an idea which has been a source of endless confusion in the exegesis of the New Testament. The truth is that such an interpretation of sacrifice is characteristic of heathen, and not of Jewish, religion. The ram sacrificed instead of Isaac is of course a case of substitution. But in the form in which the story has come down to us, the object of the sacrifice is not propitiation ; it is simply a proof of Abraham's obedience. In the New Testament, moreover, the story is never mentioned in connexion with Christ's sacrifice, although the author of Hebrews cites it as a type of resurrection.[1] Again, in the law of the first-born there seems to be another case of an animal victim substituted for a human life ; [2] and in the story of David there is an unmistakable allusion to a sacrifice intended to propitiate God.[3] But these have nothing to do with the sin-offerings of the later law. Scholars now seem to be fairly agreed that the object of the sin-offerings was expiation rather than propitiation, and that the victim was regarded as the offerer's representative rather than as his substitute. The intention was that the blood, or offered life, of a sinless victim should cleanse the offerers, or things used in worship, from the defilement of sin. The sacrifice thus changed the relation of man to God by operating directly, not upon God, but upon man.[4] Dodd has argued powerfully that the word ἱλάσκεσθαι and its cognates, which in heathen writers almost always signify propitiation and are sometimes so rendered in the English Bible, nevertheless usually

---

[1] Heb. xi. 17–19.   [2] Exod. xiii. 13.   [3] 1 Sam. xxvi. 19.
[4] I do not, of course, mean to exclude the idea that it was the blood of a life *offered to God* which effected expiation.

in the Greek Bible signify expiation.[1]   The object of the verb ἱλάσκεσθαι is usually, not God, but sin ; and in the New Testament the verb is never used with God as its object.   Be that as it may, the author of Hebrews clearly understood the object of sacrifice for sin to be the cleansing away of defilement by the blood of a sinless victim.

(b) The second reason for the failure to do justice to the theory of the atonement set forth in Hebrews is of a different kind.   As we have already noticed,[2] the austerity of the author's religious temperament makes him reluctant to use the Pauline language of love and grace in connexion with God.   Although he clearly teaches that Christ is the divine Son through whom the worlds were made, he presents the earthly life of the Son only as the life of perfect human obedience culminating in the death on the cross.   The connexion of Christ's self-sacrifice with love, divine or human, is never explicitly made, and has to be supplied by an extension of the author's thought.

What, then, is the essence of his theory ?   We may render it somewhat freely as follows.

The real intention of the old sacrifices for sin was that the blood of an unblemished victim, representing a stainless life offered to God in death, might be applied so as to remove defilements caused by sin, in order that man might draw near to God in worship, and communion between man and God be established.   In these sacrifices the victim was offered by a priest who was appointed by God to represent the people before him.   But the ordinances of the old covenant were imperfect for two main reasons.

(a) The lives of the victims were unstained by sin only because, being animals, they were innocent.   The only blood, or sacrificed life, which can really avail to take away sin is that of one who has conquered temptation. It was therefore in the nature of the case impossible that the blood of bulls and goats could ever cleanse man's conscience.

(b) The animal-victims were sacrificed against their will.

[1] See his Commentary on *Romans*, pp. 54 *sq.* ; also *J.T.S.*, Vol. XXXII, pp. 352–60.

[2] pp. 113 *sqq.*

But the only life which can really avail for cleansing, is a life which has undergone death in free and perfect obedience to God. It must therefore be self-offered. In the perfect sacrifice for sin, priest and victim must be the same person.

A further requirement for a perfect sacrifice remains to be noted. The life offered, while it must not be below the level of human capacities, nevertheless must not be strictly superhuman. Only the life which has conquered temptation *in man's own nature* can thereafter apply to that nature in other men a fully sanctifying power. The one therefore who is to be the perfect priest and victim must himself be human.

At all these points the Epistle exhibits the perfection and finality of Christ's atoning sacrifice. He is the God-appointed priest and victim who offered himself to God for us. He was a man, tempted in all points as we are, yet without sin. He was completely obedient to the Father's will even unto death. And thus he made his death to be the one all-sufficient sacrifice of the perfect human life, which, having passed through death, becomes the one availing power for sanctification. The blood of Christ's offered life is sprinkled on our sin-stained consciences. It enters our souls and cleanses them with its own triumphant purity, so that we also can draw near to God and offer ourselves in a like obedience.

Christ, then, has indeed done something for us which we could never have done for ourselves. In that sense he has suffered vicariously. But there is no hint of substitution in the thought. Christ's sacrifice avails for us because the sanctifying blood, the symbol of his offered life, is sprinkled upon us his people, and restores to us that communion with God which enables us to follow him who is our forerunner and pioneer as well as our high-priest. Nor is there any suggestion that Christ's sacrifice has propitiated God. For the perfectly obedient life self-offered avails to change, not God's attitude to man but man's attitude to God, and to remove the barrier between man and God which man's sin has erected.

Thus interpreted the theory of Hebrews supplies a firm basis for the doctrine of an *objective* element in the atone-

ment. We are enabled to see in Christ's death something
in principle more than the most appealing display of God's
love for man ; we now see it as the means whereby Christ's
offered life becomes the power of a perfect and glorified
manhood, which from the unseen world can penetrate and
transform human souls. Christ has actually opened for us
a new way into heaven, and made available a new power
to enable us to tread it. True, temptation, suffering and
death lie before the Christian still. What the Schoolmen
called the *poenalitates praesentis vitae* [1] are not removed ;
the Christian's obedience still has to be made complete by
his submission to them. Yet the atoning sacrifice of
Christ has in itself made a real and objective difference,
beyond the mere revealing of God's constant love. It
has made available for Christians communion in and with
that perfect humanity of their representative and high-
priest, which has already through its sacrifice entered the
heavenly world.

The one conspicuous point of incompleteness in the
atonement theory of Hebrews is its failure to make evident
how the whole work of atonement is from beginning to
end the act of God's love. We miss in Hebrews just that
vital element which St. Paul and St. John so clearly supply.
The reason for this defect is probably to be found, as we
have suggested, in the author's temperament. Perhaps,
moreover, he regarded his theory of the atonement as a
supplement to Pauline theology, and thought it the less
necessary to reaffirm explicitly that aspect of the truth
which St. Paul had already made unmistakably clear.

8. SUMMARY AND CONCLUSIONS

There is a real and important distinction between " subjective " and " objective " theories of the atonement. The
former see in the atoning life and death of Christ only the
demonstration of a divine love which had been real from
the beginning ; they find the saving effect of that life and

---

[1] These *poenalitates* are distinguished from the *poena*, or direct
punishment, for sin, as those " penal conditions " of life in this
world, to which even the redeemed and forgiven must submit.

death only in the penitence to which the sinner is freshly stirred by what they reveal. " Objective " theories, on the other hand, see in the atoning life and death an act which in itself effects a change in the relation of man to God ; and according to them this change is antecedent to the faith and penitence whereby the sinner is made partaker of its benefits. Each of these two broad types of theory is specially relevant to a particular conception of the nature of sin. Those theologians who think " subjective " theories sufficient are on the whole those who, like the prophets, regard sin mainly as a matter of personal *reatus*, i.e., as something for which the sinner is personally responsible as a free agent. Those, on the other hand, who maintain " objective " theories are on the whole those who see in sin a corrupting *vitium*, a moral or spiritual disease in human nature which man's will is powerless to overcome. It was as a *vitium* or taint that the priestly religion of sacrifice treated sin, though very often it failed to distinguish between a taint that really affected man's moral and spiritual being, and one that was a matter merely of ceremonial uncleanness.

It is obviously consistent with this analysis that among types of " objective " theory we should have found the most satisfactory to be that which most clearly bases itself on sacrificial ideas, and finds in the sin-offerings of the Old Testament a true foreshadowing of the atonement. Juridical theories, we have suggested, can only defend themselves against theological criticism by abandoning the claim to be " objective ". But this point is easily obscured by the failure to distinguish clearly between ideas and language which are properly juridical, and those which are properly sacrificial.

When, however, the juridical and sacrificial theories have been distinguished from one another, and each expressed in its most acceptable form, there seems to be no good reason for holding them to be mutually exclusive. The truth that the cross shows the willingness of divine love to suffer the consequences of sin in man's behalf, need not exclude the further truth that on the cross the sinless manhood was offered so that, having passed into the heavenly world, its sanctifying and life-giving power might be available to sinful man.   This latter doctrine is robbed of all unethical and quasi-magical implications, if it be recognized that the new power thus made *available* only becomes actually *availing* when it is humbly and thankfully received as God's gift.   When it is thus received, what it bestows is the grace of Christ-like life.

Taken then in conjunction with one another, the truths of the juridical and sacrificial theories do but give greater precision to the truth of the " classical " theory that by the cross God in manhood has won the victory which redeems mankind from the powers of evil.   And thus, finally, the fullest truth is found in the great principle vindicated by Abélard that the cross is the supreme demonstration of God's love for man.

CHAPTER XXII

THE LAST THINGS (GENERAL)

IN THE previous chapters we have considered the Christian doctrine concerning the evil from which man is to be saved and the relevance of the gospel of the atonement to his need. We must now turn our attention from the *way* of salvation to its *end*.

In the two great traditions of thought and experience, the Hebraic and the Hellenic, which have principally influenced Christian theology, we find two quite different ways of conceiving the relation of the perfect world to this world in which and from which we crave salvation. The first employs mainly the symbols of temporal relation, the second those of spatial.

1. TWO WAYS OF CONCEIVING THE PERFECT WORLD

No doubt the Hebrew religion, like all others, started with a spatially conceived distinction between heaven above, God's dwelling-place, and the earth below, the abode of men. Nevertheless, the notion of God's covenant and promise, which is the peculiar feature of the Hebrew religion, constantly turned the eye of faith towards the future. In the earlier prophetic writings it would seem that the hope of God's chosen is strictly temporal, and is directed to a blessed time when God will grant to future generations of Israelites the glories of an earthly empire. When this hope waxed dim, some prophets and sages tried vainly to show that God rewarded the righteous individual with happiness and prosperity before his death. But the common facts of human experience have always been too strong for theodicies of this kind. And finally, in the age of the apocalyptists, the wonderful persistence of the pious Jew's hope in Jehovah led Hebrew theology to make a new cosmic distinction of equal importance with that between heaven above and earth below, viz., that between this present age or world and the age or world to come.   This present age is that of imperfection, strife, and suffering, in which the righteous remain for the most part " poor and needy ".   But this age will come to an end, the whole world-order will be changed, and the universe refashioned by a great intervention of God. Then there will be a new heaven and a new earth.   Death will be no more.   Those who have been loyal to Jehovah in this age will rise again from the tomb to partake of endless happiness, and those who have been his enemies in this age will also rise again to an endless punishment. In this way the state of being, which in the popular language of Christianity is called " heaven ", is conceived as wholly future ; but, properly speaking, this state is to be identified, not with heaven, but with the new heaven and the new earth which belong to the age or world to come.   At the same time, the original spatially conceived distinction between heaven and earth endures in Hebraic thought and is never abolished.   For the whole hope of Israel depends on the belief that Jehovah, the creator and ruler of all, abides in his heaven throughout all ages, and thus brings his purposes to fulfilment.   It has been left for a modern philosopher to place all perfection so entirely in the future as to declare that God himself has not yet come into being.[1]

Hellenic thought, on the other hand, developed quite differently the same primitive distinction between heaven above and earth below.   The most complete and effective contrast to Hebrew eschatology is found in Platonic idealism.   To Plato there is no perfection strictly in the future.   History has no end or goal; it was indeed commonly conceived by Hellenic thinkers as consisting of an endless series of revolving cycles, each of which left things at its close very much as they had been at the beginning. Plato speaks of the perfect world as ἐκεῖ (there), opposing it to the ἐνθάδε (here) of our present experience.   But, though he does not believe in time, Plato does not take

[1] S. Alexander, *Space, Time, and Deity.*

even his spatial metaphors very seriously. His real thought is that the perfect world is the world of changeless and eternal reality behind and beyond phenomena. Of this world our spatio-temporal experience is in part a moving image and in part a veil. Salvation depends on the power of the philosopher-saint to penetrate behind its illusory appearances and to gaze on the vision of the eternal. The perfect world must be already real : it is indeed the only full reality. But the knowledge of it is still future for the individual, in so far as the latter is not yet sufficiently freed from illusion to apprehend it. And the seeker after truth may look forward to the death of his material body as an event which will deliver him from what still holds his spirit in bondage to the world of sense.

2. CHRISTIAN ESCHATOLOGY

When we pass to Christian eschatology, we find that in the New Testament at least the Hebraic type of thought is predominant. To the first generation of Christians the resurrection of Christ was the sign that he was shortly to return from heaven in glory to bring in the new age or world, and to wind up the present age in judgement. It is true that in Hebrews and St. John's Gospel and First Epistle the expectation of the second coming has passed into the background ; and in Hebrews especially there are unmistakable traces of Alexandrian Platonism. On the whole, Hebrews emphasizes the thought of Christ as our pioneer who has opened the way into the unseen world which we are to follow. St. John speaks mainly of our present communion with the living Christ which has already given us eternal life in him. Yet, even where Hellenic influence is present in the New Testament, it is only superficial. New Testament writers do not look forward to a long, still less to an unending, future of temporal history in imperfect worlds. Nor do they ever hint that the imperfection of this world makes it illusory. What to the author of Hebrews is partial or shadowy is a partial or shadowy indication of what God is hereafter to bring to pass, rather than, as it was to Plato, the veil of a reality timelessly present. The characteristic thought of the New Testament is that with the resurrection of Christ the great cosmic change, which is to be consummated in the age to come, has already begun. That is the real reason why the exact date of the end does not matter to Christians. For in their communion with the risen Lord they already partake of the life of the new world. In the Christian community the powers of the age to come are already at work. At present the powers of evil in this age are resisting desperately. But the conflict is, as it were, " too hot to last " ; and the Christian can await the issue in confident loyalty, without anxiety as to the precise length of time involved.

The actual course of history has disappointed the general expectation of the first Christians as to the temporal nearness of the end. And the eschatology of the Catholic tradition has had perforce to adapt itself to the facts. Belief in the second advent of Christ, the final judgement, the general resurrection, and the consummation of all things as the future goal of history has been retained ; but these have come to be thought of as " a divine far-off event ", indefinitely postponed. Meanwhile the note of urgency, so characteristic of the New Testament, has been preserved by a doctrine of particular or individual judgement at death. At death the destiny of the individual soul to salvation or perdition is fixed for ever. There can be no " second chance " in the hereafter. But it does not follow that the condition after death of all saved souls, nor perhaps of all lost souls, will be the same. The souls of saints are admitted at once to heaven and the vision of God, and they await the final day with Christ in glory. Others of the saved must be purified from sin by sufferings of longer or shorter duration or of greater or less intensity in the intermediate state of purgatory. On the other hand, in the case of the lost it has been found impossible to distinguish clearly between their state before and after the last day. But later theology has speculated much as to possible differences in their final condition. In the Roman Catholic Church it is now held to be at least a legitimate opinion that those who have failed of salvation without having incurred the guilt of grave sin on their own part will attain to a state of what may be called "natural happiness", though they are cut off from heaven and the vision of God.

It is evident that in all such speculations as to graded distinctions in the condition of souls after death, whether in the intermediate or in the final state, there is no word of scripture to which appeal can be made. They tend, in spite of orthodox insistence that the main issue of salvation or perdition is settled at death for every man, to make us think of the last things as but the culmination of a universal process which is now going on, and which for immortal souls is continued after death. The end then appears as that ideal state of equilibrium which would exist when every soul has reached its own fit and proper place in the universe and there is no further cause of movement. Such a notion has obvious affinity with the general thought of Hellenism that the order of the universe depends less on the personal will of a God who achieves a purpose through the history of his creation, than on an impersonal principle of reason which, as the immanent law of reality, fulfils itself everywhere. To the religion of the Catholic mystics, influenced as it was by neo-Platonism, the idea of the last day at the end of history appears to be almost wholly irrelevant.

Quite different is the fundamental idea underlying the eschatology of the New Testament. In it the end means essentially the manifest victory of God, the re-creation of the universe so as to be the perfect expression of his goodness, and the consummated glory of those whom faith in the risen Christ has already delivered from the powers of evil in this present world.

No doubt this thought of the final victory is closely connected in the Bible with that of the last judgement, and in some apocryphal writings the latter thought overshadows the former. The apocalyptists looked forward to a universal judgement, pictured as a great assize, at which God's loyal servants were to be rewarded with everlasting happiness in the new world, and the wicked consigned to everlasting torment. To some of the latest of these writers, who lived shortly before or even at the beginning of the Christian era, it seemed that the vast majority of mankind must incur the latter doom. To the author of 2 Esdras in the Apocrypha the last day appeared even more as an hour of doom for sinners than of real victory for God. Pictures of a not very different sort have found their way into certain chapters of the Revelation, and from this source they have been taken up and reproduced by orthodox artists and teachers in the Christian Church. The detailed imagery of the last day with which medieval painting has made us so painfully familiar is entirely derived, through the Revelation, from the apocalyptic writings of the later Judaism. There is nothing in it which is distinctively Christian, except what is from another point of view the least Christian feature of all, viz., the representation of Jesus Christ as the judge who consigns the bulk of mankind to everlasting torment.

Nevertheless, the really ultimate event to which the Bible as a whole looks forward is not so much a last judgement as a final victory of God. God cannot fail. In the end he must accomplish his whole purpose and fulfil all his promises. Such is the faith in which the Bible was written. The second coming is to be the manifest completion of God's universal triumph, and the final deliverance of his chosen into glorious communion with himself. Certainly this triumph involves the utter discomfiture of every enemy, and the punishment of every disloyal servant ; nor is there any hint that Christ's reign will ever be universally acknowledged before he comes again. But, outside the passages in Revelation already mentioned, the only allusion to *everlasting* punishment is in the parable of the Sheep and Goats in St. Matthew.[1] St. Paul, even when his anger against the Jews is fiercest, never speaks of anything more than " aeonian destruction ".[2] In St.

[1] Matt. xxv. 41, 46. It would be very hazardous to attribute the exact equivalent of the expression κόλασις αἰώνιος to Christ himself.

[2] 2 Thess. i. 9. The absence of any suggestion of everlasting torment is the more remarkable, because St. Paul is writing under the stress of passionate emotion caused by Jewish slanders at Thessalonica, and it is hard to deny a note of vindictiveness in his language.

Paul's mind the last judgement is clearly the penultimate, rather than the absolutely ultimate, event. The end is when the last enemy has been destroyed, and Christ shall deliver up the Kingdom to God the Father, that God may be all in all.[1] As for the teaching of Jesus, it is sufficient for our present purpose to point out that he bade his disciples look and pray for the hallowing of the Father's name and the coming of his Kingdom as in heaven so on earth. And where should we seek to learn his real mind upon this subject if not in the Lord's Prayer ?

We conclude therefore that " the last thing " for the Christian is something different, not only from the ultimate reality or perfectly rational order as conceived by Hellenic idealism, but also from the future world as pictured by Jewish apocalyptists, in which the endless felicity of some human souls is made to correspond with the equally unending misery of others. Final judgement there must be ; but there must also be something beyond it, viz., the fulfilment of God's purpose in a universe which in every corner mirrors and expresses the praise of his goodness. That purpose cannot finally be fulfilled in a world where the sentences of pain decreed by justice are equally unending with the gifts of love. We must picture the final world as one in which every enemy has been destroyed, rather than one in which enemies are kept perpetually alive by God's judgement in order to be perpetually cut off from his mercy. The world to come must be a world in which judgement and penalty are *past*.

3. THE PROBLEM OF THE FUTURITY OF THE WORLD TO COME

The obvious difficulty—and indeed impossibility—is to find any terms in which the ontological relation of the world to come to this world can be adequately expressed. The life of the world to come must be future in more than that purely subjective sense which is suggested when we suppose that that life can be entered at any time by a soul sufficiently purified to apprehend the eternal. For the

---

[1] 1 Cor. xv. 24–8.

Christian this supposition is but a half-truth. For, though
God is indeed eternal and communion with him is possible
for his saints at any time, yet the full glory of the world
to come does not exist to be apprehended until God's
purpose in his whole creative and redemptive work has
been fully achieved. On the other hand, the world to
come cannot be simply future, in the sense that its arrival
can in principle be dated, though the date is unknown.
For in that case the world to come would be thought of
simply as another temporal world, and not really as eternal
at all. What is eternal cannot be related to what is
temporal in simply temporal terms. Yet a Christian, who
believes in the reality of the eternal God's purpose and
work through time, cannot dispense altogether with
temporal terms when he thinks of their accomplishment.

4. THE MEANING OF THE WORD " LAST "

We are thinking about " the last things " ; and there
is an ambiguity in the meaning of the word " last ", of
which we may do well at this point to remind ourselves.
It may mean " last in time ", and this is at least part of
the meaning which we usually give to it in speaking of
" the last things ". But it only needs a little reflexion
to show that the notion of something which happens
strictly last in time is self-contradictory. For if we think
of it as happening in time at all, we must go on to think
of a time when it will have happened, and therefore of
something coming after it. Yet the notion of an unending
series of events in time is equally unthinkable, if we try
to give to the notion a concrete and not a merely mathe-
matical significance. It is really only a negation which
marks our inability to think of something absolutely last.
No doubt we may agree to call " last in time " any event
which our minds at their furthest stretch cannot penetrate
beyond. But even then, so long as we think of that
event as in time, it remains one among all the other events
which have happened since the world began. There seems
to be no reason why what is last in time should as such have
any special priority in importance. Suppose a millennium

or golden age is going to arrive on earth at some future date, let us say A.D. 100,000, and that we agree not to ask what is going to happen afterwards : why should this age, because it comes afterwards, be supposed in any way to outweigh or make worth while all the other ages of suffering and toil and sin which went before ? I have never heard a serious answer to this question attempted by any of those who make a religion of mere social reform or revolution. Nor on the other hand do I understand how far those who believe in a literal second coming of Christ on earth really regard this event as one historical happening, viz., the last, among all others. They certainly seem to attribute to it an importance which merely as an event in time it cannot carry.

There is, however, another and a fuller meaning which the word " last " bears in common speech. Like the word " final ", it may refer not simply to that which comes after everything else, but to that which completes a process by bringing it to its purposed end. In so far as the last event in a series is the one which fulfils the purpose which has directed the series throughout, it ceases to be merely one event among the others, and acquires a unique importance of its own. But clearly it derives that importance from what is beyond the mere series of events considered as such, and the nature of the special relation which is thus established between the last event and the others is determined by the nature of the purpose in the fulfilment of which the series ends.

Two illustrations will make clear the application of these abstract statements. The last or finishing touch given to a work of art does not at all derive its special importance from the fact that it happens to come after all the others, but from the fact that it completes the whole. In this case the purpose is only fulfilled if all the touches from the first to the last make a *simultaneous* contribution in their effects to the whole work which they have produced. Thus the series of acts by which a work of art is made, if it is considered merely as a temporal series of events which succeed one another, cannot account for the work of art at all. The second illustration is of a different kind. Suppose a man who is in London purposes to get to Edinburgh. His travelling from one place to the other is again a series of successive events of which the last, viz., his arrival in Edinburgh, may be said to have the special importance of fulfilling the purpose. But in this case the particular events which preceded the last make no present contribution to that fulfilment. If the man arrives in Edinburgh, his purpose of getting there is fulfilled, no matter which of the many possible routes he may have followed. The journey is a mere incident of the past, which has no further importance for the purpose as soon as Edinburgh is reached. We may express the difference between the two kinds of purpose exemplified in the two illustrations by saying that while the artist's purpose is *expressive*, the traveller's is merely *efficient* : the process of the artist's work aims at *expressing* something, whereas the process of the traveller's journey aims merely at *effecting* something. But both cases have this element in common. The last event or act, which achieves the purpose, is as much a beginning as it is an end. It does not really achieve the end, unless it *initiates* a fulfilment : that is why it derives its special importance from what is *beyond* the series of events of which it is the last. A work of art destroyed in the moment of completion could hardly be said to fulfil the artist's aim. A traveller who dropped dead as he set foot on Waverley platform could hardly be said to have achieved his purpose in going to Edinburgh.

We may therefore formulate the following conclusions. When the word " last " is used in relation to purpose, " the last thing " does not denote simply or mainly the thing which comes after all others in a series, but that which fulfils the purpose of the whole. And fulfilment means not merely the end of a series, but also the beginning of that state of achievement or perfection which is relative to the purpose of the series. The things then which Christian theology calls " the last " are so called mainly because they fulfil the purpose of this world-process by bringing into existence that state of perfection which the Creator originally designed. Whether or no they may be in part regarded as being themselves events in the temporal or historical series, they derive their importance from what is beyond that series; and their relation to all events, or all other events, in the series is determined by the nature of the Creator's purpose. For man they mark the transition from temporal effort or imperfection either into the full fruition of eternal life or into the irrevocable loss of it. It is not for nothing that the last and most eschatological book of the Bible closes with the vision of the *new* Jerusalem.

5. SUGGESTIONS OF A CHRISTIAN METAPHYSIC

What, then, a Christian metaphysic asks of us is to try to conceive the whole reality of the time-process in relation to the Creator's purpose, the inception and fulfilment of which lie beyond that process. Time is real, not an illusion, because God really has a purpose in creation, and really works to fulfil it. But, because the purpose and work are God's, they have an absolute fulfilment which is beyond time. The fulfilment of human purposes is always in time, which is only another way of saying that it is always relative and imperfect and never final. Every such fulfilment is the beginning of another purpose, and no satisfaction is complete or enduring, while life goes on. The artist who has finished one work, loses interest in it and puts it aside to begin another. The traveller who wants to go to Edinburgh, wants to do something else as soon as he gets there. God, we humbly believe, wants to do something in and with this world; the doctrines of impassibility which will not permit such an affirmation, we must reject. So far, therefore, time is real even to God. But God's work must reach a fulfilment and satisfaction which are absolute and complete; and therefore we must say, in spite of the apparent contradiction, that time is not a *final* reality to God.

The relation of "the last things" to the historical process and events of this world is determined by the nature of the Creator's purpose. His purpose is to express his own goodness in the created world. Therefore in the fulfilment of his purpose the past events of the process are not simply left behind, but abide in making their contribution to the goodness of the final whole. Nevertheless, this world being infected and corrupted with evil, the divine purpose can only be achieved by an act of re-creation and through the breaking up of this world-order in order to establish another. On the other hand, this breaking up cannot be an act of sheer or absolute destruction ; for even the first imperfect and sin-stained creation must enhance the glory of the perfect world which is to be—God does not fail, and he *saves* this world, though he judges and condemns. It is this fundamental antinomy which the Christian doctrines of redemption, final judgement, and resurrection strive by their symbolism to reconcile. This temporal world is a world of growth, which is in itself good and expressive of its creator's goodness, and is yet marred by evil everywhere. At the last therefore the growth must be altogether cut off, so that the harvest may be garnered and the tares burned. There can be no gradual evolution or transformation of this world into the next, or of the temporal into the eternal. And yet the harvest of eternity is the harvest reaped and garnered from this world, in which and for which the Son of God was content to die. And those who by faith in him are willing to surrender all this world's life and goodness in the spirit of his love, are those in whom the life and fellowship of the world to come are already real. Thus by the act of willing sacrifice, which is the supreme expression of love, the inevitable death, which is the judgement on this world's universal and sinful imperfection, is converted to be the means of *resurrection* into the glory of the world to come, which includes the restoration and perfection of all that in this world's life was truly God's creation.

Meanwhile we have to remember that *real* time is measured, not by clocks or calendars or astronomical statistics, but by the process of God's work. According to Genesis the " days " of creation are constituted by what God does in them, and in the Bible generally the word " day " often, means, not the interval between the rising and the setting of the sun, but rather some notable occasion, especially one on which God's work is revealed. The greatest of God's works revealed to us, the work which takes all the time of history, is in his dealings with man. The greatest " moments " or " days " of that work are marked by the creation of man in God's image, by the incarnation and resurrection of the Son of God, and by the final establishment of God's perfect kingdom in which the redeemed are glorified for ever.

If we may take the foregoing paragraphs to represent in more abstract terms something of the truth which the eschatological imagery of the Bible symbolizes, it is evident that the notions of a last day and a second advent in the future are not to be understood literally at all. Nevertheless these notions stand for a vital truth which Platonism can never express, viz., that the end of salvation is achieved by God's completing act in a fellowship of redeemed souls in a universe which is at once a new world and the perfection of the old. And what Christ has revealed as the nature of God's purpose throws some light on the problem of the futurity of the world to come. From one point of view the end must be *deferred*, until the fruits of Christ's atoning work in this world can be fully reaped, or until, to use St. Paul's words, the πλήρωμα τῶν ἔθνῶν be brought in.[1] But on the other hand the *imminence* of the end, which is more constantly emphasized in the New Testament, symbolizes that for each individual and generation " the time is short ". Men must repent and accept the gospel, or the opportunity of salvation will have gone by for ever. If we measure the duration of God's whole work by our reckoning of historical time, it seems that it takes a length of time which perhaps hardly even astronomers can compute. But we may not therefore infer that there remains for each generation of human souls, even if we postulate life after physical death for them all, an indefinitely long future in which further opportunities will be given or other avenues to salvation

---

[1] Rom. xi. 25. The Greek words, meaning " full number or complement of the Gentiles or peoples ", are not exactly translatable into English.

opened.   Just because the life of the world to come transcends all human measurements of temporal sequence or
relation, the end, which in general human history is
indefinitely distant, is in spiritual reality incalculably close.
For God's final appeal and offer of salvation have been
made in Christ.   No further opportunity can be imagined.
Response must be immediate, or it may be too late.   In
spiritual reality time is to be measured by God's work.
And in the cross and resurrection of Christ his last act for
man's redemption has been wrought, his last word spoken.
There remains on man's part either acceptance or else
rejection of a work of love, which, because it is final and
all-sufficient, can never be repeated or renewed.   However
long history may last in years Anno Domini, the eternal
world has drawn finally near to man in Christ.   Because
there is nothing left for God still to do in redemption, " the
last time " has already begun ; and the true duration of
its opportunity is not to be measured in terms of general
history, but rather by the fact that in the risen victorious
Christ the world to come already confronts the soul.
Nevertheless, we may still say that, as long as the time of
this world endures for any soul, its opportunity endures
also ; for the God revealed in Jesus will never remove
the chance of penitence from those who in time may still
be changed.

CHAPTER XXIII

JUDGEMENT AND FINAL CONDEMNATION

LET US agree that all Christian teaching about " the day of judgement " has the value of a parable, and not that of so-called " literal truth ".   Nevertheless, the theologian is not absolved from the duty of seeking to determine, as closely as he can, wherein the essential truth of the parable consists.

1.   THE   NOTION   OF   TRIAL   INAPPLICABLE   TO   THE LAST DAY

How far is imagery derived from human law-courts at all applicable to God's final treatment of human souls ? The operation of justice in a law-court contains three distinct stages.   First, there is the *trial*, in which the actual facts concerning which judgement is to be passed are as clearly as possible established.   Secondly, there is the *verdict*, which is the judgement proper, pronouncing the guilt or innocence of the person or persons whose conduct is being tried.   Thirdly, there is the *sentence*, which enforces the verdict by the punishment, more or less severe, of the guilty party.

The moment we seek to draw any analogy between such legal proceedings and God's final action towards men, one fact is immediately evident.   The trial, as a process separate from the facts to be tried, is necessary only for the due information of judge and jury.   It is needed only because judge and jury are men limited in knowledge and discernment.   Where God is judge, no such trial is thinkable at all.   And it is to be remarked that in the gospel-parables which are usually supposed to have an application to the last judgement, there is no hint of any trial at all, except that sometimes the accused person's own words are made to manifest the justice of the verdict. In the parable of the Wheat and Tares it is assumed that at the time of harvest there is no difficulty in separating the tares from the wheat ; and in that of the Sheep and Goats the story begins with the separation of those to be condemned from those to be saved already made. According to the general teaching of the New Testament the real time of human trial is *now*. In so far as it is concerned with trial, judgement is present rather than future. The gospel inevitably tries every soul to which it is brought, and the soul is inevitably discriminated towards salvation or condemnation according to its response. The real trial is not a process which takes place after the facts of the case have happened ; it is a process which accompanies the facts as they happen, constitutes their eternal meaning, and determines their abiding consequences. Once the process of human response to God is complete, once its character in any human soul is finally fixed, there is no place left for anything but God's verdict. And the verdict is inevitable ; it must be what it is. To talk of a merciful *verdict* is nonsense. The God of love cannot treat the ultimate rejection of love as though it were not rejection. Otherwise he would be as unloving as unrighteous.

2. VERDICT AND SENTENCE

The relation of verdict to sentence raises a more difficult problem for theology. How far can we suppose that the verdict of the last judgement may issue in a sentence of punishment ? In order to answer this question, we must first ask, what is the significance and function of punishment in human society ?

In human society unchecked wrongdoing inevitably leads not only to general unhappiness but finally to the dissolution of the society itself. It is arguable that a similar result follows in the case of the individual wrongdoer. In so far as it does so, spiritual pain and death may be regarded as consequences of sin, in the same way that physical pain and death are consequences of disease. But this analogy between the physical and the moral life, though it may be true, is incomplete. For sin, being a moral and not a physical phenomenon, is not related to its results simply as cause to effect. Sin, in so far as it involves guilt (*reatus*), is a free act of choice on the part of a responsible agent. And therefore its disastrous consequences, in so far as they fall upon the sinner, may be viewed, not merely as effects of his wrong action, but also as just punishment or retribution for it. And they may still be so viewed, even if they are at the same time natural effects of the sin, and do not arise from the intervention of any agent who has the express purpose ·of punishing. When a self-indulgent man suffers from the results of his self-indulgence, or a habitual liar finds that others will not trust him, the suffering is in each case truly a punishment for sin, though it is also a natural and inevitable consequence of it.

On the other hand, punishment inflicted by a deliberately punitive act differs from the " natural punishment " just described in having something about it which is at once artificial and dramatic.[1] It is not in the same way an effect produced by wrongdoing ; and the pain inflicted seems to be a sort of symbolic representation of that inevitable consequence which will righteously overtake the wrongdoer in the long run, if he persists in wrongdoing. Because lawfully inflicted punishment always has this artificial and dramatic character, it can never be justified solely as retribution. Retributive indeed it must be : otherwise it would not be punishment. But, in order to be justified, it must have some other aim as well. That aim may be to deter the wrongdoer from his evil way, while there is still time to save him from pursuing it to the end. Or it may be to deter others from following his bad example, and so to safeguard the society of which he is a member. Or it may be publicly to declare that the society as a whole is on the side of righteousness, and is

---

[1] I am conscious that my whole discussion of punishment, and in particular this and the following sentence, owes much to what I have learned in conversation from Sir Walter Moberly, who, it is to be hoped, will soon give us the fruits of his long study of the subject.

able to maintain its cause.   But in every case the justification for the inflicted punishment is incomplete, unless the punishment has some purpose looking towards a future in which the cause of righteousness needs vindication.   If there be no such purpose, if punishment be solely retributive and looks only towards the past, then there is no justification for any artificial or dramatic infliction of it. Apart from the forward-looking purpose of punishment, the wrongdoer had better be left to suffer in the end from the consequences of his own acts.

Now punishment which is absolutely final, as is that associated with the last judgement, cannot have any forward-looking purpose.   Being therefore wholly right and just, it must be simply the inevitable consequence of the sinner's own acts and of the character which they have formed in him.   Thus there can be no thought of any intervention of God to punish at the last day.   God's final verdict, because it is final, must be also his sentence.   The verdict of condemnation does but declare the truth, and its consequences, whatever they may be, need no further act to enforce them.

3.   THE NEW TESTAMENT ON DIVINE INTERVENTION

It is fundamentally in accordance with the theology of the New Testament to affirm that the purpose of God's intervention in human affairs is always to save and deliver, although the salvation and deliverance may involve the condemnation and destruction of those who resist God. St. John states a great principle of doctrine in the words " God sent not his Son into the world to condemn the world, but that the world through him might be saved." [1] Professor Dodd has argued convincingly [2] that St. Paul, on the whole, understands the divine Wrath, not as the personal attitude of God towards sinners, [3] but rather as a sort of dramatic symbol for the operation of those divinely ordained laws of the universe according to which sin brings

---

[1] John iii. 17.   [2] See his note on Rom. i. 18.
[3] 2 Thess. i. 6 to 10, seems to be an exception, though the word ὀργή does not occur there.

punishment upon itself as its consequence. Dodd's argument is based on St. Paul's use of the word ὀργή. His general conclusion may be supported by pointing out that whereas St. Paul can speak of the end of sinners as being the death which sin " works " (i.e., produces), or which is " the wages of sin ", he could never speak of the end of the redeemed as being a life which anything in them either produces or deserves. On the contrary eternal life and salvation are the free gift of God's love, the direct result of his personal action in intervening to deliver. Passages which seem to attribute to God a similarly personal activity in intervening in order to punish, must surely be understood as expressing in a vivid and dramatic way the truth that by the operation of the spiritual and moral order of the universe sin must in the end bring the punishment of destruction upon the sinner's head. Even the medieval doctrine of hell might be justified as a dramatization of this sort, were it not that its pictures of unending torment seem to suggest a directly false idea of God. Such pictures have certainly proved to be on the whole ineffective. It is really impossible to make Satan cast out Satan, even by using him to terrify men out of their sins. St. Paul, it is to be noticed, only speaks of delivering a sinner to Satan as a disciplinary measure with a remedial purpose.[1]

The significance of Christ's own teaching upon this subject must be estimated by its general tenor, due allowance being made for the doctrinal tendencies and interests which are characteristic of each evangelist.[2] On the whole our Lord seems to have accepted the eschatological imagery with which his hearers were familiar, and certainly to

[1] 1 Cor. v. 5 ; 1 Tim. i. 20.

[2] A good example of the kind of allowance needed occurs in the use of the phrase about " weeping and gnashing of teeth ". In Luke xiii. 28, the expression is clearly part of an *ad hominem* retort to Pharisaic opponents. " There shall be *the* weeping and gnashing of teeth (with which you threaten others) when you shall see . . . yourselves thrust out." In St. Matthew's Gospel the phrase seems to have become a piece of general eschatological imagery inserted by the editor whenever he thinks it appropriate to enforce the point of a saying or parable.

have avoided all appearance of palliating the terrible consequences of sin or of minimizing its danger. But his main
purpose seems to have been to change radically men's ideas
of what the sin is which God's judgement most utterly
condemns. He sought, not to make God's punishment
of sin seem less real or terrible, but to convince men that
it is sins against love which are most in danger of it. It
was those, he suggested, who were most willing to consign
others to God's wrath, who in reality themselves stood
nearest to its doom. Such sayings as " Forgive, and ye
shall be forgiven ", " Condemn not, and ye shall not be
condemned ", represent the main principle which he strove
to bring home to man's conscience.[1]

We conclude, therefore, that the ultimate issue of the
rejection of God's love must be God's final abandonment
of the soul to the consequences of its own corruption. In
the Gospel of St. Matthew God's final doom on his unrepentant people is pronounced in the words, " Your house

[1] A hindrance to our understanding of the New Testament arises
from the fact that in English the words " damn " and " damnation " (when they are not simply " bad language ") are restricted
to an exclusively theological and eschatological meaning. There
are no such words in the Greek New Testament. But the full
truth is not conveyed by the substitution of the words " condemnation " and " condemn " in English versions, so long as
these words are still contrasted in the reader's mind with the
theological terms they have displaced. From a theological point
of view it would have been better (though on literary grounds it
was impossible) if the Revisers had written the words " damn "
and " damnation " *wherever* the Greek words occur which are
now rendered " condemn " and " condemnation ". In that case
they could have rendered the saying in Luke vi. 37, " Damn not,
and ye shall not be damned ", and, though the Greek word is
καταδικάζειν and not κατακρίνειν, perhaps the rendering would have
brought out an aspect of our Lord's real meaning.

Special difficulty is also caused by Mark ix. 43-8. Here the
language about the worm and the fire is borrowed from the concluding verses of Isaiah, where it depicts a horrible state of corruption, but not of torment. Our Lord's words seem to suggest
a parable, that, just as the refusal to amputate a diseased limb
may result in the corruption of the whole body, so the refusal
of self-denial (in the ordinary sense of that word) may result
in the total corruption and dissolution of the personality. In
any case there is no suggestion of everlasting torment.

is left unto you ", ἀφίεται ὑμῖν ὁ οἶκος ὑμῶν.[1] And the
prayer of Charles Wesley's hymn, " Leave, ah, leave me
not alone ", is not to be distinguished in meaning from the
petition of the Litany, " From everlasting damnation, good
Lord deliver us ".   The soul which suffers that doom will
inevitably perish in the final passing away of the sin-
tainted world with which it has chosen to identify itself.
It is only man's failure to appreciate the terrible meaning
and possibility of such a fate, which excuses the Church
for painting it in the most lurid colours it could devise,
even at the risk of marring its own gospel.

4.   THE DOCTRINE OF UNIVERSALISM

But is the death of final separation from God a *real*
possibility ?   This question brings us face to face with the
doctrine of universalism, i.e., the doctrine that since no
soul can have been created for final condemnation, no soul
can in the end be lost.

The Christian arguments for this doctrine are powerful,
and must be fairly heard.   They depend, not, as opponents
of the doctrine usually suggest, upon sentimental humanitarianism, but on logical inference from the sufficiency of
the atonement.   If the cross is really " a full, perfect, and
sufficient sacrifice for the sins of the whole world ", then
universal salvation *must* be a real possibility.   And, if it
be a real possibility, must it not ultimately be a fact ?
The really ultimate purpose of God, as we have already
argued, is not judgement but victory ; and his victory
means the redemption of creation, the refashioning of it
into a new world which perfectly expresses and embodies
his goodness.   To that end he sent his Son into the world,
not to condemn but to save it.   In so far then as the final
result is not salvation but condemnation, is not his purpose
frustrated ?

It is no answer to say that still God's righteousness may
be vindicated in condemnation.   For the essence of the
atonement is to reveal the power of a love which is more

[1] Matt. xxiii. 37.   The word " desolate ", ἔρημος, was almost
certainly absent from the original text.

than righteousness.   The Christian must think of the world
to come as that state of being in which the self-sacrifice of
Christ is ultimately found to be not in vain but triumphant.
How can that consummation be fully realized, if any soul
finally reject God's love, so that Christ died for it in vain ?
Or, if it were not for all men that Christ died, where is the
catholic gospel ?

Moreover, when we turn to Scripture, it seems that St.
Paul's great argument from history, sketched in Galatians
and elaborated in Romans, leads to something like universalism as its logical consequence.   The argument is
that, since God's promise of salvation was given *before* the
law, fulfilment of the law cannot be a condition of receiving
the promise, and the condemnation, which the law justly
brings upon man, cannot make the promise of none effect.
In other words, since God's *first* word is promise, not law,
his *last* word must be salvation, not judgement.   Perhaps
this interpretation of St. Paul's logic may seem to go too
far beyond what he actually says.   But it is at least
remarkable that, whenever St. Paul draws a comparison
and contrast between the effect of Adam's sin and that of
Christ's atonement, he cannot help dwelling on the superior
power and efficacy of the atonement in a way which leads
straight to a universalistic conclusion.   " As in Adam all
die, even so in Christ shall all be made alive." [1]   " As
through the one man's disobedience the many were made
sinners, even so through the obedience of the one shall
the many be made righteous." [2]

Nevertheless, it cannot fairly be said that the main
trend of the New Testament is towards universalism.   Its
writers and, according to their report, Jesus himself are
far too constant in their warning that men may finally
reject even the universal gospel which Christ brought and
the apostles proclaim.   And the warning that the gospel

[1] 1 Cor. xv. 22.   The universalistic implication can be avoided
by interpreting the words to mean, " As in Adam all that are in
Adam die, even so in Christ shall all that are in Christ be made
alive."   But the antithesis would rather lose its point, if only a
tiny fraction of those who are in Adam will ever be in Christ.

[2] Rom. v. 19.

may finally be rejected seems often to pass into the prog-
nostication that many will finally reject it. In any case
it would contradict the very essence of the gospel to suppose that God will ever compel a soul to salvation ; and
therefore the presentation of his final offer of salvation in
Christ must impose upon the soul an absolutely critical
choice. It is on the critical character of that choice, as
well as on the reality of God's forgiving and redeeming
grace, that the New Testament principally insists. Christ
would return no direct answer to the question, " Are there
few that be saved ? " But he did say that the gate was
narrow, that it was not the many who were finding it,
and that to postpone the effort to enter might be fatal.[1]

In view of what can be said on both sides, we must con-
cede to the universalist that it is at least legitimate to
hope that no soul will finally be lost, and that the final
issue of God's work will be, not the redemption of some
souls out of the world, but the redemption of the whole
world which is the object of his love. Such universal
redemption may be said to be the antecedent purpose of
God's atoning work in Christ, and we dare not set limits
to what the cross may achieve. Nevertheless, we must
also admit the reality of the possibility, and the justification
for the fear, that God's antecedent purpose will never be
achieved fully. For, in the nature of the case, the fullness
of achievement must depend upon a response in each
individual soul which can never be compelled and which,
so far as our present experience goes, is being by many
definitely refused. No doubt the very fact that even in
those who do respond the response is still imperfect, is a
ground for believing that in those who refuse to respond
the refusal is still incomplete. Further, we may surely
affirm with confidence that God would never have created
man, if the main issue of that creation were to be the
condemnation of man. But, for the rest, we must leave
ultimate possibilities open in the case of individual souls,
and retain only the certainty of our faith in God's power
and goodness. Even confidence in the ultimate triumph
of God's love does not entitle us to regard as assured truths

[1] Matt. vii. 13, 14 ; Luke xiii. 23 *sqq.*

all the inferences which our limited logic may draw from it. Hope is not knowledge, and it is only perfect love which can legitimately cast out fear.

CHAPTER XXIV

THE HOPE OF RESURRECTION

EVEN THE summary account of Christian eschatology which we are here attempting requires us to say something further in explanation of the Christian affirmation of belief in the resurrection of the dead. For no article of the Creed is more liable than this to offend the intellectual conscience, especially in an age which finds such difficulty in believing in any life after death at all for the individual soul.

1. TWO PRINCIPLES IN CHRISTIAN BELIEF

The essential meaning of the Christian affirmation in this matter involves two fundamental principles or postulates which we will discuss briefly in turn :

First, that the object of ultimate hope is communion with the eternal God, and not any prolongation of human lives as such.

Secondly, that the way in which this hope is to be finally attained, as well as the true significance of its attainment, are more adequately symbolized under the figure of resurrection, than by any doctrine which asserts simply the immortality of the soul.

2. LIFE AFTER DEATH AND THE RELIGIOUS DOCTRINE OF IMMORTALITY

In dealing with the first of these two principles, we must begin by making an important distinction. When we say that we believe in " life after death ", we may have either of two quite different ideas in mind.

(*a*) We may be thinking of the answer to the question, does the soul or personality of a man go on existing when the body dies ? This is a perfectly intelligible question but it has no self-evident connexion with any particular belief about God. Many believers in God reject belief in the immortality of the soul. And on the other hand some have believed in the immortality of the soul, while rejecting belief in God. Moreover, it is to be observed that to say that the soul survives the death of the body is not necessarily to say that it is immortal; for it is quite conceivable that it might perish afterwards. The evidence for and against survival, as distinct from immortality, may be investigated from a strictly scientific standpoint, which excludes both metaphysical and religious presuppositions altogether.

(b) On the other hand, it is possible to regard belief in human immortality as a religious belief founded upon some faith in the being of God. And when we thus approach the subject from the religious side, the fundamental question which we ask about life after death has a quite different context and significance. Almost all religions attribute immortality or eternity to the God of their worship, while at the same time they indicate to man some way of entering into some sort of communion or fellowship with God. And thus the thought is bound to arise that man himself may somehow be made partaker of the immortality or eternity which is properly divine. The question then asked about life after death ceases to be, Is the human soul by nature such as to survive the death of the body ? and becomes rather, Is the human soul capable of rising into or receiving a higher kind of life which is somehow akin to God's ? In the affirmative answer to that question we reach the religious doctrine of immortal or eternal life for man. It is not based upon the nature of the human soul simply as such, but upon a relation which exists or may exist between the human soul and God. Nor could it be proved to be true by the most complete evidence conceivable that in fact every human soul survives the death of the body.[1]

---

[1] The most such evidence could do would be to remove one *a priori* objection to the religious doctrine of immortality, viz., the objection that, since the soul or personality must perish with the body, no kind of immortality for man is possible. Whether this objection ever *ought* to be removed in this way, is another question.

3. THE TEACHING OF THE BIBLE ON LIFE AFTER DEATH

Having made this distinction clear, we turn to the teaching of the Bible. Its most obvious feature perhaps is the lack of any positive information as to what happens to the human soul when the body dies. In the Old Testament indeed there are many passages which roundly deny that the human soul continues after death in any life worth having. And even the New Testament, for all its emphasis on the glorious hope of resurrection, gives no kind of answer to the questions asked by those who are interested in spiritualism or what is commonly called " psychical research ".

Why is there at first so much negation, and at last so little information, in the Bible ?   The question has deeply perplexed sincere Christians who long for some definite knowledge about the condition of dear ones departed.

> When Lazarus left his charnel-cave
> And home to Mary's house returned,
> Was this demanded—if he yearned
> To hear her weeping by his grave ?
>
> " Where wert thou, brother, those four days ? "
> There lives no record of reply,
> Which, telling what it is to die,
> Had surely added praise to praise.
>
> Behold a man raised up by Christ !
> The rest remaineth unrevealed ;
> He told it not ; or something sealed
> The lips of that evangelist.[1]

Tennyson's question is certainly not to be answered by suggesting doubts as to the historical value of the Fourth Gospel. But the distinction previously drawn between survival and eternal life may afford us more help. From first to last the Bible is chiefly concerned to teach us that our faith and hope must be in God, that it is on God's Kingdom, not on personal survival and its particular phases and circumstances, that our aims and affections should be set.

[1] Tennyson, *In Memoriam*, XXXI.

Already in the Old Testament it is very significant that when the psalmists deny most explicitly any value to the life of the departed spirit, they immediately pass on to declare that just for that reason their hope is more firmly fixed on God.[1]　There seems to be good reason for thinking that the picture of Sheol as a prison for unsubstantial wraiths, a picture which represents the orthodox belief of Israel before the Captivity, was originally intended to discourage a false spiritualism or cult of departed spirits which led men away from the worship of Jehovah.　It was to Jehovah's seers and prophets, not to the witches and wizards who professed to raise the ghosts of the dead, that the loyal Israelite should go for guidance.　It was when Saul could get no answer from God through prophets, dreams or divination, that he turned in despair to the witch of Endor.[2]　Only after the Captivity, when idolatry and necromancy have ceased to be dangers, do we find a new hope of the after-life taking shape dimly in the Hebrew mind.　And this new hope is based wholly on the all-pervading presence and power of Jehovah.　The faith is at last dawning that never and nowhere in the universe can the faithful be really " cut away from God's hand ", not even by death or the bars of Sheol itself.　" Though I walk through the valley of deep darkness, I will fear no evil ; for thou art with me." [3]

In the New Testament Christ's reply to his Sadducean questioners carries on the same line of teaching.　That there is life beyond the grave, he tells them, is proved when God says to Moses, " I am the God of Abraham, Isaac, and Jacob " ; for God is not the God of the dead, but of the living.[4]　In other words, a man has abiding

---

[1] See, e.g., Pss. xxx. 9–11 ; xxxix. 6–8.

[2] 1 Sam. xxviii. 6.

[3] Ps. xxiii. 4.　See also Pss. lxxiii. 22–5 ; cxxxix. 7–11, and Job xix. 25 (R.V. Margin).

[4] Matt. xxii. 31–3 ; Mark xii. 26, 27.　Luke (xx. 38) makes an addition to the saying, which is apparently a gloss derived from 4 Macc. vii. 19 ; xvi. 25, and which obscures the point.　The words added are " for all live unto him ".　But the point is not that all live unto God, but that those who are truly God's must have abiding life.　See Easton's Commentary, *ad loc.*

life, in so far as the living Jehovah is really his God. For God's faithful servants, therefore, there can be no imprisonment or empty existence among the shades. For " the gates of Hades " (or the bars of Sheol) do not prevail against the life and fellowship of God's own ecclesia.[1] This is the great conclusion which the Bible reaches. The immortality of man is the gift of the living God who conquers death. Of that the Bible assures us ; but it does not answer our questions about what happens to the soul when the body dies. And it would be difficult to cite any text outside the Apocrypha which suggests that the soul of man is by the necessity of its own created nature immortal.

4. RESURRECTION

And yet, if we are content to leave at this point our account of the Christian hope for the individual, we shall still have almost ignored what is perhaps the most characteristic feature of the Christian gospel. For we have said nothing of the difference made to the religious doctrine of immortal or eternal life by the Christian teaching of the resurrection.

No leading idea in human religion has had a more complicated and paradoxical history than that of resurrection. In pagan thought it is connected with myths of a dying and rising god or goddess, which apparently have their origin in the cycle of the seasons, the death of winter followed by the rebirth of spring. But such legends as that of Persephone seem to have little direct relation, either historical or ideological, to Christian belief. The latter springs out of Judaism. And in Judaism the religious idea of resurrection appears in its crudest and most

---

[1] This surely is the most natural explanation of the saying to St. Peter in Matt. xvi. 18. I cannot resist the speculation that this whole saying, recorded only by St. Matthew, represented originally words spoken by our Lord to St. Peter when he appeared to him after the resurrection. Placed in that context, the saying gains a clearer and greatly enhanced significance. It is on St. Peter as penitent and believing in the resurrection that Christ founds the fellowship of his Church against which the gates of Hades shall not prevail. But this is of course only a speculation.

materialistic form. It came into being as part of the eschatological expectation conceived by Jewish apocalyptists at a time when all hope of a national redemption wrought by natural means seemed destined to final disappointment. The apocalyptists sought to re-establish faith in God's guidance of history with visions of a purely supernatural event. They spoke of a great theophany at the end of the age when men were to rise again with their material bodies from the tomb in order to receive the reward of their deeds in everlasting felicity or torment. Compared with such fantasies, the language of Psalm cxxxix and the Platonistic teachings found in the Book of Wisdom seem to convey a much more worthy and spiritual idea of immortality. And at first sight it appears to be merely a disaster that the Church should have felt herself obliged to repel the most sympathetic minds in the pagan world by retaining in her creed a clause which speaks of the resurrection of the body or the flesh. Doubtless that clause was retained because of the Church's belief that her Lord's body had actually been raised from the tomb. But was that belief itself originally due to a misunderstanding, inevitable perhaps to minds brought up on Jewish notions of eschatology, but none the less fatal to a truly catholic interpretation of the gospel ?

Such a conclusion is only superficially attractive. Of course as long as resurrection is understood, as it was understood by Jewish apocalyptists, to mean simply the restoration of life by divine fiat at some moment of time *after* death, it remains a crude and primitive notion, on a lower level altogether than the nobler forms of the Hellenic belief in the immortality of the soul. But when an attentive reading of the New Testament has enabled us to perceive that Christ has given to the idea of resurrection the quite new meaning of life restored and glorified *through and by means of* death, we see also that he has made it the symbol of a deeper truth than any which a doctrine of mere immortality can express. Christianity must indeed sublimate and spiritualize the belief in resurrection which was part of its heritage from Judaism. And yet the Jewish notion, crude and fantastic as it originally was, contributes through Jesus a vital element to Christian faith and hope which the Hellenic doctrines of immortality wholly lack.

For this belief in resurrection, throughout its strange and chequered history, stands for the great truth inherent in Jewish eschatology, that the change from earthly to heavenly life is not and cannot be a gradual process of ascension, in which the falling away of the material body is merely a further liberation of the soul ; rather it is a process of increasing tension and conflict leading to a crisis in which the earthly man must wholly die in order wholly to receive life. What is true of this whole age or world-order, which must pass away in the new creation of the world to come, is true also of the individual organism which is a man—it also must wholly die in its present earthly state in order to receive from God that full and heavenly glory of which its created nature has made it capable. The gateway to the heavenly and eternal life is the self-sacrifice which Christ first accomplished only through his death, and in which he enables Christians to follow him. And thus in Christ the universal fact of physical decay and death becomes for man, as it were, the sacrament of the inward and spiritual truth that life must be wholly surrendered before it can be wholly won.

To use the now fashionable term, the progress of the earthly life towards the heavenly is inherently *dialectical*. In the more concrete and illuminating language of the gospel, it is a story of exaltation won through humiliation, of gain through loss, of having through giving, of power through suffering, of victory through defeat, of joy through sorrow, of holiness through common sharing, of glory through shame, of life through death. And the reconciliation of all these antinomies is in the simple yet world-transforming fact that God is love, the love which decrees that the Son of Man, who is also the Son of God, must suffer in order to reign and save. That is the supreme truth which Jesus taught ; and Calvary, the empty tomb, and the visions of the glorious body bearing the marks of the cross, mean that in his own person he has proved the truth to be true indeed.

That is why the resurrection of Christ has a truly eschatological significance. It is the sign, not that a holy manhood survives death, but that by the humiliation and self-sacrifice of the Son of God the deadliness of death has been overcome, and the kingdom of heaven opened to all believers. In the crisis which that gospel inevitably brings to every soul which hears it, the world to come itself, together with its living Lord, are already at the doors.

From another point of view the essential difference between believing in the resurrection of Jesus and believing merely in the immortality of his personal spirit or soul, is clearly seen the moment we seek to apply to his case the language which the author of the Book of Wisdom uses about the souls of the righteous. "In the sight of the unwise," he writes, "they seemed to die", and he implies thereby that their death was apparent only. Can we imagine St. Paul using such words of Christ? If he had done so, his gospel would certainly have caused no scandal in the Gentile world. On the contrary it would have been received with much sympathy, not least in philosophical centres such as Athens. To suggest that Christ's death was an appearance, and not a full or ultimate reality, would have removed all the offence of the cross ; but it would have removed also the essence of the gospel. For to the Christian the death on the cross, with all its circumstances of shame, was not less real, not less vitally important for faith, than the resurrection of which it was the condition. The reality of the resurrection balanced and transformed the reality of the death ; both realities were equally essential to the new salvation that was in Christ. Therefore the fullness of the gospel required the emptiness of the tomb. And it was better that the intelligentsia of the Gentile world should continue to be alienated by crude beliefs about the final resurrection, which St. Paul and St. John [1] failed to banish from the Church, than that the gospel should be lost by being

[1] The author of Hebrews hardly says anything explicitly about the resurrection ; but his teaching in ii. 5–9, is well worth examining in connexion. (See above p. 120.)

assimilated to religious philosophies which had no room for the true value of Hebraic eschatology.

Christian theologians to-day are still in quest of a metaphysic which will do full justice to the Easter-gospel. But, in the light of the experience and thought of the centuries, they should be able to see rather more clearly than their forefathers what is the real heart of the problem.[1] So far as it concerns the destiny of the individual soul, the essence of the Easter-gospel consists in declaring in Christ the correlation between the completeness of the surrender of life to God and the completeness of its restoration in glory. By that great correlation or antinomy (whichever we like to call it) the Christian's hope of life eternal is determined. All that lives in this world must really die. But this fact of mortality may be made the opportunity for entering into the service and the self-surrender of the Son of God ; and, by so entering, this mortal personality of ours, and not any supposedly undying part of it, must at the last through death put on immortality. To be made partaker of Christ's life here and hereafter, as in heaven so on earth, is what the Christian means by life eternal. Only through Jesus Christ, yet through Jesus Christ in the commonest as well as in the holiest things, he claims to have fellowship with the eternal God. We dare not say how far on the other side of physical death a soul may have opportunity for completing a self-surrender which on this side it hardly seemed to have begun—just as we cannot say how far Christ's greatest saints had been received into the life of heaven even before in the body they crossed the narrow stream. But this much surely we know, that whenever, and not until, a man's surrender of himself to the God of love has been altogether accomplished, he attains the end of his being ; and that end is not death but life.

[1] The Christian metaphysician who seems to me to penetrate most deeply to the root of the matter is N. Berdyaev, *The Destiny of Man*, Pt. III, c. I.

PART IV

THE HOLY SPIRIT AND THE CHURCH

INTRODUCTION

THE CONSIDERATION of the doctrine of the Holy Spirit brings into the mind a multitude of the theological problems, very various from one another, yet all of them vitally important to Christian thought. Controversies about authority and freedom, dogma and experience, the ecclesiastical and personal aspects of religion, the relation of the Church to the world, and the distinction between the sacred and the secular, must all find their solution somewhere in the truth of which the doctrine of the Holy Spirit is the expression. Small wonder that it should be often said that the greatest need in the theology of our time is for a clear and comprehensive exposition of this doctrine. Yet neither perhaps is it any great wonder, if it is impossible to point to any single treatise on the subject which can satisfy our requirements. The Holy Spirit is the Lord, the giver of life. And the nature of all life, and therefore of its giver, can only be learned gradually by living. In its widest range, the doctrine of the Holy Spirit is nothing else than the doctrine of the manner and method of the presence and activity of the living God in his created world. And how can any knowledge of man discern or express clearly the being of him who is not even its object in the same sense that the incarnate Son is its object, but is himself the source of vital knowing and the light in which objects are truly known ? Here, then, the theologian is at a great and special disadvantage. He may be well content if he can help both himself and others to avoid false simplifications of doctrine and to enter a little more fully into the Spirit's fellowship.

I need hardly say that, in the brief sketch which is all that I can offer here, I shall not attempt even to touch on all the questions which require discussion. I shall seek only to draw out certain implications of scriptural teaching which the Christian needs specially to bear in mind as he confronts the confusions and perplexities of the modern world. And to two subjects I. shall give particular attention. The first is the relation within Christianity of religious to secular activities, and the second the doctrinal foundations on which rests the Christian conception of the nature and function of the Church as a society upon earth. The first suggests a problem specially urgent in an age which tends to regard religion as a special department in man's increasingly many-sided life, while misunderstandings and differences of view as to the second are a principal hindrance to that Christian reunion towards which the Holy Spirit to-day is surely directing our efforts. Perhaps also it will appear that the two subjects, in spite of their difference, are not unconnected. For each leads to the consideration of a special aspect or expression of the Spirit's unity.

CHAPTER XXV

THE RELATION OF THE NEW TESTAMENT TO THE OLD IN THE DOCTRINE OF THE SPIRIT

THE GREEK word translated " spirit " in the English New Testament is of course πνεῦμα, and the same word in the LXX represents " spirit " in the English versions. In classical Greek πνεῦμα means wind, air, or breath, most commonly the last. Occasionally it is used in a metaphorical sense, as we use the word " spirit " to-day, for a temper or state of mind. But it has no special connexion with anything divine or supernatural, nor is it set in opposition to matter. Classical Greek has no word corresponding in significance with what we mean by " spiritual ".

1. THE MEANING OF THE WORD " SPIRIT " IN THE OLD TESTAMENT [1]

In the Greek Bible, on the other hand, the word πνεῦμα has from the beginning different associations. In the LXX it is used to translate the Hebrew *ruach*. *Ruach* means originally wind ; but in the earliest documents of the Old Testament it means wind as the manifestation or sign of a mighty invasive power, not human but supernatural. Dr. Wheeler Robinson writes, " The primitive and fundamental idea of spirit (*ruach*) in the Old Testament is that of active power or energy (ἐνέργεια, not δύναμις), power superhuman, mysterious, elusive, of which the *ruach* or wind of the desert was not so much the symbol as the familiar example." [2] Originally, indeed, it was

---

[1] I am not myself a Hebrew scholar, and am indebted throughout this section to Dr. Wheeler Robinson's *The Christian Experience of the Holy Spirit*, pp. 8-14. See also the same author's *Religious Ideas of the Old Testament*.

[2] Wheeler Robinson, *op cit.*, p. 8.

the idea of power supernatural or dæmonic, rather than
strictly divine. Its operation was seen in all phenomena
in which men or creatures seemed to exceed their natural
powers, whether for good or evil. Its essential character
is perhaps best understood in the saying of Isaiah that the
horses of the Egyptians are flesh and not spirit.[1] *Ruach*
is responsible for the feats of judges, the inspiration of
prophets, the skill of Bezalel, the wisdom of Joseph, the
faithfulness of Caleb.[2] But it is also evil *ruach* that divides
Abimelech from the Shechemites, and makes a people
unfaithful to its God.[3] The only place where *ruach* is
quite clearly personified is in the story of Micaiah, where a
lying spirit is said to have deceived the optimistic prophets.[4]

When the Hebrew people attained to a clearly conceived monotheism, all supernatural powers were believed
to be under the sovereign control of Jehovah. *Ruach*
then comes to be thought of more definitely as the activity
of the one living righteous and merciful God. And, since
for the Hebrew God's presence always means God's activity,
the Spirit and the presence of God are in the later parts
of the Old Testament almost identified, whether the presence is thought of as universal or in particular relations.
Thus in the fifty-first Psalm the prayer, " cast me not
away from thy presence ", has as its parallel clause, " take
not thy Holy Spirit from me ". In the one hundred and
thirty-seventh we read, " Whither shall I go from thy
Spirit ? Or, whither shall I flee from thy face ? " In
one or two passages of the prophets the presence of God
with his people is understood to imply that his Spirit
dwells in their midst.

The Hebrew words for the breath and " breath-soul ",
which constitute the principle of life in man, are *neshamah*
and *nephesh*. There are one or two passages in the early
documents of the Hebrew Bible where the word *ruach*
is applied to purely human energy,[5] but even there it
means *energy*, and not soul. After the exile, when it had

[1] Isa. xxxi. 3.
[2] See Exod. xxxi. 3 ; Gen. xli. 38 ; Num. xiv. 24.
[3] See Judges ix. 23 ; Hos. iv. 12, and v. 4.
[4] 1 Kings xxii. 21.   [5] Judges xv. 19 ; 1 Kings x. 5.

become established doctrine that Jehovah was the creator
of man and had breathed into him the living soul, the
word *ruach* becomes to some extent synonymous with
nephesh, but it still conveys some suggestion of its old
associations with the supernatural.

2. PRINCIPAL POINTS IN THE OLD TESTAMENT DOCTRINE OF THE SPIRIT

Four points in the Old Testament conception of the
divine Spirit are specially important for our purpose.

(a) The Hebrew *ruach* is as far as the classical-Greek
πνεῦμα from suggesting our modern contrast between spirit
and matter. We have already noticed Isaiah's contrast
between " spirit " and " flesh " in reference to the Egyptian
horses. He implies not that, if the horses had been spirit,
they would not have been tangible and material, but that
in that case they would have been endowed with supernatural powers which in fact they lack.

(b) The original associations of the word *ruach* are with
a definitely supernatural energy, not with anything natural
or merely human.

(c) In connexion with God the word *ruach* always suggests energetic action rather than immanence. It represents an invasive, rather than a pervasive, power. Even
in Psalm cxxxix., where the omnipresence of God's Spirit
is clearly affirmed, the conception of it is different from
that which appears in the Hellenistic Book of Wisdom in
such sayings as " Thine incorruptible Spirit is in all things ",
and " The Spirit of the Lord hath filled the world." [1] The
psalmist is thinking of God's care and guidance of the soul
in all conceivable situations, not of a divine element within
the being of all creatures.

(d) While the word *ruach* has no definitely Messianic
associations, there are passages in the Old Testament which
prepare the way for them. Once or twice prophets speak
of God's Spirit as dwelling with or among the chosen
people to guide and direct them.[2] At an earlier point [3]

[1] Wisd. xii. 1 ; i. 7.
[2] Hag. ii. 4 *sq.* ; Isa. lxiii. 10 *sq.*   [3] See above, p. 85.

we noticed that the Bible often applies the same language
to the whole people of God that it does to the person of
the Messiah.   And in at least two passages of Isaiah [1] the
Spirit of the Lord is represented as resting upon an individual king or prophet in a special manner, which may
be said to invite Messianic interpretation.   Finally, there
is one most noteworthy passage where the Spirit is mentioned in an eschatological connexion, and it is promised
that God at the last will pour out of his Spirit upon all
flesh, and even upon the servants and handmaids among
his people.[2]

In conclusion, a few words may be added upon the use
of the adjective " holy " in connexion with " spirit " in
the Old Testament.   The expression " holy spirit " occurs
only thrice in the canonical books.[3]   Throughout the Old
Testament the word " holy " denotes primarily the awful
separateness which is characteristic of God and of the
things or persons which are set apart to belong to him
in a special way.   In connexion with " spirit " therefore,
it may be said to emphasize the essentially divine and
supernatural character of the spirit, and the separateness
of its activity from everything common or ordinary.

3.   CONTRAST OF THE NEW TESTAMENT WITH THE OLD

It is from Hebraic rather than from Hellenic sources
that New Testament writers derive their fundamental
conception of what the word $\pi\nu\varepsilon\tilde{\upsilon}\mu\alpha$ means.   So much,
in the light of modern scholarship, may be taken for
granted ; and later on we shall have occasion to notice
how the associations of the word *ruach* cling to early
Christian thought about God the Holy Spirit.   Nevertheless, the most striking characteristic of the New Testament
doctrine of the Spirit is one which sets it in contrast with
that of the Old.   In the Old Testament the Messianic connexions of the doctrine are dim and slight.   In the New
Testament, on the other hand, it is broadly true to say
that there is no teaching about the Spirit of God except

---

[1] xii. 1 *sq.* ; lxi. 1.   [2] Joel ii. 28 *sq.*
[3] Ps. li. 11 ; Isa. lxiii. 10, 11.

in direct connexion with the life and work of the Messiah Jesus. The suggestion of the omnipresence of the Spirit which we find in Psalm cxxxix., to say nothing of the Book of Wisdom, has no parallel in the New Testament. It is only in connexion with the Logos, as in the Prologue of St. John's Gospel, that universal presence and activity are there spoken of. The Holy Spirit is mentioned only in three connexions ; first, as the Spirit who brought about the conception of Jesus, and at his baptism descended and thereafter abode upon him ; secondly, as the inspirer of the prophets who foretold his sufferings and triumph as the Messiah ; thirdly. as the guide, teacher and source of power in the fellowship of the Church and in its individual members.

It is this apparent limitation of the Spirit's activity which is the cause of such grave difficulty to the liberal-minded Christians of modern times ; and it may have seemed hardly less unreasonable to intelligent Jews and pagans of the first century. But at least nothing bears clearer witness to the profound and entirely unique impression produced by the life, death and resurrection of Jesus upon those who first believed in him. And we shall best understand the true significance of the New Testament doctrine of the Spirit, by examining more closely its relation to the person and work of Jesus in the thought of the two great theological apostles, St. Paul and St. John. It is only in the light of their thought that the fragmentary indications of the Synoptic Gospels, and the rather naïf affirmations of Acts, become intelligible.

CHAPTER XXVI

THE HOLY SPIRIT IN ST. PAUL'S THEOLOGY

1. ST. PAUL'S PHILOSOPHY OF HISTORY

To ST. Paul the outpouring of the Spirit in the Christian community through the resurrection of Jesus Christ is a great fact which takes its place in the philosophy of history which is unfolded in Romans.[1] St. Paul thinks of history as the story of the operation of God's purpose to redeem and save fallen mankind in Jesus Christ. From the first God's method is the choosing or calling out of certain individuals and their descendants to hold a special place of trust in preparing the way for the salvation which is to come when the time is ripe. Pre-Christian history is the record of repeated restrictions in the number of the elect by the rejection (whether due to their own fault or not) of many of those who at first sight seemed to have been chosen. Originally the promise is given to Abraham that in his seed all nations shall be blessed. The choice of Abraham and his seed implies the present rejection of the Gentiles; yet the promise looks forward to their ultimate salvation. Next, the successive rejections of Ishmael and of Esau make it clear that only some even of Abraham's descendants are to constitute the chosen people. Afterwards, in the period of the prophets, it appears that even among the children of Israel the majority is rejected, and only a faithful remnant left to carry on the true succession. Finally, even the faithful remnant is reduced to but one man, Jesus, who is the promised Saviour. Thus all fail and fall under condemnation. Jesus alone, the Son of God who was born of

---

[1] I must acknowledge my indebtedness in this paragraph to Dodd's Commentary on Romans (Moffatt Series).

Abraham's seed according to the flesh, is perfectly obedient to God's will even unto the death of the cross. And in him and through him God's original promise of blessing to all the nations is now being fulfilled. By his resurrection Jesus has become the head of a new redeemed humanity and people of God, who in him receive the promises, and are destined to bring blessing and salvation to the whole human race previously rejected for its sin. The history of God's dealings with men, which up to Christ's coming had been mainly a story of successive rejections and exclusions is now to become a story of successive inclusions and incorporations through the preaching of the gospel. There is still a process of divine selection. But now it is seen to be a selection mainly towards equal acceptance and salvation, and not towards equal rejection and condemnation.

Such is the theological interpretation of history which in St. Paul's mind formed the *rationale* of his missionary labours. And bound up with it is his whole conception of the gifts and work of the Holy Spirit. " The Holy Spirit " meant to him primarily the active principle and power of that supernatural order which will be fully revealed and expressed at the last day when all things will be transfigured into conformity with it in the world to come. By the resurrection of Christ manhood in him has already entered into that order. This is the beginning of the fulfilment of God's promise to man. Its immediate effect is a wholly new outpouring of spiritual life and power among the believers who constitute the new redeemed mankind, the head and representative of which is Christ. Through this power of the Spirit flowing from the risen Christ, the spiritual world, the world to come, is in one way already present. " We have," says St. Paul, " the first-fruits of the Spirit." [1] But on the other hand, as regards their bodies at least, Christians are still in that flesh which belongs to the natural, unredeemed, unspiritual world. *That* flesh Christ has left behind ; Christians as yet have not. Therefore their resurrection is still only partial at best. They wait in hope for the fullness of

[1] Rom. viii. 23.

spiritual transformation. Meanwhile the manifestation of
the Spirit in the Church marks the fact that God's purpose
has reached the penultimate stage of its fulfilment. The
gospel of God's grace in Jesus Christ is carrying with it
round the world the present advent of that new life in the
Spirit, into which God's forgiveness now freely incorporates
those who under his righteous law had previously been
condemned.

2. THE RELATION OF THE SPIRIT TO THE GLORIFIED CHRIST

It is against a background of such ideas, Jewish in origin
yet transformed by Christianity, that St. Paul's theology
of the Spirit is to be viewed. I cannot think that it is of
very great importance to settle the vexed question whether
St. Paul thought of the Holy Spirit as a divine being
personally distinct from Christ. On the whole, it is probably truer to say that he did than that he did not. St.
Paul often uses language which personifies the Spirit;
and, although the presence of Christ and the presence of
God's or Christ's Spirit in believers seem to be for him
practically synonymous and interchangeable expressions,
he yet avoids any actual identification of the Spirit with
Christ. There is indeed one passage where this identification appears to be explicitly made; but its obscurity
and the uncertainty of the text make it a very unsafe
foundation on which to build any interpretation of St.
Paul's thought.[1]

The truth is that the questions which agitated later
theology in its endeavour to define the relation of the
Spirit to the glorified Christ do not seem to have interested
St. Paul. What matters to him is that, since in Christ's
resurrection man has been recreated and raised into the
fully spiritual order of the new world, the Spirit of God
has now begun to exercise in the society of the redeemed
that new immanence and transforming power which will
finally be manifest in the whole universe. The Spirit

---

[1] 2 Cor. iii. 17, on which see commentators. Hort's conjectural
emendation, οὗ δὲ τὸ πνεῦμα κύριον, is extremely probable.

brings to men the powers and gifts of the new world into which Christ's manhood has been raised. At present, it is true, man's body and, as I think St. Paul would have added, his natural soul (ψυχή) also are still fleshly, and belong to this present unspiritual world. But there is also in man's nature a spiritual element, a πνεῦμα, which it retains from its creation by God, although in unredeemed man this spiritual element is overpowered by the flesh. As man's spirit by faith responds to the call of the gospel, the Spirit of God takes hold of it in the power of the new creation, so that the man is now enabled to live *after* the spirit, even though he still has to live also *in* the flesh, as long and in so far as he is in this world. In the end will come to pass " the redemption of the body " also, i.e., its complete spiritualization, " which means our full sonship ".[1] Meanwhile, to live in Christ is to live in and according to the Spirit ; [2] the body of which the believer is a member being Christ's, and the Holy Spirit being the animating power which unites the body and all its members to Christ whose body it is.

3. THE KOINONIA OF THE SPIRIT

So far we have been dealing mainly with the meaning of the term " the Spirit " in St. Paul's theology. But perhaps his most important teaching is concerned with the concrete nature and content of the Spirit's work in the Christian society. In what definable way does the life of that society differ from that of the old Israel, and reveal its newness because of its possession of " the first-fruits of the Spirit " ?

The answer to that question is, I believe, essentially contained in St. Paul's great phrase, ἡ κοινωνία τοῦ ἁγίου Πνεύματος, the communion of the Holy Spirit. The phrase may be translated in various ways, and more than one meaning may well have had a place in St. Paul's thoughts. But at least the idea of a common sharing in the Holy

---

[1] Rom. viii. 23 (Moffatt's translation).

[2] Strictly to preserve St. Paul's thought, I should perhaps write " in the Spirit and according to the spirit ".

Spirit is not to be excluded ; and it is that idea which supplies the answer to our present question.

In the Old Testament the Spirit of God is usually thought of as a power coming suddenly upon men and leaving them again. Sometimes it is suggested that the Spirit remains more permanently with an individual leader ; and, as we have seen, one or two passages in the prophets indicate a continuous dwelling of God's Spirit among his holy people.[1] The nearest approach to the thought of a common sharing in God's Spirit is to be found in the eschatological prophecy of Joel already referred to, which we find quoted in Acts as having begun to have its fulfilment at Pentecost.[2] It is indeed a striking fact that the early Church should thus have found the fulfilment of this prophecy in its own life. But to St. Paul the idea of the koinonia of the Spirit means something more profoundly new even than the appearance of abnormal gifts among the humble rank and file, " the servants and the handmaids ", of God's people. St. Paul's central thought seems to be that the new presence and power of the Holy Spirit constitute the very life of the Christian society as a corporate whole.

Modern scholars suggest that the use of the word " body " (*corpus*, σῶμα) to denote a society or " body corporate " is originally derived from St. Paul's conception of the Church as the Body of Christ.[3] Be that as it may, St. Paul certainly does think of the Christian ecclesia as really constituting a body, and as such living with a single life which is the gift of the Spirit. It is significant that nowhere in the New Testament, except in a single text of St. Luke's Gospel,[4] is it suggested that Christians ought to pray *for* the Spirit. It is assumed that Christians have the Spirit (by his aid they pray), and the receiving of that gift is essential to membership of the Church. From Acts we should gather that the laying-on of hands, by which the gift was normally imparted, was accompanied by some

---

[1] See above, p. 276.   [2] Acts ii. 17 ; Joel ii. 28.

[3] See Dr. A. E. J. Rawlinson's essay, " *Corpus Christi* ", in *Mysterium Christi*.

[4] Luke xi. 13. Matthew's version of the saying (vii. 11) contains no reference to the Holy Spirit.

distinct experience or phenomenon which made the fact
of the reception unmistakable. But to St. Paul the
koinonia of the Holy Spirit means something more, and
something other, than the reception of a particular and
immediately recognizable gift by each individual Christian.
It means, as can be seen from a study of 1 Corinthians xii.
and xiii., that the Spirit permeates the whole body or
organism which is the Christian society, so that all endow-
ments, offices and functions which are useful in the life
of the community, and not only those which seem in
themselves to be supernatural, are lifted to a new and
higher status because they are to be traced to the same
Holy Spirit as their source and to be exercised by his
power. Every member in a body, even the least " comely "
or conspicuous, must live with the same life ; and in the
Christian body that life is wholly the gift or the presence
of the Spirit himself. It is manifested, not only in the
apparently supernatural, but also in raising the apparently
natural and commonplace to a new spirituality and dignity,
because what is natural and commonplace also has its
necessary and appointed place in the whole body of Christ,
who is the head of the new humanity.

Moreover, having in 1 Corinthians xii. emphasized the
diversity of gifts which the one Spirit bestows, St. Paul
proceeds in the next chapter to speak of " the more excellent way " of love. He does not say that love is one, even
the highest, among the Spirit's gifts. Rather it is the
universal accompaniment of all, apart from which none
can be truly spiritual. For it is love, and love alone,
which makes each spiritual gift to be, not a mark of some
special superiority or privilege in its possessor, but a contribution which the individual supplies to the common
life of all. Thus it is love which makes possible a true
koinonia of the Holy Spirit, because it makes the results
of his special gifts to be common property for the good of
all. Therefore, whatever of the Spirit's gifts may prove
to be temporary or variable, love must endure the same.
And, because it is the very spirit of community itself, it
will be less transformed in its final fulfilment even than
faith and hope. Therefore it is greater than they.

Finally, it is because the koinonia of the Holy Spirit is to him the essential characteristic of the Church's new life, that St. Paul, especially in Colossians, so strenuously resists the gnostic type of heresy which would have divided Christians into two classes, the one of *illuminati* or really spiritual mystics, and the other of still carnally minded believers who could only be taught the truth in parables and made to obey ceremonial rules. To admit a double standard in Christian faith or conduct seemed to St. Paul a fundamental contradiction of the gospel. The common possession of the Spirit made all Christians equal. But this equality did not, in St. Paul's mind, invalidate the principle of authority in the Church, whereby some were divinely appointed to rule over others. For the same Spirit who set apart some to rule and teach sanctified others in learning and obedience, while all together learned and obeyed in Christ.

4. KOINONIA AND HOLINESS

We have spoken of what St. Paul meant by communion in the Spirit of God. But we have not yet penetrated to the paradox which lies in the fact that the Spirit, whose presence and gifts are thus *commonly* shared, is and remains *holy*. The paradox is fundamental in Christian thought and life, whether or not St. Paul was himself fully aware of it.

Just as in English the words " communion " and " common " are cognate, so in Greek the word κοινωνία is allied to κοινός, which means " common " or " unclean ", the very opposite of ἅγιος, " holy ".[1] And the connexion is not purely verbal, but has a basis in ideas. In the Old Testament the notion of the holiness which is the essential characteristic of God excludes the notion of a common sharing. The holiness of God means his awful, mysterious separateness. The holiness of God's chosen people meant that they were separated and set apart from all the nations. The holiness of the inner shrine in the Temple meant that

---

[1] Cf. Jer. xxxi. 5 (R.V. with margin) for the double meaning of the Hebrew verb translated " enjoy (as common) " or " profane ".

it might not be entered by all and sundry even of the holy
people, but only by the high-priest once a year.   But
a careful study of Biblical theology shows that, with the
gift of the Holy Spirit to the Church, the whole connotation
of the term " holiness " has undergone a subtle but far-
reaching change.   The characteristic of the Christian
society is common participation in the Holy Spirit.   Thus
within the Church the fencing off of the inner shrine has
disappeared.   And this change, which so profoundly affects
the relations of God's chosen people to one another and to
God, affects also their relation to the world outside.   For
the holy people no longer in principle excludes the Gentiles,
or no longer only suffers them to enter if they first become
Jews by circumcision.   It is a company in which all, Jew
and Gentile, bond and free, Greek and barbarian, are to
stand on a common and equal footing, first as alike sinners,
and then as redeemed members of Christ's body to which
the Spirit gives its common life.   It is on this conviction
that St. Paul's conception of the catholic mission of the
Church depends.

   With this thought in mind we can perhaps interpret
more widely the Pauline philosophy of history which we
have already described.   Christ's resurrection followed by
the gift of the Spirit is the great turning-point in God's
historical dealings with men.   At this point, as it were,
the movement of holiness changes its direction.   Before,
it was a movement away from the common world towards
the awful separateness of God.   God's Spirit came upon
certain men chiefly to separate them from others, and
though he gave them a message to other men foretelling
future redemption, the message in the immediate present
was mainly one of condemnation.   This movement of
holiness is typified by the fact that in the Old Testament
the centre of religious interest is in journeyings towards
Jerusalem, and the establishment of the holy people with
their separate worship in that holy and separate place.
But after Pentecost all is changed.   The earthly Jerusalem,
which was before the centre of religious attraction, now
becomes a centre of diffusion or a base of operations, which
is soon left behind for good.   Missionary journeys into the

Gentile world take the place of pilgrimages towards the holy place where God has caused his name to dwell. The representatives of the twelve holy tribes have become twelve apostles sent out with a gospel to mankind. The movement of holiness has become a movement from God through his apostolic Church out into the common world. That is the difference which Pentecost has made.

And what was the cause of Pentecost? The New Testament teaches us to find it in the incarnation. The changed direction of the movement of holiness has its origin in the fact that in Jesus Christ the holy God took upon him the common flesh of the sons of Adam. God the Son himself came forth, as it were, from his separate heavenly shrine into the common world to tabernacle among men, and to suffer with them and for them. From that act of divine love the new koinonia of the Holy Spirit is ultimately derived.

CHAPTER XXVII

ST. JOHN'S DOCTRINE OF THE SPIRIT

IN ALL essentials the identity between St. Paul's and St. John's teaching about the Holy Spirit is remarkable, the more so because the language which each apostle uses to express it is so distinctly characteristic of himself.

1. THE AGREEMENT BETWEEN ST. JOHN AND ST. PAUL

Corresponding with St. Paul's suggestion that God's election was at last narrowed down to the one person Jesus Christ who entered a universally sinful world to become the head of a new spiritual humanity, we have the teaching of St. John's Gospel that before the crucifixion the Holy Spirit abode upon Jesus alone, and that it was only after the resurrection that the Holy Spirit was given to the apostles. Both St. Paul and St. John agree in assuming that all true Christians have the Spirit as Christ's gift ; both teach that the Spirit is the living means of communion with the risen Lord, that the gift of the Spirit implies the present indwelling of Christ, while yet the Spirit is in some measure personally distinct from Christ, and that the most essential mark of spiritual communion with Christ is love rather than more apparently supernatural phenomena—of which latter indeed St. John makes no direct mention. All this unanimity is indeed striking. And Bishop Gore has asked whether some such teaching of Jesus about the Spirit as is recorded in the fourteenth and fifteenth chapters of St. John's Gospel must not have been already current in the Church when St. Paul wrote.[1]

One very familiar passage in St. John's Gospel requires a special mention at this point, because it is often taken to

---

[1] *The Holy Spirit and the Church,* p. 113 *sq.*

imply the universal presence or immanence of the Spirit in all sincere seekers after God—a notion which, whatever its truth, is, as we have already seen, quite foreign to the pneumatology of the Bible as a whole. "The hour cometh and now is, when the true worshippers shall worship the Father in spirit and truth; for such doth the Father seek to be his worshippers. God is spirit; and they who worship him must worship in spirit and truth."[1] Preachers on this text often seem to forget two points which are essential for its correct interpretation. Jesus is clearly speaking of a time to come in the immediate future when true worship will be possible in a way in which it has never been possible before. The new possibility will come with the gift of the Spirit, a gift, which as St. John's Gospel clearly teaches, was not bestowed until Jesus had been glorified on the cross, and was then bestowed only on those who had believed on Jesus. Again, just as "spirit" here means a divine gift of the crucified and risen Christ, and not an attitude of the human heart or mind, so "truth" (as always in St. John) means the divine, transcendent, and Christ-revealed reality, and not human sincerity of intention. *God* is spirit, and *God* is truth. It is only those who are in God who can fully worship God; and only those are in God who come to him through Jesus Christ, and receive thereby the power to be his sons. These will soon worship the Father in spirit and truth in every place to which the gospel spreads. But neither the Temple at Jerusalem nor the holy mountain of the Samaritans will remain centres of God's worship. The Samaritans worship blindly. The Jews have a knowledge of the true God; but they will soon seal their rejection of him whom God has sent to them. Therefore, although salvation starts from the Jews, it will not remain with them.

The main point, then, of this discourse is, in St. John's mind, not the delocalization of worship (though this is implied), but its coming transformation and spiritualization through the gift of the Paraclete who will establish Christian believers in a relation of sonship towards God. The

[1] John iv. 23 *sq.* See also the two preceding verses.

whole thought is thoroughly in accord with St. Paul's interpretation of history, although the language in which it is expressed is not Pauline.

2. THE PARACLETE AS INTERPRETER OF THE INCARNATION

There are however important points at which St. John's doctrine of the Holy Spirit differs in emphasis from that of St. Paul. These correspond to the different points of view from which the two apostles regard the incarnation. The first concerns the work of the Holy Spirit in interpreting the incarnate life of Christ.

Early Christian apologists were constrained to account for the fact that, although Jesus Christ was not only the Messiah but actually the divine Lord of the Church's worship, the truth of his person and mission had not been recognized until after his death. In the third century Celsus could still use the taunt against Christians that their Jesus during his lifetime has not been able to persuade even his own disciples. In St. Paul and St. John, respectively, we can trace clear indications of the two ways of dealing with this difficulty which Christian theology must always employ.

To St. Paul, as we have already seen, the earthly life of Jesus was in itself a veiling, rather than a revealing, of the Godhead.[1] The revelation proper begins with the resurrection, when Christ is known " after the spirit " and no longer " after the flesh ". During the earthly life the divinity was concealed, because the divine glory had been put off in that unimaginable act of loving self-humiliation whereby he who was before " in the form of God " took upon him " the form of a servant ". This is the line of thought which is carried to extremities in Kierkegaard's doctrine of " the divine incognito ".

St. John suggests a different way of expressing the truth. To him, Jesus the incarnate Logos was already in his earthly life the full revelation of the Godhead. He who had seen him had seen the Father. Yet the meaning of the revelation could not be grasped in any full way until

[1] See above, p. 95.

290 ST. JOHN'S DOCTRINE OF THE SPIRIT [PT. IV.

the Paraclete had come to enable those who had already believed on Jesus to know him truly. And this gift of the Spirit could not be bestowed until Jesus had been glorified on the cross and gone back to the Father. Not until then could the disciples be in Christ and he in them, as all along Christ had been in the Father and the Father in him.

But, according to St. John, now that the Spirit is given, his work is to enable the Christian with the spiritual eye to see God not only in Jesus exalted to heaven but also in Jesus as he lived in Palestine under Herod and Pilate. That is why St. John wrote his " spiritual Gospel ".[1] The earthly life of Jesus is not to St. John, as apparently it was to St. Paul, a necessary stage in God's redemptive work which has now been left behind ; it remains for ever that which has revealed, and still reveals, the eternal Word of God to men. Jesus is not changed even by his resurrection ; he is but withdrawn from outward sight, so that the Spirit may enable believers to know him better as he both was and is.

Thus it comes about that St. John emphasizes more than St. Paul the personal distinction of the Holy Spirit from Christ. To St. John he is definitely "another comforter ", ἀλλὸς παρακλητός. For it needs another helper, sent by Christ and as divine as himself, to enable the human soul truly to apprehend Christ as God and Friend. To St. John the Christ of the flesh has not passed into the Christ of the Spirit, as St. Paul's language might sometimes seem to suggest : rather, it is the Spirit, another than Christ, who enables the believer, in contemplating the past facts of the visible outward incarnation, to realize the abiding presence of the incarnate.

3. THE SPIRIT, THE CHURCH, AND THE WORLD

Another contrast which the student of the New Testament cannot but feel between St. Paul's and St. John's theology of the Spirit, lies in the absence in St. John of that note of missionary urgency which is so characteristic

---

[1] The purpose here attributed to St. John accounts for many of his alterations in detail of St. Mark's narrative.

of St. Paul.   The absence of this note in St. John is clearly
connected with his comparative disregard of time and lack
of interest in the future.[1]   Not a word is said in the
Johannine books about any duty of Christian love towards
those who are outside the Christian brotherhood.   " The
whole world " is painted in the blackest colours as " lying
in the evil one ".   Christians are forbidden to love it,[2]
and even in the great high-priestly prayer of the seven-
teenth chapter of the Gospel, Christ himself excludes the
world from the scope of his petitions, and prays only for
those whom God has given him out of the world.   As to
any work of the Holy Spirit outside the Church neither
St. John nor St. Paul gives any hint whatever.

Yet this apparent restriction of the love which is spiritual
life only represents one side of the Johannine picture.
It is St. John who wrote, " God so loved the world . . ."
In the next verse we read that " God sent not his Son
into the world to judge the world, but that the world
through him might be saved ".   This affirmation is repeated in the solemn discourse which concludes and sums
up Christ's public teaching, and it is reiterated in the
First Epistle.   Again, in the Gospel Christ declares, " I, if
I be lifted up, will draw all men unto me ", and " I give my
flesh for the life of the world." [3]

We cannot escape the contradiction.   We may solve it
practically, as St. Paul solved it, by trusting to God's work
in time.   We may think of the Church as a small body
chosen out of the world, yet destined somehow to include
it.   We may think of God's love focused or concentrated,
as it were, at particular points, so that its power from
those points of concentration may operate the more
widely and effectively.   But St. John does not think in
these temporal and practical terms.   He states the contradiction flatly, saying that the world is what God loves
and sent Christ to save, and yet that Christians must not
love it, that Christ at the last did not pray for it, and that
he saves his loved ones from it.

[1] See above, pp. 103 *sq.*   [2] 1 John v. 19 and ii. 15.
[3] John iii. 16 *sq.* ;   xii. 47 ;   1 John iv. 14 ;   John xii. 32 ;   vi. 51.
Cf. also 1 John ii. 2.

The only positive suggestion which St. John makes about
the missionary activity of Christ's Church is that it is an
activity of attraction. The light of grace and truth
shining from Christ through his Church into the world
draws men to itself; and those especially who " do the
truth " will come to it. But the parable of the shepherd
going out to seek the lost is not Johannine; and St.
John gives little hint of that great change of direction in
the movement of holiness, which we found to be indicated
in St. Paul's interpretation of history. The truth is that
St. John is not interested in the *movement* of history at
all. Or rather, perhaps, we should say that for him the
incarnation has manifested once for all the whole meaning
and end of that movement. It is the Spirit's work, not to
complete or change the movement, but to interpret the
already given revelation of its meaning and end.

4. THE SPIRIT AND THE FLESH

But it would be a great mistake to suppose that, because
St. John shows such a strong tendency to view history
sub specie aeternitatis, he is really any nearer in his thought
than St. Paul either to Platonic or to Cartesian idealism.
To him the word πνεῦμα is still primarily a translation of
ruach, that mysterious supernatural energy, the conception of which was derived from the desert-wind. And
to him the fact that the Spirit abode upon Jesus in the
flesh is not less important than the fact that the Spirit
was imparted only after Jesus had been raised from the
dead.

St. John's use of the term " the flesh ", though from a
certain point of view it is more ambiguous than St. Paul's,
nevertheless avoids a difficulty which must have confronted St. Paul, if he had worked out more fully his
doctrine of the incarnation. St. Paul uses the term to
denote " unredeemed human nature ", usually with a
suggestion of its hostility to " the spirit ". Because " the
flesh " suggests to St. Paul something inherently sinful,
he does not speak categorically of Christ having come in
the flesh, but uses a phrase such as " in the likeness of

sinful flesh ". Clearly St. Paul has no intention of conveying any docetic suggestion, that our Lord's material flesh was unreal or not fully natural and human ; but, owing to his own habitual use of terms, he cannot speak simply of Jesus coming in the flesh without seeming to imply some sinful element in him. And there is here a real difficulty for the Pauline metaphysic, with which St. Paul never directly deals. For according to him the flesh in which Jesus lived his earthly life was free from taint of sin, and yet it was the flesh of this world and not of the world to come. St. John, on the other hand, though he does use the term " the flesh " to denote unredeemed nature, or nature unquickened by the Spirit, nevertheless never speaks of it as being in itself sinful, and therefore he has no difficulty in laying the greatest emphasis on the unqualified statement that Jesus came in the flesh.

At this point the discourse to Nicodemus [1] is of crucial importance for understanding St. John's doctrine. " The spirit (or wind) bloweth where it listeth, and thou hearest the sound thereof, but canst not tell whence it cometh or whither it goeth. So is everyone that is born of the Spirit." As commentators point out, the saying, in its context of teaching about spiritual re-birth, is strikingly reminiscent of the words of Ecclesiastes, " As thou knowest not what is the way of the spirit (or wind), nor how the bones do grow in the womb of her that is with child, even so thou knowest not the work of God." [2] Just before Jesus has said to Nicodemus, " That which is born of the flesh is flesh, and that which is born of the Spirit is spirit."

Now, whether St. John did or did not believe in the fact of the Virgin Birth, he must unquestionably have believed that Jesus was born of the Spirit. But equally certainly he did not believe that, while the Lord's spiritual personality was born wholly of the Spirit, his natural body was born simply of the flesh. To St. John no such dichotomy was conceivable. To him everything was spirit which comes from the Spirit and moves with Spirit-given life ; and this description might apply to material as well as to immaterial things. " The flesh " when

[1] John iii.   [2] Eccles. xi. 5.

contrasted with " the spirit " is just nature as yet unquickened by the supernatural *ruach* of God. As the
instrument or expression of " spirit ", " flesh " may or
may not be what we should call " material ". According
to St. John Christ's body before the resurrection was
certainly material. In the post-resurrection appearances
he seems to suggest that it might reassume on occasion
the characteristics of materiality. In the discourse in
which Christ speaks of his flesh as the heavenly bread,
what is meant by " the flesh " is certainly something
immaterial, except in so far as the eucharistic element may
possibly be referred to.

Christ's words to Nicodemus, therefore, as understood
by St. John, mean that his whole life on earth, because it
was Spirit-born and Spirit-led, was wholly mysterious in
its origin, movement and goal to those whom the same
Spirit had not quickened. That is why Christ is so completely misunderstood by the Jews, only somewhat less
completely by Nicodemus, and even misunderstood to a
great extent by the believing disciples. " Ye know not
whence I come, nor whither I go," says our Lord to the
Jews ; and even when he speaks differently to his disciples
just before his passion, he receives the reply from one of
them, " Lord, we know not whither thou goest, and how
know we the way ? " [1] But with the gift of the Spirit
the illumination of the disciples' minds begins. The
meaning of sayings, obscure when they were first uttered,
is understood afterwards by the Spirit's help. And by
the same help the disciples recognize Jesus " come in the
flesh " to be not only the Messiah of the Jews but the
eternal " Word ", and " God only-begotten ".[2] Thus the
Spirit-born life of Jesus, which to the natural man re-
sembles only the force of an aimless wind blowing he
knows not whence or whither, appears to a man caught
up into its movement by the same Spirit, not as a wind,
but rather as a steady light shining in a dark world, a
light which the darkness could not overtake or over-
power, because it shines from the eternal reality.

[1] Cf. John viii. 14 with John xiv. 4, 5.
[2] Almost certainly the right text in John i. 18.

Nevertheless the light is still Jesus *come in the flesh.* To that truth the true Spirit is witness, and no spirit which does not confess it is of God.[1] Thus St. John rejects all gnostic heresy. And the truth implies that fellowship with Christ is to be found not so much in mystical experiences as in the acts of righteousness and, above all, of brotherly love in which the disciples obey their Lord's command.

[1] 1 John iv. 2, 3.

CHAPTER XXVIII

THE DOCTRINE OF THE SPIRIT
IN THE MODERN WORLD

IN MODERN times the expressions " the religion of the
spirit " and " spiritual religion " have usually been
connected with one or both of two general ideas.[1]

1. MODERN CONCEPTIONS OF THE RELIGION OF THE SPIRIT

The first is the idea of a general movement in human
life towards the realization of other and higher values than
the biological values which may be denoted by such
phrases as " the survival of the species or race " or " the
control of physical environment ". Philosophy, art, and
morals, the quest of truth, beauty, and goodness, are in
some sense universal activities among men. And these are
felt to be in a special sense activities of the spirit, lifting
man above immediate interaction with physical environment into a realm where he seeks to realize something of
eternal worth. Moreover, the comparative study of
religions has shown that these activities of the spirit are
almost inseparable from notions about God or a divine
being, which take very various forms and yet seem to
show at least a certain unity of movement or appetition in
man's soul towards a life higher in kind than that of his
physical nature. From this point of view, then, the
phrase " religion of the spirit " may denote all man's
effort after the higher life through any and all of his
spiritual activities, with whatever theological doctrines or
beliefs these may happen to have been associated.

Those who take such " a religion of the spirit " to be the
true religion of mankind cannot accept any exclusive claim

[1] In this section I have tried to develop thoughts suggested
by Bishop Gore, *The Holy Spirit and the Church*, pp. 1-7.

made on behalf of any one religion to present any unique
or final revelation.   To them every creed expresses more
or less imperfectly some partial aspect of truth, and every
sage or saint or creative artist some partial aspect of the
Spirit's life.   Jesus may indeed hold the first place among
the religious geniuses of the world.   But to speak of Jesus
Christ as " the one name given under heaven whereby we
must be saved ", or to think of him as the only-begotten
Son of God is to confine the spirit's activity in a quite
unjustifiable way.   Christians, it is suggested, should
abandon their exclusive and intolerant attitude, and be
content to join on an equal footing with the adherents of
other creeds in the common search after the fuller truth
and the higher life.

There are however many to whom the expression " the
religion of the spirit " conveys a rather different idea or
set of ideas.   To them it speaks not so much of a universal
movement in human nature as of a universal opposition
in religion between the inward and the outward, the
spiritual experience and the ritual form.   Among those
who make much of this opposition are many who would
quite clearly make for Christianity an exclusive and para-
mount claim such as is rejected by those who see in Christianity only one example among many of a universal
movement of the human spirit.   The opposition between
inward and outward, between the freedom of personal
religion and the authority of ecclesiastical forms and
rules, constitutes the very *raison d'être* of certain Christian
Churches or denominations, such as the Society of Friends.
But many also, who understand the expression " religion
of the spirit " in essentially the same way, are but loosely
attached to any form of what is known as " organized
religion ", and some would not call themselves " Christians " at all.

We have then here two distinct objections which are
brought against the main tradition of Christian orthodoxy
in the name of " the religion of the spirit ".   The first,
brought forward by those whom we may call " imman-
entists ", accuses orthodoxy of seeking to *limit* a divine
activity and self-revelation which are present everywhere

in the spiritual effort and quest of man. The second, brought forward by those whom we may call " anti-formalists ", accuses orthodoxy of seeking to *mechanize* a divine activity which is essentially living, free, and personal. No doubt the two objections are often found to coalesce, or to be confused, with one another. But the distinction between them is important. The first has a pantheistic tendency by no means generally characteristic of the second, which is associated rather with individualism. Moreover, immanentism readily allies itself with doctrines of evolutionary progress, and is by no means indifferent to the general movement of history—it has been much influenced by the philosophy of Hegel. On the other hand, anti-formalism, being in the main individualistic, has no similar interest in history. To it, Christianity means following the teaching of Jesus as interpreted by itself ; and to that interpretation the Old Testament is mainly an embarrassment. In this sense anti-formalism may be said to be radically unhistorical.

Finally, we must notice a third way of understanding the phrase " spiritual religion ", a way which has arisen within the tradition of Christian orthodoxy itself. This way is especially characteristic of the piety developed by the Counter-Reformation in the Church of Rome. But it has its counterpart in the reformed Churches, and its special features have been accentuated by the modern tendency to regard human life and activity as consisting of a number of autonomous, separate, and more or less independent departments, of which religion is one. The kind of piety of which I am now speaking seeks to train and develop " the spiritual life " as something in principle quite separate from all secular or " worldly " activities. It does not at all disparage the outward forms and ceremonies of religion—rather it emphasizes their importance. But it uses them mainly in order to strengthen and cultivate a purely religious or spiritual experience, which exists as something complete in itself over against all man's natural and human relationships towards his fellows. It tends to think of communion with God, when the phrase is used in the strict and proper sense, as being confined to this devotional experience, and not as something to be realized *in* all the relationships of human living. No doubt those who thus think of the spiritual life are generally eager to maintain that it cannot flourish apart from Christian conduct in natural relationships, and that the Christian vocation of many is in secular affairs. But they suggest that, since such relationships and affairs belong to this world, what is done in them can influence the spiritual life of devotion only from outside, however beneficial and indispensable the influence may be, whereas in the devotional life alone are we permitted to enter the divine communion which is the true and other-worldly end of human living. This doctrine is in extreme opposition to the tendency of more secularly minded Christians to regard religion mainly as a means of helping men to do their duty in their ordinary avocations. And it thus creates a special kind of antithesis between religion and morality, the supernatural and the natural, the life of the spirit and the life of the world, which seems to demand a more attentive consideration from Christian theologians than it has so far received.

2. THE CHALLENGE TO ORTHODOX THEOLOGY

Thus in many different ways modern conceptions of spiritual life and spiritual religion offer a challenge to the Church's doctrine of the Holy Spirit. And it is a challenge which traditional expositions of that doctrine hardly enable us to meet. When we survey the history of the Church's theology, we find that the doctrine of the Holy Spirit, when compared with Christology, plays on the whole a minor and, in regard to the questions we are now asking, a not very illuminating part. In patristic times discussions of the doctrine seem to have been largely concerned with attempts to define the dogma of the Trinity, which lead us into a region where all human thought is baffled, as indeed the Fathers themselves were well aware. Later on, at any rate in the West, the doctrine tended to become identified with theories of ecclesiastical order and authority, which to those who reject the dogma of

infallibility cannot appear, whatever their value, to do justice to the truth concerning the Holy Spirit's guidance of
the Church.   The special application of the doctrine to the
inspiration of Scripture raises questions with which we
need not here concern ourselves—except to say that in no
connexion is it more obvious that views, once universally
held and authoritative, have had to be revised.   And,
finally, we cannot forget melancholy records of religious
movements which seemed to manifest the Spirit's operation, and yet were crushed into insignificance or driven
into heresy or schism, because an ecclesiastical system
left no room for the exercise of their gifts.

It is indeed difficult to deny that the perplexing nature
of the problems which confront Christian theology to-day
is due in no small measure to the long-continued failure of
orthodoxy to give adequate expression in thought and
action to that doctrine of the Holy Spirit which it has all
along acknowledged to be one of the chief articles in its
creed.   It may be that one of the chief tasks of the theologian to-day is to go back to the New Testament and seek
to reinterpret the apostolic message concerning the Holy
Spirit's work.

3.   THE SPIRIT AS INTERPRETER OF CHRIST

Let us consider first the objection raised by immanentism, that Christian orthodoxy seeks to confine the
Spirit's operation by the exclusive claims which it makes
on behalf of Jesus Christ.

It is undoubtedly true, as we have already seen, that the
New Testament does speak as though the presence of the
Holy Spirit were a gift passed on by Jesus Christ only to his
Church, which thus enters upon a quite new life in him.
On the other hand, the New Testament not less clearly
affirms a universal presence and operation of the same
God who through Jesus Christ has given the Spirit to
believers ; and a chief work of the Holy Spirit himself
is to enable them to see the Jesus of history as the self-
manifestation in the flesh of the eternal Word who is
God's agent in creation and the universal light of men.

Both these complementary truths are emphasized by St. John ; and at this point he especially must be our teacher.

In speaking of revelation, the theologian must distinguish between the *revelatio*, or act of revealing, and the *revelatum*, or reality revealed. Considered as an act of revealing, the Christian revelation has a definite beginning at a particular time and place in history, and continues to operate through the historical life of a particular society. The act begins in the historical life of Jesus, and is continued through the operation of the Spirit in the Church. On the other hand, considered as reality revealed, the content of the Christian revelation has no beginning, end, or limits in space and time. For what is revealed both by the historical life of Jesus and by the Spirit in the Church is nothing other than God's eternal presence and his perpetual work in all times and places. Now, when we consider this antithesis between the revealing act and the revealed reality, the historical life of Jesus Christ appears, according to St. John, on *both* sides of it. On the one hand it is the beginning of the great divine act which reveals God's eternal nature and constant operation in and towards his created world. On the other hand, through the Holy Spirit it is itself revealed as the life in the flesh of him who is identified with the eternal Word and only begotten Son of God. But the work of the Holy Spirit is thought of as belonging only to the revealing act. The Holy Spirit is revealer, not the revealed. That is why his work appears as starting only from the historical life of Jesus, and as being in this way historically limited.

Thus a double truth is safeguarded, and two opposite errors avoided. If, because we acknowledge the historical Jesus to be the revealer of God, we seek to hold and contemplate him only as he was in Palestine, then we are, like Mary Magdalene in the garden, endeavouring to cling to him only as he was, not as he eternally is ; we are trying to rest in that faith which the disciples had before the crucifixion, and we are rejecting his own gift of the Spirit who would lead us into all the truth. This has been the error of much medieval devotion to the Crucified, and, in a different way, of much Liberal Protestant devotion to

" the Jesus of history ". It is that error which gives its
sting to historical criticism of the Gospels. But if, on the
other hand, we claim to have the Holy Spirit's revelation,
without acknowledging that this revelation starts from the
historical life of Jesus only and that the Spirit is his gift,
then by implication we deny God's absolutely single and
final act of self-manifestation in this world. Forthwith,
then, we are at the mercy of vague or occult doctrines of
divine immanence ; the light is not in us ; and we can
retain no firm grasp of the truth that God is *agape*. This
is the more deadly error of gnosticism, immanentism, and
much Catholic modernism.

With the prologue of St. John's Gospel before his mind,
the Christian must always attach a high value to the
comparative study of religions. In every quest and
achievement of the human spirit, not only even in religion,
the same God is partially and dimly apprehended and
revealed ; and the Christian will expect that the Holy
Spirit will teach him, through his comparative study, a
fuller understanding of his own faith in Christ. But,
apart from the life of Jesus, the eternal Word is apprehended apart from his own great and final self-revealing
act. The Christian therefore cannot place his own creed
on a level with others, as though, like them, it were but a
partial and relative expression of truth. For it is only the
light of Jesus who gave the Spirit and whom the Spirit
ever more fully reveals, that enables the Christian to
discern and judge and learn from the partial truths in other
faiths. Even if his study obliges him in candour to
abandon a traditional doctrine which previously seemed to
belong to Christianity itself, he will abandon it only
because of the Spirit's interpretation of what the cross must
mean to him in the sphere of the intellect. If the cross
itself be not the light of the eternal and absolute truth,
then the Christian's whole standard in judging what is
partial, and his whole inspiration in seeking to learn, are
made illusory and void. Christian breadth of mind is
born of no easy-going or sceptical relativism, but of that
sure knowledge of Christ through the Spirit, which enables
him to see signs of his presence and work in hitherto

unrecognized and unlikely places. Did not the Spirit himself teach St. John the meaning of the fact that in his historic incarnation the Son of God seemed to come out of Nazareth, and was only rejected in Jerusalem? How many would-be orthodox teachers have forgotten, and still forget, St. John's warning to orthodoxy! The Church's most searching critic will always be the Spirit whom Jesus gave to be her inward guide and the interpreter of himself.

4. THE HOLY SPIRIT AND HISTORY

We turn next to consider the objection of anti-formalism, that Christian orthodoxy seeks to mechanize the operation of the Holy Spirit by associating it with outward forms. With part of this objection we shall be concerned in the succeeding chapters. Part of it belongs to the subject of the theology of the sacraments, which is outside our scope. But in part also it is an objection in principle to the idea that the operation of God's Spirit is to be found in his selection of a particular people or outwardly organized society to be in its historical development the guardian of his spiritual gifts and the dispenser of them to mankind. The anti-formalist gives an essentially individualistic application to the principle of the free operation of the divine, life-giving Spirit. Everywhere, at all times, in all varieties of historical circumstance, and apart from membership in any particular society, God's Spirit touches the individual heart and raises it to fellowship with himself. The life of Jesus is the supreme manifestation of this universal truth. To this manifestation the legacy of Judaism in the Church is a hindrance rather than a help. We understand the message of Jesus best, when we take it out of the merely Jewish context which was inevitably its historical setting. And to the spiritual Christian the true Church on earth should appear, not as a society of baptized persons acknowledging a particular creed or confession, but rather as the company of all individuals, some of them perhaps quite isolated, who have realized the great truth that Jesus in his loneliness came to teach, that God is their Father and men their brothers.

This kind of anti-formalism is not acceptable to the Biblical scholars of to-day, who are apt rather to ignore the precious half-truth which it contains. But to answer it in terms merely of Biblical scholarship inevitably begs the fundamental question which it raises. We may perhaps find a more profoundly relevant answer in a free rendering of the thought which underlies the historical philosophy of Romans.

God works out his universal purposes of love and grace through history, through historical movements and events, and not merely by illuminating individual souls. In a sinful world this truth implies that he selects particular peoples and societies as chosen vessels to which he commits a special gift of spiritual life, so that, when the gift has been developed for a time within its vessel, the vessel itself may be broken, in order that the treasure within may be more widely diffused. But since the chosen vessels are themselves, with one exception, made up of imperfect and selfish humanity, they in part refuse their office. The natural consequence of this refusal must be the progressive loss and disappearance of the gift itself; for the talent buried to be retained must in the end decay. But the divine love does not suffer this process to complete itself. Always through the breaking up of one culture or order or civilization, and the apparent loss of its gifts, it brings about a fresh concentration of its gifts in a new vessel from which a greater spiritual treasure may be diffused.

The process in many manners and degrees repeats itself ceaselessly in history. But in one particular historical process the meaning and end of all history are revealed. This is the process of which the Bible is the record, and that which the Bible records is the very sacrament of God's historical dealings with mankind. The people of Israel was God's chosen vessel, the Christ-nation, above all others. To it " the oracles of God " were entrusted, so that, when it had learned in its isolation the truth of what had been committed to its charge, in the end all nations of the earth might be blessed through the disappearance of its own separate entity and the diffusion of its gifts. But God's people, so the story runs, did not live up to their high calling. They desired the promised greatness for themselves ; but they refused submission to the law of God's righteousness, which was the condition of true attainment. So the prophets and their followers within Israel are made " the holy remnant " of a people which has forfeited its holiness. But even the prophetic message itself is confused with baser elements, and, after proclaiming confusedly a future hope of redemption, it dies away. The more uncertain voice of the apocalyptists succeeds that of the prophets, and the Pharisaic movement maintains the observance of God's law with a narrow-minded zeal which in the end only obscures God's purpose. God's gift to his people seems to be lost. Then, and not till then, the great miracle can happen. God's own arm in history brings salvation, where man has failed. The treasure of God's grace, lost among his people, is wholly concentrated in the one man Jesus, who is God's Christ indeed, not only an individual but the one human representative of all God's people. And now God's love has created the one human vessel which completely expresses and embodies it. Those to whom Jesus comes—so the terrible logic of sin works itself out—reject or, at best, forsake him. The chosen vessel is broken in death. But the breaking of that vessel, willingly accepted by it, is the sacrifice which is God's victory. In Jesus God's purpose for man is at once revealed and fulfilled. And from his glorified manhood the power of the Spirit comes to found a new society, a new people of God on earth, which can carry the redeemed life of fellowship with Christ to all mankind. Because that society arises out of the incarnation and still works in this world, it must have its outward organization and external limits ; the Church on earth is still a historical and a visible institution. Through and in it, though not confined by it, Christ's Holy Spirit works. But, as indwelt and guided by the Spirit, the Church knows once for all the end of history, the end of the world, and the end of its own being, that by its fellowship in Christ's self-sacrifice to God mankind should be redeemed. Corrupted by sin and torn by schism, the

Church on earth still knows, and can never wholly forget, whence it comes, whither it goes, and ᵂhat it exists to do. It exists that the world may know that the eternal God who once for all in history revealed himself, suffered, and triumphed in the Christ who created it, is the God of love.

5. THE KOINONIA OF THE HOLY SPIRIT IN THE CHURCH

There is, however, still a final question to be asked ; and, as we consider it, we must bear in mind all three conceptions of " the religion of the spirit " or " spiritual religion " which we have described as current in the modern world, and especially perhaps the third, which we said was characteristic of the piety produced by the Counter-Reformation. What is the peculiar treasure recognizable within the body of the Church, which can justify us in speaking of the Church even now on earth as the society of the redeemed humanity living with the life of " the world to come " ? Imperfect as that Church is, and full of the sins which have always marred all other humanity than that of Christ himself, how can we say that in it alone the Spirit dwells with his gifts of the new and heavenly life ? To answer that question we shall turn once more to St. Paul's great phrase, the koinonia of the Holy Spirit.

One essential paradox of Christianity consists in the fact that, although when viewed from outside it is one of the religions of the world, when it is known from within, it is not *a* religion at all, nor even the true *religion* only, but something inherently more than religion ; it is a whole social life of communion in God among men, a communion which embraces both sacred and secular activities and is altogether transfigured by the pervading presence of God's love. The life of heaven itself is the life of perfect community and communion. In a sinful world, on the other hand, the life of the holy soul is *primarily* one of separation.[1] Because it lives in communion with God, it is

[1] If we try to conceive the life of this world, as it might have been apart from sin, the life of souls in it would still be relatively a life in separation. For the initial separateness of the finite

separate from sinners ; and, because the God whom it serves is the lover of all, that separation brings with it pain such as no sinner can experience. This separation of holiness, and the pain which it brings, were realized in Jesus the crucified in whom God's Spirit fully dwelt. But, because the self-surrender of Jesus was complete, his manhood has been raised to heaven, and, with a new operation derived from that manhood, the Holy Spirit establishes among men a new communion and fellowship on earth, in which the members realize not only their separation from the world, but also, though dimly and partially yet truly and positively, the communion which will be fulfilled in the world to come. The sin of the world has entered deeply into the society in which that communion and fellowship have begun to be granted. Sometimes it has dragged down that society to lower levels than any to which natural society can sink. The sin of the world in the Church is blacker than the sin of the world outside. Yet still the principle of the Church's life is supernatural. It binds all kinds of men together in an equal fellowship, where each *through love* contributes something to the good of all, *because*, not *in spite of*, his special gift, calling, and characteristics.

True, the differentiation of functions subordinated to the common good is a principle which even Plato thoroughly understood. But the love which sees in every fellow-citizen a brother for whom Christ died, and in every differentiated function a gift of the one Spirit whom Christ imparts—that Plato could not understand, because Jesus had not yet been glorified, nor the Spirit given. Therefore in *The Republic* the philosopher-saints, who are the aristocracy of Plato's ideal state, are obliged reluctantly to leave the contemplative pursuits in which their real interest lies, in order to do the practical work of government. Plato suggests that they will govern disinterestedly, just because they are reluctant and govern only from a

self is a condition of that free self-surrender whereby alone it can enter eternal life. It is this initial freedom of separateness or freedom of *choice* which also makes possible *sin*, the wilful refusal of self-surrender.

sense of duty, while their hearts are elsewhere. Such other-worldliness, though it has sometimes played a not ignoble part within the Church itself, is fundamentally non-Christian. There is quite literally a world of difference between Plato's Republic and St. Paul's conception of the body of Christ. And however little the real fellowship of the body has prevailed even in the Christian Church, it is clear that apart from the Church it could not exist. The operation of the Spirit in the Church is not identical with the omnipresent activity of the creative Word; it is the operation of the Holy Spirit who has now become the life of a fellowship which is common as well as holy, because he unites men to the Christ who has redeemed common manhood and raised it into the heavenly world.

6.   THE KOINONIA AS SPIRITUAL

What then precisely do we mean by the word " spiritual ", when we use such phrases as " spiritual life " and " spiritual experience " ? To many the answer to that question will seem plain enough. To them spiritual life and experience constitute that particular part of all human life and experience, in which God or divine being is the direct object of consciousness : or, to say the same thing in other words, the spiritual life of man is that part of his life in which he is apprehending, or seeking to apprehend, God's presence and reality in direct relation to his own soul. Some such definition is indeed perfectly legitimate, and even, for certain purposes, necessary. Its main point is to make spiritual life and experience one clearly distinguishable activity among the many which make up the life and experience of man as a whole. It may be that some men lack spiritual capacity, either completely or almost so, as some men appear to lack a moral sense. But it would of course be grotesque to suppose that spiritual life and experience, thus understood, are confined to the adherents of any one religion.

On the other hand, the Christian theologian, though he will accept and use for certain purposes some such definition as that just suggested, still cannot be content with it.

His faith is that God's own supreme revelation of himself
to man does not consist in any disclosure made in the
" spiritual experience " of men in general, or of some
particular men, or even of one. That revelation took
place when God by the action of the Holy Spirit became
incarnate in the whole life of one whole man ; and, as the
result of that incarnation, the same Holy Spirit joins one
body of men in and through all their activities to him who
was incarnate and is now their head. Therefore in the
Christian community, and there alone, *all* human life is
in principle made spiritual. All definitions of " spiritual
life ", which make it one activity among others, begin to
break down. And in that fact precisely consists the truly
supernatural character of the Church as belonging to God's
new creation. In " the world to come " there can be no
separability of sacred from secular, spiritual from material,
supernatural from natural. And the Christian Church
reveals and prophesies the life of the world to come just
in so far as in it already such separations are transcended.
It is inherently impossible that the lives of those who are
called technically " religious ", or even religion itself as
one activity among others, should in themselves be sufficient for the task. The separations of which we have
been speaking can only be overcome (in so far as here
below it is possible to overcome them at all) in a community where men of different callings, sacred and secular,
are together sanctified in Christ's love which penetrates
to every corner of human life.

To sanctify secular avocations or occupations in the
Christian way is not to ignore, nor even to diminish, their
inherently non-religious character. The artistic and
scientific work of Christians ought not to be disguised
sermons, though of course there must be in the Church
a religious kind of art, just as there must be a scientific
study of religion. Christian art and science and industry
and any other right and useful activity we can name, are
those which fulfil that distinct and proper function in
the whole fellowship which God's love has appointed for
each. It is in their non-religious character that the Holy
Spirit sanctifies them and those who engage in them,

" as he distributes his gifts to each man severally as he will ".

In this world religion must always remain one distinct function and activity among others within the community, if only because it differs from the rest in representing the ultimate goal and significance of all. And just for that reason there must always be some, and only some, who find in religion their special vocation ; although none can be genuinely a Christian in his non-religious activity, unless he also shares personally in Christian prayer and corporate worship. It is only in heaven, or in the world to come, that there can be no *temple* at all, since there the universe is God's *Church,* and all distinction between sacred and secular obliterated. Here below it is otherwise. Yet even here below it is the Church's task, precisely because it is " other-worldly ", to make non-religious activities into holy callings, *in* which (and not merely by means of which) communion with Christ is to be sought and found. The κοινωνία ἁγίων (communion in holy things), which is the Church's glory, is but a vain glory apart from the ἁγίασμος κοινῶν (sanctification of common things) which it implies. But all the time we must remember that lives spent mainly in non-religious affairs could not be thus " in Christ " without the witness borne by those other lives of ascetic or missionary or pastoral devotion in which the same love makes more manifest the marks of its cross.

7. THE CHURCH AS EXCLUSIVE TO BE INCLUSIVE

Perhaps the cardinal error in what has passed for orthodoxy, both in the Middle Ages and in the Counter-Reformation and also sometimes in the reformed Churches, has been to emphasize the reality of the supernatural (which is sometimes almost identified with the spiritual) in such a way as to fix the dividing-line between it and the natural. Thus it is that to-day orthodoxy finds itself confronted by philosophies which deny that any real difference exists, and suggest that the supernatural and the natural (and perhaps the spiritual and the material) are but two universal aspects of one world—a doctrine which leads many theologians to disparage or condemn philosophy. But Christian philosophy would teach that in Christ and in his Church the supernatural, in order to redeem the natural, crosses the dividing line and will finally abolish it.

It follows from this philosophy that the Church must be exclusive from one point of view, but only because it is inclusive from another. Only in the Christian community is that operation of the Holy Spirit found which derives full redeeming power from the incarnation and the cross of Christ. Only there can exist the true κοινωνία ἁγίων which is also the ἁγιασμός κοινῶν. But because it is in this respect that the Church is exclusive, the Church is seen to be potentially all-inclusive also. For there is nothing in nature which cannot in the Church's fellowship be made into a holy and acceptable offering to God. The Church's supernatural life is in itself a holy communion ; its sacrament is a holy act which is also a sharing in common. And therefore its relation to the world is expressed by the similar paradox of its titles " holy " and " catholic ", separate and yet all-inclusive. The Church can be in truth both holy and catholic, because it is also apostolic, sent from God into the world with the gospel of the world's redemption. In this world its holy fellowship exists for the sake of those who are still outside it.

CHAPTER XXIX

FREEDOM AND AUTHORITY IN FAITH

THE MODERN revolt against the recognition of authority in the sphere of religious belief is a remarkable phenomenon. For it is evident that in matters of belief, no less than in matters of conduct, freedom is inseparable from the acknowledgment of law. In conduct an unrestricted licence of the individual to do what he pleases issues in an anarchy where no one is free to have a life worth living. And, indeed, the very notion of moral freedom implies some conception of a law of right which is valid for all. Similarly, in the sphere of belief the refusal to admit the authority of any universal law of truth destroys the meaning and possibility of intellectual freedom. For if there be no one truth imposing its own inherent authority upon all, every protest made in the name of reason against the tyranny of dogma loses its point, and there is no essential sin against truth, when a government, whether ecclesiastical or secular, seeks to produce a unanimity convenient to itself by a rigid control of education and all the means of disseminating information to the people.

1. THE GENERAL RELATION OF AUTHORITY TO FREEDOM

It is to be noticed that in a society where a body of unanimous belief is thus manufactured, the principles of authority and of freedom disappear together. For the true exercise of authority is inherently different from compulsion. Authority operates not by compulsion but by obligation. And compulsion and obligation, far from being synonymous terms, really exclude one another. In so far as I am simply compelled to believe or do anything, that belief or action has no obligation for me ; it is mean-

ingless to say that I ought to believe or do it. In so far
as I have been compelled to make a promise, the question
whether I ought to have made it cannot arise, and no
moralist would say that I am under any obligation in
respect of its fulfilment. It is true that, when the obligation imposed by authority is disregarded, authority may
be supported by force. But force is at most the sanction
of authority, not its proper exercise. On the other hand,
obligation, which is imposed by authority as such, presupposes a certain freedom or spontaneity on the part
of him who obeys it. Authority and freedom therefore
are strictly correlative.

2. RELIGION AND DOGMA

Such a statement of abstract principles, however, does
not take us far towards the solution of any concrete
problem. Our immediate concern is with the sphere of
religion. And here it must be observed that the exercise
of authority in matters of faith is characteristic only of
those higher religions in which personal belief is held to
be more important than mere cultus. Primitive religion
on the whole is content with prescribing correct procedure
in worship, and concerns itself very little with what the
individual may or may not actually believe. And, when
primitive religions are developed in a polytheistic civilization, this comparative indifference to personal belief
readily becomes the basis for an apparently broad-minded
toleration. The religion of classical Athens, for instance,
knew nothing of dogma. It is difficult to suppose that the
orthodox Aristophanes really believed in Zeus even as
much as did Socrates the heretic. Later on, the Roman
Empire extended religious toleration more widely than the
city-states of Greece. It was for external non-conformity
rather than for any theological conviction that both Jews
and Christians found themselves suspect even under a
government which sheltered so many varieties of religious
experience and creed. The imperial authority would not
have concerned itself about their personal beliefs, if they
had readily conformed to the accepted rituals, especially

those connected with Emperor-worship. But Christianity at least could not reconcile itself to a religious toleration based upon a divorce between faith and cultus. And in this respect Islam followed in the same steps. When a religious society claims to be the trustee of a revealed truth which imposes an obligation upon the belief of all men, it must exercise a definite authority in matters of faith which can make no terms with an easy-going Rimmonism. Dogmas are products of catholic and evangelical religion ; and such religion cannot but produce them.

3. AUTHORITY AND FREEDOM IN CHRISTIANITY

The specific nature of Christianity, however, gives special characteristics to its insistence upon the principles of authority and freedom in faith, characteristics which we can trace clearly within the New Testament itself. On the one hand, the essence of its gospel is the report of certain facts, attested by witnesses, together with a theological meaning attributed to those facts. For this reason Christianity is bound to attach a peculiar importance to the element of authority in faith, since it must present an authoritative message concerning facts to be accepted and believed on the word of apostolic testimony. That is why its truth cannot rest either on strictly logical demonstration, or on a merely spiritual vision or mystical insight which is independent of any particular happening in history. It is for the same reason that the authority of the apostles as witnesses and messengers of the gospel was of necessity a fundamental element in the faith of the primitive church. On the other hand, it is no less certain that part of the essential content of the primitive gospel was the imparting of the gift of the Holy Spirit to all believers. There was one Spirit, as there was one body and one Christ. It was the Spirit who gave the Apostles utterance, and made their message to be the word, not of men, but of God. It was the Spirit who confirmed the word with signs following. But the gift of the Holy Spirit was shared by all ; it was bestowed through the word

and work of the Apostles, but it was in no sense confined
to them. The reception of the Holy Spirit by all was the
very sign, prophesied by Joel,[1] of the coming of the new
age, with which the gospel of the Messiah was concerned.
Thus it is that the balance of apostolic authority in the
New Testament is balanced by the doctrine of the spiritual
liberty of the Christian. The gift of the Spirit to uncircumcised believers declares their deliverance from bondage, not only to sin, but also to the Mosaic Law. From
the Spirit they receive manifold new powers, illuminations
and guidances, which the apostolic authority must teach
them to discern and recognize, but not disparage or restrain.
The Spirit in the Christian laity must not be quenched.

4. ST. PAUL'S CORRELATION OF AUTHORITY AND FREEDOM

Such were the conditions of the problem with which we
can still watch St. Paul grappling as we read his epistles.
He must at all costs maintain his authority as the divinely
appointed trustee of the gospel, inferior to no other. Any
attempt to discredit his commission, or to alter the essential
content of his gospel, must be unsparingly denounced.
But it is precisely that same gospel, and nothing else,
which gives spiritual liberty to men. Christian freedom,
expressed in the cry, " Abba, Father ", is the only true
freedom ; and it is limited only by the fact that it is
Christian. The law of Christianity is that no inspiration,
however apparently supernatural, can be genuine, which
denies the Lordship of Jesus or offends against love. On
the other hand, all activities, however lowly, which serve
the life and welfare of the Christian body, are to be esteemed
as spiritual gifts. In thus interpreting the meaning
and application of the gospel, St. Paul claims apostolic
authority ; for it is only under the law of such a gospel
that Christian freedom can exist. To the principle of
religious toleration, as understood by the Roman or the
British Empire, St. Paul would never have dreamed of
applying the word " freedom " at all. True, he acknowledged and prized a secular freedom, his Roman citizenship.

[1] See Acts ii. 16 *sqq.*

But this freedom meant to him a precious privilege, enjoyed under Roman law, which slaves and many others had not. In the same way his Christian freedom meant an infinitely greater treasure of heavenly citizenship, which those not in Christ inevitably lacked. It did not occur to him to interpret freedom negatively as characterizing a sphere in which authority refrains from operating and regards variations as indifferent. To him the spheres of authority and freedom were the same.

5. OPPOSITION OF AUTHORITY TO FREEDOM IN THE LATER CHURCH

The correlation between the two principles, which St. Paul thus attempted to establish in the Christian Church, was no doubt always imperfect, and did not long endure. Very soon the conviction of the Spirit's presence in the whole body of Christians, and the vivid sense of new liberty which that presence gave, began to fade. The Church began to include multitudes for whom St. Paul's conceptions of the koinonia of the Spirit and of the freedom with which Christ set us free, meant but little. Still, the Church maintained its unity and extended its frontiers by loyal adherence to its bishops as guardians of the tradition of the faith. But the bishops did not regard their apostolic ministry in quite the same way as St. Paul. They were not for the most part missionaries creating new churches with the gospel of a new age. They were trustees concerned mainly to keep intact the tradition committed to them, and to define it further when compelled to do so by the misinterpretations of heretics. Hence faith came gradually to be identified less with the laying hold on a new life in Christ than with orthodoxy, or correct opinion, concerning him. The test of such orthodoxy was assent to propositions. The authority of the bishops, and finally of the Pope, determined the form of the propositions to which assent should be required. In these circumstances freedom was no longer felt as the release from external ordinances into the glad consciousness of being at home in the universe, the God of which had adopted Christians as his children. The freedom of faith came rather to mean the right or licence of the individual to speculate wherever authority had not already prescribed the answer to the question asked. And the Spirit's guidance was normally identified with the authoritative definition, not with the free speculation. Thus freedom and authority, instead of being correlative, became opposed to one another. Their provinces were conceived as mutually exclusive ; and the covenanted guidance of the Spirit was found within the province, not of freedom, but of authority. Such was the position already approached in patristic times and definitely reached in the Middle Ages.

It would take far too long to discuss the relations between authority and freedom in faith as they were variously conceived in the bodies which severed themselves from the Roman communion at the Reformation. Suffice it to say that any return to the model of the New Testament was largely illusory or transient. Most of the reformed Communions, though not all, quickly established an ortho-doxy of their own, according to which assent to formulæ remained the necessary test of faith, although the formulæ of course differed in content from those which the medieval Church had imposed.

6. MODERN LIBERALISM AND THE REACTION AGAINST IT

What is from our present point of view a much more radical revolution took place in the nineteenth century, when a thoroughgoing attack upon orthodoxies of every kind was made in the name, not of free faith, but of free thought. " The truth shall make you free " is the scrip-tural saying which had expressed the ancient notion of Christian liberty through the Gospel. " Freedom shall give you truth " was in effect the motto of the new Liberal-ism. Its immediate aim was to import into theology those principles and methods of experimental science which had recently established the great doctrine of evolution. Let the Church cease to bind the intellect with any creed or dogma ; let the human mind be encouraged to regard nothing as fixed or certain in the sphere of belief ; then the truth will gradually emerge out of a healthy conflict of unfettered opinions among those who acknowledge themselves to be only seekers. Such was the new gospel which challenged the Church's right to exercise any authority in faith at all. The opposition between authority and freedom which orthodoxy itself had created was turned against it, somewhat as in the parable the separation which Dives made between himself and Lazarus was turned against him in the end. The provinces of authority and freedom remained separate ; but now the operation of the Spirit was found to be wholly within that of freedom. Unfortunately, even the Christian exponents of undogmatic religion failed to perceive that the liberty which they proclaimed to the captives of dogma was something very different from that which the Bible had associated with the acceptable year of the Lord.

To-day it would be waste of time to dwell on the mistakes of Victorian Liberalism. We should be concerned rather to acknowledge and maintain those elements in Christian truth which it re-emphasized. For in any case events since the great war have remorselessly exposed the futility of its pathetic trust in human nature unevangelized and unredeemed. In the last twenty years the pendulum of human inclination has swung violently back again from the side of evolutionary democracy to that of revolutionary despotism. Many have found in the iron discipline of Communist or Fascist parties something of that sense of freedom in common self-dedication which characterized original Christianity. Meanwhile the reformed Churches themselves seem to hesitate, bewildered between a pacific humanism which neglects the element of supernatural judgement or crisis in the gospel, and a prophetic zeal which would purge from it the last trace of the " sweet reasonableness " (ἐπιείκεια) commended even by St. Paul.

7.   A RETURN TO FIRST PRINCIPLES

We must go back to first principles. The claim of Christianity to make men free depends upon the truth of

its gospel.   That gospel is essentially a message concerning
certain historical facts and their meaning in relation to
God and man.   The Church exists to declare that message
to mankind and to manifest the new life of freedom and
fellowship which belief in it makes possible.   The message,
because of its nature and content, can only be accepted
by what St. Paul called "the hearing of faith"; and
correspondingly there must be apostolic authority in the
Church to make clear what the essential and permanent
content of the message is.   In one sense at least it is true
that salvation is by faith only; but it has been left for
the non-Christian psychologist to explain the meaning of
that great principle to be that it does not much matter
what a man believes in, provided that he believes in it
enough.   The Christian message is that to believe in Jesus
Christ, crucified and risen, sets free the soul; and the
freedom depends on the divine authority of those who
declare the message.   It is, moreover, a freedom in the
communion of the same Spirit who, according to Christ's
promise, will always maintain in his Church the authoritative witness to the truth of the gospel, which is Christ
himself.   Creeds and dogmas are but formulated statements
which are needed as visible signs of the continuity and
permanence of the witness.   Apart from the interpretation
given to them by living minds which they guide, they
would have no authority, and indeed no significance,
at all.

8.   FUNCTION OF CREED AND DOGMA IN CHRISTIANITY

If, then, creeds and dogmas are to be rightly used as a
means of enabling Christians to stand fast and grow in their
liberty, two principles must constantly be remembered :
   (a) Creeds and dogmas are not the object of faith, but
its expression with reference to its object.   What they
express is *faith* in God and in what through Christ he has
both revealed and done, not *assent* to a number of several
propositions.   In the past a cardinal mistake of orthodoxy
has been to treat creeds, not as standard expressions of
the Church's faith, but as test-formulæ to be imposed on

individuals for their assent. Now it is inherently impossible to test faith by assent. A man may genuinely assent to any number of these propositions about God without having any spark of faith in God at all. So far as assent goes, as St. James grimly pointed out, the devils also believe. No doubt the majority of those who have found the Christian creeds easy of assent are not devilish persons at all, but only unthinking or conventionally minded. Yet it is not good that these should be readily welcomed into the Church's fellowship, while those whose intellects are active and possibly over-scrupulous should be excluded, because they cannot conscientiously assent to some particular proposition which a formal creed either contains or implies. The Church ought not carefully to strain out gnats of intellectual orthodoxy while it eagerly swallows whole camels of worldliness and spiritual pride —the leaven of the Sadducees and Pharisees. The wrong thus indicated is widely recognized. But so long as creeds are regarded as tests for assent, there is no remedy for it, except to substitute for the creed some vaguer formula to which everyone who desires to call himself a Christian can assent without difficulty. And such a formula would certainly be even more valueless as a test of faith in the gospel to which the Church exists to bear witness.

On the other hand, if creeds and dogmas generally are regarded as standard expressions of the Church's faith, then the Church can gladly welcome into and retain in her fellowship anyone who honestly desires to live and grow in the knowledge of the gospel which these standards define and safeguard, even though certain particular propositions in them may at present excite dissent rather than assent in his mind. It may well be that such dissent must disqualify the individual in question from being accredited as a teacher of the faith. But there is no reason why he should not be recognized as a faithful disciple, if he sincerely intends to take Jesus for his Lord, and, as a member of the Christian society, to learn more of the faith which it professes. The creeds and dogmas of the Church then challenge his understanding to enter more deeply into the mystery which they declare. If the Chalcedonian formula had never received authority, the mystery of the gospel might long ago have been explained away.

(*b*) The second principle is more directly concerned with the koinonia of the Holy Spirit. There must be men of apostolic authority in the Church who are specially com-missioned to maintain, in its fullness and purity, the essence of the gospel which the Church declares. But Christians ought to acknowledge also a spiritual gift in those who criticize traditional doctrines, either with the moral zeal of an Amos or with the intellectual acuteness of a Socrates. There is no valid reason why the authorities concerned to maintain the truth of the gospel should take disciplinary action to silence such men in the Church, even if they consider their teaching mistaken, provided it proceeds from sincerity of faith in Christ, and claims only the authority which belongs to it as such.

There is indeed a Christian justification for the criticism of tradition, viz., the conviction that the intellect, as well as the heart, is called to take its proper share in the self-sacrifice which is the way of salvation. The true sacrifice of the intellect consists, not in cutting reason's throat with the knife of revelation, but rather in the loyal acceptance of unpleasant and even disturbing facts in the ultimate assurance of faith that all truth, however unedifying at first sight, must in the end reveal the same God who was manifest once for all in Jesus. It is exactly by submitting itself to learn and take account of facts as they are, without imposing upon them its preconceived ideas of what they ought to be, that the Christian intellect is trained in the self-denial by which it also enters God's Kingdom. If the intellect has not the utterly sincere love of truth, it can never learn the full truth of love. And just for that reason there must be those within the Church whom the Spirit of Jesus himself inspires to follow the love of truth first, even when the truth of love seems for a while to be endangered thereby. Criticism so inspired, even when it challenges doctrines that seem to many Christians funda-mental, can have no taint of pride or desire for notoriety. It is part of the cross of the Christian critic that he should be lauded in the public press for his courage and candour.

The courage of the surgeon, who hurts because he would heal, craves no praise from men. Simply because its inspiration is Christian and acknowledges Christ's law of love, room must be found for drastic criticism within the spiritual liberty and communion of the Church, even at the cost of difficulty and tension. The Spirit operating in the whole body will prove its truth or falsehood when patience has had its perfect work.

It is indeed manifest in history that the most effective and thoroughgoing criticisms of apparently catholic doctrines and practices have appealed to the principles of Christianity itself. Christians have often been, and still are, effectively attacked for not being Christian enough, never for being too Christian. The fact that Christianity is always its own severest critic is one proof that it is indeed the final and perfect religion for mankind. And the way for the Church to keep and manifest her divinely ordained authority in faith is not to adopt measures of repression whenever the critic's voice is raised, but rather to trust the one Spirit to reconcile within the freedom of his own fellowship the diverse gifts of which he is the author.

CHAPTER XXX

THE HISTORICAL FOUNDATION OF THE CHURCH

U P TILL now we have been dealing mainly with the spiritual nature of the Church as constituted by the koinonia of the Holy Spirit. We must now turn our attention to questions more closely connected with its outward organization. For the Church of Christ on earth and in history has always a religious organization with a system of government, appointed officers, and characteristic rites. We can have no complete doctrine of the Church until we have related this fact to the spiritual essence of the Church's being.

Considering the Church then as a historical and organized society, we must first ask the question, who founded it, and when ?

1. THE PROBLEM RAISED BY HISTORICAL CRITICISM

Up till quite recent times no Christian would have hesitated in his main answer to that question. Jesus Christ himself, he would have said, founded the Church by giving a definite commission to his apostles before his ascension, and by fulfilling his promise to bestow the Holy Spirit. And, if we trust the historical accuracy of every statement in the Gospels, there can be no doubt whatever about the matter. The words to St. Peter, " Upon this rock I will build my Church ", those to the Eleven, " Go ye and teach all nations, baptizing them in the name of the Father and of the Son and of the Holy Ghost ", the high-priestly prayer in St. John's Gospel, and other texts, furnish explicit evidence which is abundantly sufficient.

The historical studies of modern scholars, however, require us to make allowance for the fact that in some cases the traditional record of the Lord's words has been influenced by the desire and need of the early Church either to claim dominical authority for its institutions or to explain the relevance of Christ's teaching to a situation which arose subsequently. And this influence is most clearly traced in the First and Fourth Gospels. Few scholars would now maintain that the bulk of the Johannine discourses represents exactly reported words of Jesus. The evidence that in the primitive Church baptism was performed in the name of the Lord Jesus makes it very unlikely that Christ actually commanded his apostles to baptize in the name of the Trinity. And many would regard it as almost equally improbable that during his ministry on earth he used the actual expression " my Church " with the meaning implied in the saying which St. Matthew records as uttered to St. Peter.

2. DID ST. PAUL FOUND THE CHURCH ?

Such considerations, combined with the modern tendency to emphasize the eschatological element in the teaching and thought of Jesus, have led some students of Christian origins to a conclusion absolutely contradictory of the Church's main tradition.   Jesus, they say, had no thought of founding any Church on earth at all.   His whole mind was dominated by the expectation of the almost immediate end of the world.   He never even considered the need of making provision for a society to carry his gospel out into the world.   We must therefore suppose the true founder of the historical Church to have been St. Paul.   St. Paul professed to derive his commission and his gospel entirely from the risen Christ.   To the Lord's historical ministry prior to the crucifixion he attached, it is alleged, but little positive importance.   Because he was the first Catholic as well as the first Protestant, he involved himself in bitter controversy with the original disciples, who regarded their religion merely as a form of Judaism which claimed that Jesus was the true Messiah.   On the main issue of the controversy Paulinism triumphed.   Thus it was that Christianity, which had originally been a special form of

Jewish Messianism, became the new religion of a new Church. The next generation of Christians glossed over the breach between the Christianity of Jesus and that of Paul, by attributing to Jesus himself such words and acts as would represent him to have been in historical fact the founder of the Church and the religion which bore his name.

No doubt this theory, in the precise form in which I have stated it, is already old-fashioned. The most recent scholars are generally agreed that the controversy between St. Paul and St. Peter, of which we catch echoes in Galatians, cannot have been concerned with such fundamental issues as the old Tübingen School of critics suggested. St. Paul's attack upon St. Peter was based on the contention that St. Peter's action at Antioch in giving way to the Judaizers was false to his own acknowledged principles. All the evidence both of Galatians and Acts goes to show that St. Peter and St. Paul were in principle on the same side in the Judaistic controversy. Moreover, it is perfectly clear that a Gentile-Christian congregation had been founded at Antioch before St. Paul went there. The admission of uncircumcised Gentiles to the Christian body was originally the work of St. Peter and St. Stephen, and not of St. Paul. Finally, as we have already seen, it involves a radical misunderstanding of St. Paul's whole teaching to suppose that he attached little importance either to the ministry and sayings of Jesus before the crucifixion or to the central tradition about Jesus which he had received from " those who were in Christ before him ". The idea that St. Paul inaugurated a new religion, essentially different from that of the original disciples, is seen on examination to be entirely baseless.

Nevertheless, the atmosphere of scepticism produced by attempts radically to reconstruct and rewrite the whole story of Christian origins still persists. And, although it is impossible here to deal in any adequate way with the problems of strictly historical study, it belongs to our doctrinal purpose to sum up the basic evidence on which the Christian belief must rest that Jesus Christ in historical fact founded his Church on earth. For the nature of this evidence must affect our doctrine of the Church's nature.

3. IN WHAT SENSE JESUS FOUNDED THE CHURCH

When the New Testament is re-examined in the light of modern studies with such absence of bias as a Christian can command, the following conclusions seem to emerge.

(a) The theory that the whole substance of Christ's teaching was determined by the expectation of the immediate end of the world will not stand the test of fair-minded criticism. In fact, it is St. Paul and not our Lord who occasionally allowed such an expectation to influence his ethical teaching. St. Paul enforced his regulations about marriage by emphasizing the shortness of the time now left.[1] Jesus based his condemnation of divorce on a divine law which existed before Moses. Similarly the most " unworldly " principles of conduct laid down in the Sermon on the Mount are commended not at all on the ground that the end is near, but on the ground that in following them Christ's disciples will be acting as their heavenly Father has always acted from the beginning of time towards both the good and the evil among men. It may be added, though it would take far too long to discuss the point, that much of Christ's teaching about the Kingdom, both in his parables and elsewhere, can only be made consistent with an exclusively eschatological outlook by a strained and artificial exegesis.

(b) On the other hand, there is singularly little direct indication that Jesus regarded it as part of his mission to found any religious organization upon earth which would supersede the institutions of Judaism. The Judaistic controversy in the apostolic Church is witness that the apostles themselves were in doubt how far and in what sense Christianity must form a quite new organization which could dispense with the ordinances of the Law and the institutions of the synagogue ; and this hesitation is quite intelligible, if the main substance of Christ's teaching was what the Gospels represent it to have been.

But this consideration is double-edged. For it also shows how little the Pauline conception of the Church has been allowed to influence the record of Christ's words and

---

[1] 1 Cor. vii. 29. Contrast Mark x. 5 *sqq.*

acts. It is really remarkable that documents which reached their present form so long after St. Paul's victory had been definitely won, should show so little trace of any attempt to claim the direct authority of Jesus for the positions St. Paul had maintained in controversy. The very fact that the Gospels make no attempt to show that Jesus gave any definite or explicit teaching as to the future Church and its relation to Judaism, should make us more confident in relying upon the evidence which they do provide that Jesus founded the Church.

(c) The evidence of St. Paul's Epistles and of Acts supports the Gospels in their affirmation that Jesus appointed a group of twelve men to be specially near to himself and to be his missionaries to others, and that these twelve were at the beginning chosen out of a larger body of disciples, and were assumed, at any rate after the Lord's death, to possess special authority within that body. The significance of the number is not really lessened by doubts which exist as to one or two of the original names, by the peculiar authority of James the Lord's Brother in the Jerusalem Church, or by the fact that St. Paul claimed an authority not inferior to that of the Twelve. The number is an indication of the fact, manifest in many ways all through the Gospels and in the New Testament as a whole, that in claiming to be the Messiah, the fulfiller of God's promises to Israel, Jesus knew himself sent to reconstitute the chosen people, Israel, on the basis of a new relationship to God which must supersede the Mosaic Covenant. The choice of twelve means that the new Israel, the Israel which has received the Messiah, is making a fresh start from the twelve apostles, as the old Israel started its history from the twelve sons of Jacob.

(d) The word *ecclesia*, translated " Church " in the English New Testament, was not a new one to Jewish ears. In the LXX it meant " the congregation " of Israel, and it is so used in St. Stephen's speech in Acts. Nor did the Christian Church ever claim to be a quite newly founded society. By St. Paul, as doubtless by all other Christians, it was identified with Israel, the chosen people, living under a new dispensation now that the Messiah had appeared.[1] There were doubts how far the old dispensation was in practice to be regarded as obsolete before the final appearance of the Christ in glory. The Judaizers, though not St. Peter, appear to have thought that the Mosaic Law must still remain binding upon Christians for the present. But all Christians made the tremendous claim that they, in recognizing Jesus to be the Messiah, from henceforth constituted the true Israel, and were the inheritors of the promises made to the fathers. The Jews who rejected Jesus were no longer to be recognized as true Israelites at all. In this sense at least the Christians from the beginning claimed, and rightly claimed, to be the new Church or ecclesia of God, historically founded by Jesus Christ himself, with the appointment of the Twelve.

Having made this affirmation we may be quite ready to admit that the further organization of the Church as a society quite distinct from the old Israel was a matter of subsequent development, as to which no express directions were given by the incarnate Lord. We can trace the initial steps of this development in the Pauline Epistles and in Acts.

4. CONCLUSION AS TO THE CHURCH'S NATURE

What then we can be sure of is this. From Pentecost onwards the Christian ecclesia existed under apostolic leadership as constituting the true Israel of God which had begun to receive the promises made to the fathers. It was a spiritual society in that it had received, and continued to confer upon fresh converts, the gift of the Holy Spirit from the risen Lord. The common sharing of this

---

[1] Professor Dodd points out to me that the Messianic idea is always correlative with the idea of a Messianic community which is " the people of the Saints of the Most High " (Dan. vii. 27), the people of the New Covenant (Jer. xxxi. 31 *sqq.*). The numerous sayings of Jesus implying the rejection of the old Israel which rejected him, make it necessary to postulate a new Israel. And the reference to the " twelve thrones " (Mt. xix. 28, Lk. xxii. 30), and that to " the covenant " at the Last Supper (Mk. xiv. 24), almost prove that in some sense or other Jesus intended his apostles to be the nucleus of the new Israel.

gift by all its members was a distinctive mark of its new life as the ecclesia of the new age, the company of those who were already being saved (σωζόμενοι). It soon became apparent that Jew and Gentile alike were to be made recipients of this gift, and that Gentiles were not to be brought first under the old covenant by circumcision and observance of the Law.

The Church, however, was not "a purely spiritual society ", if that expression is taken in its modern sense as implying that all outward rites were optional, or that leadership in it was not an office but a matter of occasional inspiration. The Church practised baptism and the laying on of hands as its ceremonies of initiation. It observed the breaking of bread or the Lord's Supper as a solemn memorial of, and means of communion with, the Lord Jesus Christ; and its acknowledged ministerial leaders were the apostolic company which Jesus had at least begun to constitute before his death, and which he afterwards accredited as witnesses of his resurrection.

CHAPTER XXXI

ORDER, ORDERS AND UNITY IN THE CHURCH

W E HAVE argued that the Church from its original foundation was not " a purely spiritual " society, but in a real sense an organized body, however elementary that organization may have been at the start. The further doctrine of the Church's nature, which is more and more clearly seen to be the main issue whenever possibilities of reunion between the existing Churches are discussed, depends upon the answer to the question : What is the essential relation between that outward structure which makes the Church an organized society in the view of the world at large, and the spiritual reality which all agree to be, in the deepest and most ultimate sense, the Church itself ? Or, more particularly, do any outward unity and continuity of organization in any way *constitute* the unity of the Church, or are they *outward* even in the sense of being external to that unity ?

1. UTILITARIAN AND ORGANIC VIEWS OF CHURCH ORDER

Many and voluminous as are the answers given to that question, there are, I believe, only two which do not ultimately evade it. These two are quite opposed to one another, and the essential contrast between them can be quite shortly expressed by the use of a rather crude analogy. The first answer conceives the relation of the Church to its external order or organization to be somewhat analogous to the relation of a man to his clothes. The second answer conceives that relation to be analogous rather to that of a man to his body.

The point of each analogy requires some amplification. A man, we may say, always needs clothes of some kind ; and some kinds are more convenient than others. Moreover some are more suitable for one occasion, some for another. A man therefore is well advised to change his clothes according to the occupation of the moment or according to the climate in which he happens to be living. Again, clothes wear out from time to time, and need to be renewed with some change of form and material. In the same way, there are many Christians who hold that some form of outward order or organization is indeed always necessary for the Church on earth, but there is no one form and no external continuity which ought to persist always and everywhere. There is no need for unity and continuity of external order, save as a matter of expediency ; and variation at different times and in different places in also expedient. There are many types of Church order or " polity " in the world to-day. But it is quite wrong to dispute about them as though any one type could represent a sacred principle to which the Church is bound in all circumstances to adhere. For episcopalianism to claim a special divine authority for all time, is merely disastrous. It may well have been the best form of polity to hold the Church together in the early centuries, and as such it may claim to have had a divine sanction. But it does not follow that it is the only right form of Church-polity to-day.

On the other hand, let us consider the relation of a man to his body. It is evident that a man *is* his spiritual and mental self in a stricter sense than he actually *is* his body. It is evident again that the spiritual element in a man's being is infinitely more important than the physical. Moreover, the range of a man's spiritual and mental activity is not wholly confined by his material body ; for otherwise he could not even be aware that his body limits him. Finally, we must admit that the body develops and grows with the man. And yet the man's very life is bound up with the body, and his unity with its unity, in a way which makes his relation to his body quite different from his relation to his clothes. Any breach in the unity and continuity of the living body is a maiming or mutilation of it, and an injury to the man himself. There are many Christians who conceive in some analogous way the relation of an outward order and organization to the spiritual essence of the living Church. They do not identify the Church's being with the outward order in the same sense that they would identify it with fellowship in Christ. They do not regard the unity of the outward order as comparable in importance with the unity of the spiritual fellowship. They do not confine the spiritual fellowship within the limits which the outward order necessarily marks out. They admit that the outward order has developed to a great extent and elaborated itself in history ; they will readily agree that in subordinate matters there must and ought to be wide variation in polity and ritual, and that to many of these the analogy of " clothes " is entirely applicable. But they still maintain, even to the scandal of those who do not agree with them, that the Church was originally founded as an organic unity upon the ministerial government of the apostles, and that to preserve an outward unity of order in unbroken continuity with the original apostolic constitution is essential to the Church's very being. Breaches in that unity and continuity have now manifestly taken place ; but these are comparable to lesions in a body, rather than to changes of clothing. Therefore it is an imperative duty to restore the broken unity in outward things.

2.   THE ORGANIC VIEW TO BE PREFERRED

We have then two different conceptions of the relation of the Church's outward order or organization to its spiritual being. Let us call the first the utilitarian view and the second the organic. The utilitarian view can be made extremely persuasive, and I do not think that it can be actually disproved by Scripture. It is not excluded either by the Johannine allegory of the vine and the branches or by the Pauline simile of the body and its members. It is widely held to-day by Free Churchmen, though hardly by a majority in the reformed Churches, and it is implied in the doctrine held by many Anglicans that episcopacy is of the *bene esse*, but not of the *esse*, of the Church. Nevertheless, apart from deeper considerations of philosophical theology, there are two objections to the utilitarian view which appear likely to prevent it from ever becoming the view of more than a minority in the Church as a whole. The first objection is constituted by the mere historical fact that the view was hardly even thought of before the Reformation, and on questions of the fundamental nature of the Church the appeal to history cannot but remain powerful. In the second place, historical studies are constantly confirming the conclusion that the utilitarian view can claim no direct and positive support from the New Testament. As we have seen, the Church did not in fact come into being as a purely spiritual society for which all matters of external polity and organization were questions simply of occasional expediency. Such a notion was as completely absent from St. Paul's mind as it was from that of his Judaizing opponents. And the utilitarian view presupposes a radical separation between " inward " and " outward " of a kind which, whatever its justification, is foreign to the thought of the New Testament as a whole.

3.   TWO INTERPRETATIONS OF APOSTOLICAL SUCCESSION

If then we are to take what we have called the organic view of the Church's outward order, we are obliged to give some positive answer to the question, What in the history of the Church appear to be those essential elements in the unity and continuity of its organization, which must be loyally preserved or restored in any genuinely catholic scheme of reunion ?   And at this point we are bound to recognize an undeniable fact, that from the second century onwards to the Reformation the outward sign and guarantee of the Church's unity was acknowledged to be the succession of bishops, holding office by due appointment and consecration, who safeguarded the tradition of faith handed down from the apostles and were in a true sense their living representatives.   At the present time perhaps a majority of the Christians in the world still maintain the importance of this succession of bishops as constituting one essential feature in the continuous unity of the Church's order. This recognition of episcopacy as essential need not necessarily imply that Churches of non-episcopal polity have not retained or restored other elements in the Church's true and catholic order which have been lost or obscured where the episcopal succession has been kept. But it is at least extremely difficult to maintain the " organic " view of the Church's order, unless one is prepared to admit that episcopacy is *in some way* essential to that order. And in order to determine in what way it is essential, we must examine in some detail the doctrine generally known as that of " the apostolic succession ".

The phrase " apostolic succession " is in itself obviously vague ; and in fact two quite different meanings have been given to it, which it is vital to distinguish :

(*a*) According to the first interpretation the succession is primarily a transmission of duly constituted authority in the Church, an authority exercised by those who hold office in a continuous line reaching back ultimately to the apostolic authority of the apostles themselves. By those who hold this interpretation the transmission of authority is of course believed normally to carry with it a more personal gift of divine grace to enable the bearer of the office to exercise it in accordance with Christ's will. But the essential succession is a succession in spiritual office and authority.

(*b*) According to the second interpretation the succession is primarily the transmission of a peculiar gift to the individual by means of a particular sign, viz., the act of episcopal consecration, whereby the gift and the power to transmit it have been handed down in an unbroken line from one of the original apostles. Those who hold this interpretation of course believe that the gift normally carries with it both the authority of an office in the Church and the grace to exercise it in accordance with Christ's will. But the peculiar gift itself is neither a divine grace nor the authority of an office in the Church. By scholastic theologians, as we shall explain later, it was defined to be an *indelible character*, which could not be lost, and might therefore always be transmitted, by one who had once received it.

For convenience, let us call the first interpretation the *authoritarian,* and the second the *indelibilist,* view of the gift transmitted in apostolic succession.   It is not difficult to show that it makes a great deal of difference to our whole doctrine of the Church which of these two views we hold.   The difference is chiefly seen at two points :

(*a*) If we take the first or authoritarian view, obscurities as to what exactly happened when the monarchical episcopate established itself at the end of the first century, do not greatly matter, and do not affect the reality of the succession.   All that the view obliges us to suppose is that there was some sort of transmission of authority from the apostles to men who were to be responsible after their death for maintaining the purity of the faith and the order of the Church.   The evidence certainly seems to show that something of this kind took place.   This transmission of authority was directly or indirectly the historical origin of the episcopal government which was universally recognized in the Church before the end of the second century. And it may be reasonably argued that the episcopal order, handed down from the second century, still represents the true organic continuity of apostolic authority in the Church.

If on the other hand we take the second or indelibilist view, then a breach at any point in the actual line of consecrations starting from the apostles, destroys the succession.   And if we are to hold that that succession still exists in the Church to-day, we are obliged to maintain an assurance as to what happened in the apostolic and sub-apostolic period, which the historical evidence does not appear to warrant.

(*b*) Again, if we take the authoritarian view, then clearly the bishop's whole power to act episcopally depends upon the office he holds within the one body of the Church.   He may lose that office, if he falls into schism or if for any valid reason he is deposed.   And, according to the authoritarian view, when the office is lost, the power to exercise the functions of the office must be lost also.   In the extreme case, if a bishop becomes apostate and is severed from the Church's body, it is, from this point of view, monstrous to contend that he can still perform valid sacraments and ordinations. For validity of orders depends upon the unity of the whole body within which holy orders are conferred and exercised. The succession of authority in the continuous line of bishops is the very mark of the Church's outward and visible unity. If the unity is broken by schism, the authority cannot continue unimpaired in two separated lines of succession. And if a bishop be deemed to have been cut off from the one body of the Church altogether, he cannot be deemed to retain anything of the authority which he received through his place in the succession.

On the other hand, if we take the indelibilist view, very different conclusions follow. According to this view the essential thing which the bishop received at his consecration in the apostolic succession is a mysterious gift or power which henceforth is irrevocably his. Neither schism nor apostasy nor excommunication can affect his possession of it. And since it is this gift or power which enables him to exercise truly episcopal functions, he can continue to exercise them, even when he is in schism or excommunicate. Thus it is possible that another body may be originated, which is in schism from the Church of Christ, and yet retains unimpaired the valid ministry and sacraments which exist to be the very marks and organs of the Church's visible unity.

4. APOSTOLIC SUCCESSION IN THE EARLY CHURCH

In the second and third centuries the Church universally held a doctrine of apostolic succession through bishops, especially through the bishops of the great sees, such as Rome, Alexandria and Antioch ; but it had no occasion to define that doctrine with any theological precision. In general it was held that the true Catholic Church consisted of all those local Churches which were in communion with the great sees, the bishops of which were manifestly the chief guardians of the apostolic tradition. Those who separated themselves from that communion were deemed to be outside the Church. In the fourth century further definition was made necessary by controversy on the question whether those who had received baptism in schismatic bodies should or should not be baptized again when they were received back into the Catholic Church. In the third century Cyprian had held the view that schismatic bodies could not minister true or valid sacraments ; and he therefore required re-baptism. But in A.D. 314 the Council of Arles decided for the Western Church that baptism performed in schismatic bodies with due form and matter was valid, and that therefore re-baptism was wrong. St. Augustine [1] then took the vital step of extending the argument in favour of the validity of schismatic baptism so as to make it cover schismatic ordinations. He argued that, since a man, once validly baptized, cannot lose his baptism, neither can he lose his power of conferring baptism on others : and in the same way a man, once validly consecrated as bishop, cannot lose either his consecration or his power of conferring orders. The fundamental principle of St. Augustine's reasoning was that the sacraments are everywhere the same, whether inside or outside the Catholic Church, and that their validity depends, not on any worthiness in the minister, but simply on the fact that it is Christ who uses him.

Here we have the historical origin and foundation of what we have called the " indelibilist " view. Nevertheless when St. Augustine himself actually speaks of apostolic succession, he clearly means by it a succession from holder of office to holder of office, not from consecrator to consecrated. Hence, however inconsistently, he still confined apostolic succession to the one body of the Catholic Church.

5. THE DOCTRINE OF ROMAN CATHOLICISM

The doctrine which St. Augustine maintained in the controversy about re-baptism afterwards became the orthodoxy of the Western Church. Scholastic theologians have given it more precise definition and logical consistency.

---

[1] I take this brief account of St. Augustine's teaching on this subject from C. H. Turner's essay on Apostolic Succession in *The Early History of the Church and the Ministry* (Second Edition), pp. 179 *sqq.*

According to them the sacraments of Baptism, Confirmation, and Holy Orders confer not only grace but also something which is called *indelible character*. This gift of indelible character supplies the reason why the same person must never in any circumstances receive any of these sacraments twice. For the *character* is given once for all, and it is necessarily and inevitably conveyed by the performance of the sacrament. Unlike grace, its reception does not depend upon any right disposition in the recipient. And, unlike the authority belonging to an office, it cannot be lost with the loss of the office.

In the case of the sacrament of Holy Order, the *character* is held to consist in the *potestas ordinis*, the power belonging to the order. In the case of the bishop this *potestas* enables him to confer holy orders upon others ; and, inasmuch as the *character* is indelible, he retains this power unimpaired, even though he become excommunicate. It is evident that the logic of this doctrine postulates what we have called the " indelibilist " view of the apostolic succession : the essential thing transmitted by this succession is the indelible *character* of the episcopate.

Thus, while the Church of Rome maintains that only those belong to the body of the Church who are in communion with the Pope, it admits nevertheless both the possibility and the fact that many Christians who are outside that body still possess true orders and true sacraments. Such, according to Roman Catholic theologians, is the position of the Eastern Orthodox Church, but not of the Church of England ; for the Church of Rome denies the reality of the apostolic succession in the Anglican bishops, denies that they possess the *character* of the episcopate, and denies therefore that they can perform valid ordinations.

6. THE " BRANCH " THEORY OF SOME ANGLICANS [1]

Some Anglicans are so convinced of the injustice of these denials, and of the strength of the case that can be put forward on Roman Catholic principles for the validity of Anglican orders, that they are inclined to adopt those

[1] Very few, I think, now hold it in this extreme and logical form.

principles, with one modification, in order to demonstrate their case.   They would accept the principles from which Roman Catholics argue, except in so far as, being Anglicans, they are bound to reject the doctrine that communion with the see of Rome is a necessary condition of belonging to the body of the Catholic Church.   These Anglicans therefore find themselves obliged to formulate what is in fact a new doctrine of the grounds on which a Church professing Christianity is to be judged to be inside or outside the body of the Catholic Church.   Those Churches are to be judged within the body, which retain, together with the profession of the Christian faith, that apostolic succession which gives their bishops the episcopal *character* and so ensures the validity of their orders and sacraments. When two such Churches are not in communion with each other, the schism between them may be called *internal*, since both Churches belong to the one body of the Catholic Church.   On the other hand, the schism between a Church that retains the apostolic succession, and one that does not, is to be called *external*, inasmuch as the latter is outside the body of the Catholic Church altogether.

But this particular theory of Catholicity seems to be really untenable for three reasons :

(*a*) Its claim to be catholic in any historical sense is hard to justify.   There is no ancient authority to which it can appeal, and it is in fact rejected by the main tradition of both West and East.

(*b*) The theory involves the paradoxical consequence that, whereas great Protestant Communions have no valid sacraments except baptism and are outside the body of the Catholic Church, nevertheless " a wandering bishop ", who has received the episcopal *character* but holds no office or authority in any Christian body, can confer the orders of the Catholic Church upon anyone he chooses, and thereby start a new " branch " of the Catholic Church itself.

(*c*) Whereas it seems reasonable to suppose that holy orders derive their validity from being the orders of Christ's Catholic Church to which they belong, this theory must maintain on the contrary that valid orders make Catholic the Church in which they are administered.   The question

whether particular ordinations are or are not valid is first
settled apart from the consideration whether they were or
were not administered within the body of the Catholic
Church ; and then the decision on this point is made to
settle the question whether the Church in which these
ordinations were administered is or is not " Catholic ".
Such a method of procedure is fundamentally absurd.

The conclusion seems to be that, for Anglicans at least,
it is impossible reasonably to maintain the Augustinian
arguments which lead to what we have called the
" indelibilist " view of the apostolic succession.

7.   THE WAY TO REUNION

What then can be made of the alternative or " authoritarian " view ?   Two different lines of inference from it
are logically possible.

(a) The first is represented by the rigorist doctrine which
was in fact championed by St. Cyprian.   Since it belongs
to the nature of the Church to be organically one, schism
within the Church is, strictly speaking, impossible.   If the
Church appears to be divided into two bodies, actually one
of these bodies must be the true Church, and the other
not.   Therefore the " orders " and " sacraments " of the
latter are not true orders or sacraments at all.   I do
not know that to-day the theologians of any Church maintain this view strictly ;   but in the abstract its logic is
unimpeachable.

(b) The rigorist doctrine however does not exhaust the
logical possibilities of the " authoritarian " view.   We may
affirm that there *is* schism within the one body of the
Church.   Because such schism breaks the Church's outward unity of order, it is a grievous sin, and it is indeed
contrary to the very nature of the Church itself as Christ
created it and wills it to be.   But still we may admit that
such schism does in fact exist.   Just because, therefore,
the divided Churches still remain parts of the one body,
they must all alike suffer from the lesion by which they
are divided.   And part of what they suffer is seen in the
fact that no one Church, as divided from the others, can

retain or transmit in all its fullness that tradition of one
faith and one order which the apostles bequeathed to their
successors in the government of the Church.   According
to this view, the apostolic authority of every bishop is in
some degree impaired by the fact that he can no longer
act as a member of one visibly united episcopate.   To that
extent the validity of all the orders that exist in modern
Christendom is defective.   But if the apostolic tradition of
order is not retained in its fullness even by those who cling
to the succession through duly consecrated bishops, it
seems reasonable to conclude that everywhere in Christendom the retention of that order is a matter of divers por-
tions, manners and degrees.   Once it is frankly admitted
that *every* divided Church, which maintains the Christian
faith, is in schism and yet is within the body of the Church
Catholic, the hope of a genuinely catholic reunion may be
re-born.

For what, from this point of view, is the remedy for
schism ?   Assuredly not that those who still preserve
among themselves essential elements in the apostolic
tradition of order should treat them as of little account,
or regard their retention as a mere matter of expediency
and not of principle.   The remedy for schism is that the
divided Churches should take counsel together how best
they may recombine within the single order of one Church
those elements both of order and of freedom which are
characteristic of their several traditions, so that in this
way they may supply one another's defects in the restored
unity of the body.   Progress along these lines, though
slow, seems to offer the best hope for the future.   But the
main purpose of the foregoing statement has been to make
clearer some of the main issues in a problem where they
are specially apt to become confused.

BIBLIOGRAPHY

To COMPILE anything like an adequate bibliography on all the subjects treated in this volume would be a formidable task which, if achieved, would unduly prolong the length of the volume itself. The following short list of representative books is, however, offered in the hope that it may be of some help to students by way of suggestions for further reading. Not only the selection, but also the classification of the books selected, has been a matter of some difficulty. A particular book may be relevant at two or more points which my arrangement of subjects has separated from one another. I have, however, classified my list so as to correspond roughly to the different Parts into which this volume is divided, and I have put most of the more general books under the list of Part I.

PART I (AND GENERAL)

BAILLIE, J. : *Our Knowledge of God* (O.U.P.).
BERDYAEV, N. : *The Destiny of Man* (Centenary Press).
DE BURGH, W. G. : *From Morality to Religion* (Macdonald & Evans).
DEMANT, V. A. : *The Religious Prospect* (Muller).
DEVAN, E. : *Symbolism and Belief* (Allen & Unwin).
FARMER, H. H. : *The World and God* (Nisbet).
GARVIE, A. E. : *The Christian Doctrine of the Godhead* (Hodder).
GILSON, G. : *The Spirit of Mediæval Philosophy* (Sheed & Ward).
GORE, C. : *Belief in God* (Murray).
HEADLAM, A. C. : *Christian Theology* (O.U.P.).
HODGSON, L. : *The Grace of God in Faith and Philosophy* (Longmans).
HÜGEL, F. VON : *Essays and Addresses in the Philosophy of Religion*, 2 vols. (Dent).
INGE, W. R. : *God and the Astronomers* (Longmans).
MATTHEWS, W. R. : *God in Christian Thought and Experience* (Nisbet).
—— : *The Purpose of God* (Nisbet).
NYGREN, A. : *Agape and Eros* (S.P.C.K.).
OMAN, J. : *The Natural and the Supernatural* (C.U.P.).
SELWYN, E. G. (ed.) : *Essays Catholic and Critical* (S.P.C.K.).
STREETER, B. H. : *Reality* (Macmillan).
TAYLOR, A. E. : *The Faith of a Moralist*, 2 vols. (Macmillan).
TEMPLE, W. : *Nature, Man, and God* (Macmillan).
WEBB, C. C. J. : *God and Personality* (Allen & Unwin).
—— : *Divine Personality and Human Life* (Allen & Unwin).
—— : *Problems in the Relations of God and Man* (Nisbet).

PART II

BELL AND DEISMANN (edd.) : *Mysterium Christi* (Longmans).
BRUNNER, E. : *The Mediator* (Lutterworth Press).
CREED, J. M. : *The Divinity of Jesus Christ* (C.U.P.).
DODD, C. H. : *History and the Gospel* (Nisbet).
—— : *The Apostolic Preaching and its Developments* (Hodder).
FORSYTH, P. T. : *Person and Place of Jesus Christ* (Hodder).
GORE, C. : *Belief in Christ* (Murray).
GRENSTED, L. W. : *The Person of Christ* (Nisbet).
MACKINTOSH, H. R. : *The Person of Jesus Christ* (T. & T. Clark).
MOZLEY, J. K. : *The Incarnation* (Bles).
—— : *The Impassibility of God* (C.U.P.).
PRESTIGE, G. L. : *God in Patristic Thought* (Heinemann).
RAVEN, C. E. : *Jesus and the Gospel of Love* (Hodder).
RAWLINSON, A. E. J. : *The New Testament Doctrine of the Christ* (Longmans).
—— (ed.) : *Essays in the Trinity and the Incarnation* (Longmans).
SELLERS, R. V. : *Two Ancient Christologies* (S.P.C.K.).
TEMPLE, W. : *Christus Veritas* (Macmillan).
THORNTON, L. S. : *The Incarnate Lord* (Longmans).
—— : *The Atonement* (Bles).

PART III

AULÉN, G. : *Christus Victor* (S.P.C.K.).
BAILLIE, J. : *And the Life Everlasting* (O.U.P.).
BRABANT, F. H.: *Time and Eternity in Christian Thought* (Macmillan).
GRENSTED, L. W. (ed.) : *The Atonement in History and in Life* (S.P.C.K.).
HICKS, F. C. N. : *The Fulness of Sacrifice* (Macmillan).
HÜGEL, F. VON : *Eternal Life* (T. & T. Clark).
MOBERLY, R. C. : *Atonement and Personality* (Murray).
MOZLEY, J. K. : *The Atonement* (Duckworth).
RASHDALL, H. : *The Idea of the Atonement in Christian Theology* (Macmillan).
TAYLOR, A. E. : *The Christian Hope of Immortality* (Bles).
TAYLOR, V. : *Jesus and His Sacrifice* (Macmillan).
—— : *The Atonement in the New Testament* (Epworth Press).
WILLIAMS, N. P. : *The Ideas of the Fall and of Original Sin* (Longmans).
VARIOUS AUTHORS : *Man and Eternity* (Burns Oates & Washbourne).

PART IV

ADAM, KARL : *The Spirit of Catholicism* (Sheed & Ward).
BARRY, F. R. : *The Relevance of the Church* (Nisbet).
BERDYAEV, N. : *Freedom and the Spirit* (Centenary Press).
FLEW, R. N. : *Jesus and His Church* (Epworth Press).

GORE, C. : *The Holy Spirit and the Church* (Murray).

HEADLAM, A. C. : *The Doctrine of the Church and Reunion* (Murray).

HEBERT, A. G. : *Liturgy and Society* (Faber).

KIRK, K. E. : *The Vision of God* (Longmans).

RAMSEY, A. M. : *The Gospel and the Catholic Church* (Longmans).

RAVEN, C. E. : *The Creator Spirit* (Hopkinson).

ROBINSON, H. W.: *The Christian Experience of the Holy Spirit* (Nisbet).

STREETER, B. H. : *The Primitive Church* (Macmillan).

SWETE, H. B. (ed.) : *Essays on the Early History of the Church and the Ministry* (Macmillan).

WILLIAMS, CHARLES : *The Descent of the Dove* (Longmans).

INDEX

ABÉLARD, 79, 222 f.

Advent, Second, *see* Eschatology

Adventism, Hebraic, and St. John, 101

Agape, distinguished from Eros, 52 f.; power of, 65; as basis of Christology, 142

Alexander, S. A., 239 n.

Anselm, St., 79, 126, 226

Anthropomorphism, and traditional orthodoxy, 25–7; and Voltaire, 29 f.; its relation to human analogies for God, 38

Anti-formalism, 298, 303 f.

Apocalyptic, and the Messianic hope, 73, 77; its influence on Hebrews, 115; and traditional Christian eschatology, 242 f.; succeeds prophecy, 305

Apollinarius and Apollinarianism, 124, 135, 178

Apostolic Succession, 333 f.

Arianism, 124

Aristophanes, 313

Aristotle and Aristotelianism, 13, 54, 56, 143, 195

Arles, Council of, 337

Arnold, Matthew, 213

Art, creative, as analogy for divine creation, 38 f.; twofold value of, 41 f.; and time, 46 f.; its function in the Church, 309

Assent, and faith, 1–3, 8, 319 f.

Athenians, the, and St. Paul, 4, 90

Atonement, the, its connexion with the incarnation in primitive Christianity, 78 f., 108 f., 114, 121, 209; its place in Christian theology, 189–91; its connexion with eschatology, 190, 258–61; its relevance to problem of evil, 208–15; transcends morality, 209–11, 230 f., 258 f.; Old Testament preparation for, 216–20; four types of theory of, 221–37

Augustine, St. (of Hippo) and Augustinianism, 26, 36, 143, 185, 217, 337

Aulén, G., 221, 225

Aut Deus aut homo non bonus, 171

Authority, and freedom, 312–322; and creeds and dogmas, 8, 319 f.

BAPTISM, in name of the Lord Jesus, 324; and re-baptism, 337

Barth, Karl, and Barthians, 141, 143

Belief and faith, 1 f.

— in God, essential value of, 18–24

Benedictus, the, 74

Berdyaev, N., 192 f., 270 n.

Bethune-Baker, J. F., 130, 143 n.

Botticelli, 43

Bousset, W., 88

Brabant, F. H., 179 n.

" Branch-theory " of the Catholic Church, 338–40

Browning, R., 41, 179 n.

Fascism, 318
Fatherhood, as attribute of God,
    11, 25, 49–58
Finality of the Christian revela-
    tion, 131
First cause, the problem of the,
    35–8
Flesh, the, its meaning in the
    N.T., 101 f., 107 f., 117 f.,
    279, 292–5; and in the
    O.T., 274 f.
Flew, R. Newton, 58 n.
Force, its relation to power, 61,
    63 f.; its relation to author-
    ity, 313
Forgiveness, its connexion with
    the Messiahship and divin-
    ity of Jesus, 76–85; and
    morality, 210; teaching of
    Jesus on, 257
Freedom and authority in faith,
    312–22
Free will, the prophetic doc-
    trine of, 217 f.

GALILEO, 3
Glover, T. R., 130
Gnosticism, St. John's and St.
    Paul's opposition to, 101 f.,
    106–8, 112, 295, 302
Godet, F., 137 n.
" God-fearers ", 89
Gore, Charles, 82 n., 133, 137 n.,
    287, 296 n.
Gospel, essence of Christianity
    as message, 84, 94, 314

HARNACK, A., 129, 226
" Hearing " and " seeing ", as
    means of apprehending the
    divine, 71 f., 94–7
Heaven, as distinct from " the
    world to come ", 239; un-
    worthy conceptions of, 203;
    true Christian belief in,
    212–14
Hebraism and Hellenism, con-
    trasts between, 26, 68–72,
    89, 115–17, 141, 238–40
Hegel, 298
Hell, medieval doctrine of,
    241–3, 256; Christ's teach-
    ing on, 256 f.

Herrmann, W., 93, 130
History, in what sense essential
    to Christianity, 67 f., 91,
    93–8, 106–8, 146–55, 303–6,
    314 f.
Hobbes, Thomas, 199 n.
Holy, contrasted with Catholic
    and Communion, 311; see
    also Koinonia
Humanitarianism, 20, 197, 258
Huxley, Aldous, 200

IMMANENTISM, 297, 300–3
Immortality, chief characteristic
    of deity in Hellenic religion,
    90 f.; and difficulties at
    Thessalonica and Corinth,
    91 f.; and Karma in Bud-
    dhism, 196; and resur-
    rection, 212–15, 266–72;
    and life after death, 262
    f.; Bible-teaching on, 264–
    266
Impassibility of God, 122–7,
    135, 184–7
Intellect, the, and self-sacrifice,
    321
Irenæus, 80, 127, 133
Irrationalism, 11–13
Islam, 63, 151, 314
Israel, the new and the old, 85–7,
    327 f.

JUDGEMENT, final, in Christian
    eschatology, 241–4, 249–51;
    the idea analysed and dis-
    cussed, 252–61
Justice, Jewish and Roman ideas
    contrasted, 230; divine, in
    relation to love, 209–12,
    253

KANT, 210
Kenosis and Kenotic theories,
    81 f., 117, 129, 132–9, 154,
    178 f.
Kerygma, the, 84, 94
Kierkegaard, 133 n.
Kingdom of God, and Messianic,
    23 f., 73 f., 169, 181
Kipling, Rudyard, 44
Kirk, K. E., 71 n.

Printed in Great Britain by Butler & Tanner Ltd., Frome and London